Developing Distributed Curriculum Leadership in Hong Kong Schools

The book aims to explore distributed leadership in developing curriculum innovations in schools with a target of bringing theoretical underpinnings in the West in line with the empirical studies and practices in the East. It examines theoretically the roots of the curriculum leadership studies and practically empirical data and case studies in Hong Kong, which has been considered a melting pot of Western concepts and innovations in a land of Eastern cultures. The examination is framed within theoretical frameworks of activity theories, discourse analysis, and social network systems. The findings will show the impact of the cultural traditions of Eastern countries in the mediation of the direction of the discourses in teacher meetings and the effectiveness of decision making in the processes of developing school-based curriculum leadership. The book is theoretically exploratory with practically examined practices for educational leaders like schools heads and department leaders as well as teachers who aim at asserting greater influence in the educational decision making processes.

Topics discussed in the book include:

- Curriculum leadership functions and patterns of leadership distribution
- Engaging teachers in reflective practice: tensions between ideological orientations and pragmatic considerations
- Models of distributed leadership: focus, development, and future
- Initiating, designing and enacting curriculum innovations: procedures and processes

This book will appeal to researchers interested in curriculum studies, school leadership and comparative education. Those who study the theory of education and Asian education will also find this book valuable.

Edmond Hau-fai Law is Professor in the Curriculum & Instruction Department and a research fellow at the Asia Pacific Centre for Leadership and Change, The Education University of Hong Kong. He was a visiting scholar at the Universities of Twente in the Netherlands, Tokyo Gagukei and Kansai Osaka in Japan, and East China Nomal and Shenyang Normal, China. He has also served as external examiner for Ph.D. theses for the Universities of Addis Ababa, Ethiopia, Malaysia, Singapore, Twente, Brunei, and Hong Kong. He has worked for the United Nations Educational, Scientific and Cultural Organization (UNESCO) on policy evaluation and pedagogical transformation projects in the Asia Pacific region.

Routledge Series on Schools and Schooling in Asia
Series editor: Kerry J. Kennedy

Minority Students in East Asia
Government Policies, School Practices and Teacher Responses
Edited by JoAnn Phillion, Ming Tak Hue and Yuxiang Wang

A Chinese Perspective on Teaching and Learning
Edited by Betty C. Eng

Language, Culture, and Identity Among Minority Students in China
The Case of the Hui
By Yuxiang Wang

Citizenship Education in China
Preparing Citizens for the "Chinese Century"
Edited by Kerry J. Kennedy, Gregory P. Fairbrother, and Zhenzhou Zhao

Asia's High Performing Education Systems
The Case of Hong Kong
Edited by Colin Marsh and John Chi-Kin Lee

Asia Literate Schooling in the Asian Century
Edited by Christine Halse

Teacher Evaluation Policies and Practices in Japan
How performativity works in schools
Masaaki Katsuno

Curriculum, Instruction and Assessment in Japan
Beyond lesson study
Koji Tanaka, Kanae Nishioka and Terumasa Ishii

School Counselling in a Chinese Context
Supporting Students in Need in Hong Kong
Edited by Ming-tak Hue

Developing Distributed Curriculum Leadership in Hong Kong Schools
Edmond Hau-fai Law

Developing Distributed Curriculum Leadership in Hong Kong Schools

Edmond Hau-fai Law

LONDON AND NEW YORK

First published 2017
by Routledge
2 Park Square, Milton Park, Abingdon, Oxon OX14 4RN

and by Routledge
711 Third Avenue, New York, NY 10017

Routledge is an imprint of the Taylor & Francis Group, an informa business

© 2017 Edmond Hau-fai Law

The right of Edmond Hau-fai Law to be identified as author of this work has been asserted by him in accordance with sections 77 and 78 of the Copyright, Designs and Patents Act 1988.

All rights reserved. No part of this book may be reprinted or reproduced or utilised in any form or by any electronic, mechanical, or other means, now known or hereafter invented, including photocopying and recording, or in any information storage or retrieval system, without permission in writing from the publishers.

Trademark notice: Product or corporate names may be trademarks or registered trademarks, and are used only for identification and explanation without intent to infringe.

British Library Cataloguing-in-Publication Data
A catalogue record for this book is available from the British Library

Library of Congress Cataloging-in-Publication Data
A catalog record for this book has been requested

ISBN: 978-1-138-85763-6 (hbk)
ISBN: 978-1-315-71824-8 (ebk)

Typeset in Galliard
by Apex CoVantage, LLC

Contents

Acknowledgments	vii
Foreword	viii
Preface	xii

SECTION 1
Leadership approaches to curriculum development — 1

1 Introduction — 3

2 Models of distributed leadership: Focus, development, and future — 9

3 Initiating, designing, and enacting curriculum innovations: Procedures and processes — 29

SECTION 2
Case studies of curriculum leadership development teams — 41

4 Developing curriculum leadership in a primary school — 43

5 Impact of school-based curriculum innovations on teachers and students — 70

6 Effects of leadership styles on distribution of teacher participation on the mathematics curriculum development team: Discourse and social network analyses — 114

7 Managing school-based curriculum innovations in a Chinese curriculum development team: Discourse and social network analyses — 134

8 Curriculum leadership functions and patterns of distribution — 153

vi *Contents*

SECTION 3
Activity theory and curriculum leadership 175

9 Mediational functions of power and status on emergence of leadership properties 177

10 Engaging teachers in reflective practice: Tensions between ideological orientations and pragmatic considerations 200

11 Conclusion 218

Index 223

Acknowledgments

I wish to thank my parents (Law Kun, Lau Sze Mui) and my family (Sau Nga, Sung Hin William, Sung Yan Anna) for their lifelong support to my studies and career development for the past 60 years. Their dedication to the mission of the Law family has been the key to the spirit and completion of this book. Special thanks go to many professors I have met around the world, including Maurice Galton (Cambridge), Jan van den Akker (Twente), William Pinar (British Columbia), Collin Marsh (Curtin), Katsuhiro Yamazumi (Kansai), Shigeru Asanuma (Tokyo Gakugei), James Spillane (Northwestern), Zhong Qiquan (East China Normal), Li Chenzhi (Shenzhen), Hwang Jengjye (Taiwan), and Nozawa Yuki (Joestu). My special thanks also go to my colleagues at the Education University of Hong Kong, in particular Kerry Kennedy, David Coniam, Allan Walker, John C.K. Lee, and Philip Hallinger, whose support and patience have been essential to my academic work. Finally, I express my gratitude to the many teachers, in particular Sally Wan, and school heads in Hong Kong who have offered their assistance to my research activities with their heart set on the betterment of our children in the coming era.

Many of the research activities reported in the chapters in this book were supported by the Hong Kong Quality Education Fund of the Hong Kong Government as well as various types of funding resources offered to the author by the Department of Curriculum and Instruction and the Education University of Hong Kong.

The work described in this book was partially supported by a grant from the Research Grants Council of the Hong Kong Special Administrative Region, China (Project No. EdUHK 18403314).

Foreword

Leadership and management, and administration more broadly, are popular topics for academics, especially those who work in applied fields such as education and business. Much of the work has centered on "for-profit" organizations though there is also an expansive literature on non-profit organizations, especially schools. Indeed, over the past half-century, interest in leadership and management in the education sector has increased as policymakers have attempted to use various performance metrics to hold school leaders and managers accountable, a move that is often referred to as the "new public management".

Much of the work on leading, managing, and administrating in education has fallen under the rubric of school leadership and management. That is appropriate, as much of this literature has paid scant attention to teaching and learning – the core technology of schooling. In other words, with a few exceptions, most notably Hallinger and Heck's work on instructional leadership, this literature has not been centrally about leading and managing teaching and learning. Perhaps that was in part a function of the fact that there was little or no managing and leading of the core technology in schools, especially in places such as the United States where a sizable amount of this research was undertaken.

When teaching and learning did figure, it was mostly treated as an outcome variable – that is, an outcome to measure the effects of school leadership and management. This is unfortunate because teaching and learning are not simply the object of leadership and management activity in schools; they are also the *subject* of such work, and as such fundamentally shape the work of leadership and management. Indeed, it is difficult to imagine how one can systematically and comprehensively study leadership and management in schools without careful and disciplined attention to what is being led and managed – teaching and learning. Yet, teaching and learning have mostly been assigned either to the outcome role or a peripheral role in leadership and management research in the education sector. We need to change this situation.

Contrast Edmond's efforts in this book to investigate school leadership and management with teaching and learning playing a central role. This is a welcome development. Focusing on school-based curriculum development (SBCD) through research on schools in Hong Kong, the book delves into the nitty-gritty work of managing and leading teaching and learning in schools. Drawing on a rich array of conceptual tools including distributed leadership and activity theory, the book examines the work of leading and managing curriculum and its improvement on the ground using various analytical approaches. Edmond works to uncover the structural and conceptual complexities in establishing a professional culture of building communities of curriculum leaders and leadership practices as an alternative model to the hierarchical conception of SCBD in Hong Kong, an Asian city that blends Western ideas with Eastern practices (Law & Li, 2013). As such, Hong Kong offers a fascinating site for studying leading and managing teaching and learning – a fusion of Western and Eastern ideas and practices.

The focus on Hong Kong is also important because much work on school leadership and management has been carried out in Western democracies and school systems or systems that have adopted Western democratic models of governance. As a result, too often, conceptual and theoretical work on leadership and management is applied whole cloth to other contexts where it may not fit as easily as might be expected. There is always a challenge in translating leadership and management ideas developed in Western democracies and applying them in other entirely different geopolitical and cultural situations. Thus, it is important to see work, such as that reported in this book, begin to emerge in the field of leadership and management in education. We need more work of this sort so we can generate knowledge of leadership and management in different types of school systems and cultural situations, but also so that over time we can learn by comparing leading and managing practice across these different situations.

Another issue taken up in this book, one mostly missing in the literature, involves explicating relations between the practice of leadership and management on the one hand, and teaching practice on the other, including the practice of improving teaching and learning in schools. This book helps address this gap in the literature by studying the role of not only leaders and teachers, but also of artifacts in relations between leading practice and teaching practice. Further, Edmond attends not simply to change in teachers' practice but also to how teachers learn and what they learn, unpacking the teacher learning process and professional learning more broadly as it is not only teachers that need to learn but also other professionals. Just like in classrooms where the teachers' style often constrains how students participate, leaders' style in meetings can work similarly to either enable or undermine learning. In doing so, this book underscores how the schoolhouse can be an important site for teacher education and, by extension, professional learning (Hopkins & Spillane, 2014; Parise & Spillane, 2010).

The book also captures the importance of taking a developmental perspective in studying leadership and management. The challenges of leading and managing teaching and its improvement depend in some measure on where a school or school leadership team is developmentally located. At the same time, changes can be implemented, put into practice, but can fade away relatively quickly when the initial supports for implementation are removed; the changes fail to stick over time and come to little or nothing with time – hence, the importance of institutionalization. In this book, for example, institutionalizing the means that

x *Foreword*

make formal teacher involvement in curriculum decision making is one issue. Institutionalization more broadly is especially relevant here and something that merits much more attention in the literature on leadership and management in education. By institutionalization here I refer to the process by which practices become self-reproducing in organizations such as schools (Jepperson, 1991). Attending to institutionalization as a process is critical to understanding change in schools, and indeed the role of leadership and management in such efforts, as it takes us beyond whether some new way of doing things is adopted by school staff to understand how it becomes self-reproducing with time (Colyvas & Powell, 2006). A central part of this work, as suggested in the pages that follow, concerns examining how school and school systems' educational infrastructures can be redesigned and changes not only implemented, but institutionalized.

A final observation prompted by Edmond's book concerns the need for much more attention to school systems and their organizations in research on leadership and management in schools (Cohen, Spillane, & Peurach, under review). We need work that better understands the role of the school system, and its educational infrastructure in particular, in defining the practice of leading and managing teaching in schools. It is difficult to comprehend leading and managing teaching and learning inside schools without attention to a school system's educational infrastructure (e.g., the exams it requires students to take, the curriculum it prescribes and mandates, the system- and school-level organizational routines that enable and constrain interactions among staff, and so on). Further, it is critical that we think about the school system not as simply a context for leadership and management but rather as an integral and constituting component of leadership and management practice in schools. Too often in research on leading and managing teaching and learning, the school is the unit of analysis with limited attention to the school system. Such work will likely have to be comparative so that we can more fully appreciate how a school system's educational infrastructure contributes to structuring interactions among school staff in their efforts to improve teaching and learning.

James P. Spillane
Chicago, IL, USA

References

Cohen, D.K., Spillane, J.P., & Peurach, D.J. (under review). Educational reform as system building.

Colyvas, J.A., & Powell, W.W. (2006). Roads to institutionalization: The remaking of boundaries between public and private science. *Research in Organizational Behavior, 27*, 305–353.

Hopkins, M., & Spillane, J.P. (2014). Schoolhouse teacher educators: Structuring beginning teachers' opportunities to learn about instruction. *Journal of Teacher Education, 65*(4), 327–339.

Jepperson, R.L. (1991). Institutions, institutional effects, and institutionalism. *The New Institutionalism in Organizational Analysis, 6*, 143–163.

Law, E.H.F., & Li, C. (Eds.). (2013). *Curriculum innovations in changing societies: Chinese perspectives from Hong Kong, Taiwan and Mainland China* (p. 545). Netherlands: Sense Publishers.

Parise, L.M., & Spillane, J.P. (2010). Teacher learning and instructional change: How formal and on-the-job learning opportunities predict changes in elementary school teachers' instructional practice. *Elementary School Journal, 110*(3), 323–346.

Preface

Those of us who work with teachers know that they find it difficult to change certain aspects of their classroom practice. Ask them to learn a new skill, such as presenting information using a PowerPoint, or teaching them a new way of carrying out division generally entails little resistance, providing the person proposing the change can convince experienced practitioners that the new approach offers sufficient advantages from the previous way of doing things. To a degree, the same applies to aspects of classroom organization such as sitting students in groups, rather than rows or using a "horseshoe" arrangement when holding whole-class discussions.

However, when it comes to questions of "generic" pedagogy to do with the quality of questioning, the type of feedback provided or the use of formative forms of assessment, which are designed to monitor the effects of one's teaching, the would-be reformer encounters greater difficulty in promoting change, even though there may be abundant research evidence in support of what is being advocated. As a result, some educators such as Larry Cuban have described teaching as one of most *conservative* of all the professions.

There are a number of reasons for this. First, there are the external pressures on teachers to deliver high-quality results on external examinations. In Western countries, for example, the results on international tests, such as the Programme for International Student Assessment (PISA) and Trends in Mathematics and Science Study (TIMSS) rank both the USA and the UK near the bottom of the participating countries. As a result, governments in both countries have introduced "performivity" measures which see schools publically identified as failing even if they are disadvantaged by their intake. Not surprisingly, therefore, teachers tend to teach to the test.

Second, there is what has been termed a *perception gap* where what teachers are observed to do and what they claim to do are sometimes at odds. This arises because teaching is both a *coping* and an *expressive* activity. Teachers have to react to different circumstances, for example, a lunchtime disturbance may result in an unresponsive class in the afternoon and a teacher might choose to abandon some lively group activity in favor of working individually in silence. This is the thinking or head part of teaching. The expressive part involves feeling – following the sentiments of the heart. Teachers may be reluctant to give students the freedom to explore their own interests and ideas in case they lose control of the learning and are seen by colleagues as weak and ineffective. In such cases where the head rules the heart, teachers might suppress those incidents where they cut off or changes a student's ideas and replace them with their own suggestions, and will therefore continue to believe that students are expressing themselves freely, despite external evidence showing this to be untrue, and that students were given few opportunities to raise questions or express their ideas.

The third impediment to changing a teacher's generic pedagogic practice lies in the presentation of the new ideas by the tutor in lectures, seminars, or workshops. Tutors tend to generalize, base their arguments on theories and previous research, but rarely offer sufficient concrete examples of how such theory translates into classroom practice. Teachers of the course may therefore feel that the tutor is out of touch or that they don't appreciate the particular problems that might occur as a consequence of adopting the suggested changes to their current practice. They will go away, therefore, unconvinced.

For these reasons there has been a growing realization that to bring about such change requires the professional development of teachers to be undertaken within the schools themselves so that *communities of practice* are established whereby teachers plan lessons together, observe each other's lessons, and then critically evaluate the outcomes with a view to repeating the cycle with the suggested improvements incorporated. Sometimes these communities will be established on a subject basis between neighboring schools and sometimes between different year groups in a single school. A considerable amount of research has been undertaken to establish the conditions that best promote change. This book not only summarizes this evidence but also adds to it through a number of illuminating case studies. In particular, it explores, in the Hong Kong context, the role of leadership in promoting effective practice. For the author, leadership roles extend beyond the actions of the school principal and the senior management. In this view, even the most junior member of staff can be required at some point to adopt a leadership role.

However, the author does acknowledge that the role of the school principal is crucial. The opening chapter contrasts the different styles of leadership: on the one hand an approach that is authoritarian, heavily directive, and where delegation is hierarchical. In contrast is a style which rather than delegate embraces a distributive style of leadership where contributions are based on the professional knowledge of the individual and their capacity to work collaboratively with others. Chapter 2 explores this concept of distributed leadership further, both looking at the various forms it can take and its effectiveness in bringing about curriculum change.

The next chapter offers the first of the several case studies. The theme here is the role of the panel head; the two contrasting styles of leadership developed earlier are explored and the effects on the participating teachers described. Succeeding chapters continue this theme by exploring the impact on teacher and student learning of different leadership styles, looking at the ways in which teachers cope with various issues associated with East Asian traditional instructional xiv *Preface*

practices and showing in general that for communities of practice to succeed requires school leaders to provide a shared vision that is created through collaborative process, in which all views are given serious consideration and initial differences are resolved either through seeking consensus or by testing them against the effect on students' learning.

The main vehicle for conducting this analysis is the detailed examination of the discourse that takes place between the teachers, but in two of the final chapters the author revisits the evidence from the perspective of activity theory. First used to explore human-computer interactions at the interface, it has increasingly been a valuable tool in exploring the various pathways of distributed leadership. In this analysis of the process of distributing leadership we identify the preference for the use of different tools (books, discussion, expert advice, etc.) leading to a division of labor in which participants hold varied assumptions about the rules (norms and values) governing their activities. This in turn can lead to sub-groups within the community of practice being at cross-purposes, thus in effect creating more than one contradictory activity system. The analysis offers a valuable warning, therefore, about the oversimplification of the debate where distributed leadership is always best and more directive instructional approaches are less effective.

The book is timely in that Hong Kong schools are about to embrace a second phase of educational reform following the adoption of the principles of *Learning to Learn* around the time of the millennium. The first priority was to reduce the amount of teacher talk during lessons and to create more active forms of learning through improved class discussion and the use of collaborative forms of learning in pairs or small groups. However, the stage is now set whereby students need to learn how to determine the success criteria associated with a particular set of task objectives, plan and review progress towards achieving these ends, and develop alternative strategies when the likely outcomes are at variance with the original goals – in short to learn to regulate their own thinking. This is no mean task and this book will be of help to teachers in their attempts to educate their students in this way of learning in anticipation of the demands of work and citizenship that surely lie ahead of these future adults in the middle and later parts of the 21st century.

Maurice Galton
University of Cambridge England

Section 1

Leadership approaches to curriculum development

1 Introduction

A school-based approach for developing school curriculum leadership has been applied for 30 years (Law & Nieveen, 2010). The Hong Kong government took this initiative in the 1980s with a focus on building individual professional capacity for teachers, rather than following Skilbeck's (1984) recommendation of adopting a structural approach to developing school curriculum and curriculum leadership. A policy that enhances curriculum development skills among individual teachers has been implemented in the last 20 years. Through this policy, the Hong Kong government enhanced the capacity of schools in developing curriculum and curriculum leadership by establishing a senior post in leading school-based curriculum development (SBCD) in 2003 (Law & Nieveen, 2010). However, the problems with various models of SBCD have not been explored. The SBCD model originated in Western democratic countries, and to best of our knowledge, how this could have worked more effectively to achieve its original mission has not yet been explored in Hong Kong (Law, 2014). This book attempts to move the theories and practice on SBCD in Asian countries a step forward by reporting various attempts at different stages of development projects (Law & Li, 2013). Theories in distributed leadership, problem-solving approaches in learning, and activity theory in redesigned projects have been used to understand the complexity of teacher learning, structural and cultural issues within curriculum teams of teachers, and power issues with directive and collaborative leadership styles. A mixed approach in data collection and data analyses is adopted. A combination of ethnographic interviews is used to showcase teachers' deep learning, the discourse analysis of interactions in meetings to uncover the leadership functions of curriculum development teams, and the social network analysis of interactions in meetings to show patterns of leadership distribution. Finally, activity theory is used to deepen our understanding of critical features in team interactions that allow the emergence of leadership practices and the generation of new and innovative ideas or their suppression.

Chapter 2 reviews the publications by five key scholars who had major contributions in the theory building and empirical investigations of distributed leadership in various Western countries. These publications have attempted to establish a correlation between leadership and student learning but found that

4 *Developing curriculum leadership*

only a particular form of distributed leadership is related to student learning. However, other forms of leadership have indirect correlation with student learning. They found that solo and distributed leadership styles are necessary in different stages of school improvement, whereas distributed leadership is essential in the empowerment of teachers and in the development of teacher leadership. Distributed leadership has been used diversely and freely without any indication of some consensus in its understanding. Despite the differences, empirical studies in this area have assumed that leadership or leadership practices should not be the sole property of the principals or the positional leaders in the institutions. Empirical investigations have also focused on the effects of multiple leaders and how leadership functions have been distributed among members within an institution. Various studies have shown that principal leadership has a key role in the dissemination of leadership functions among members. Moreover, the influence of principal leadership would be more effective if it is widely disseminated among members regardless of the fact that it would be limited to positional leaders, delegated members, or informal members whose leadership functions emerge in practice. Distributed leadership also leads to improved professional institutional capacity of schools.

Chapter 3 outlines the mechanism and process based on a series of design-based investigations conducted at two primary schools in Hong Kong in the last 10 years. The mechanism and process were repeated at two schools to triangulate the findings and enhance their reliability. The model of change and its mechanism were based on the theory about the cycles of expansive learning proposed by Engestrom. This model was part of his activity theory about social change and innovation. This chapter shows that engaging teachers in the cycles of expansive learning, which include reviewing, planning, implementing, and reflecting on curriculum practices, has enhanced spaces of learning and the individual capacity of teacher leadership. However, the effectiveness of this expansive learning model has been restricted by the leadership style of the chair or the coordinator. A directive style restricts the spaces of teacher learning, whereas a collaborative style has a more powerful effect on teacher learning. Skilbeck's problem-solving model for SCBD in 1984 should consider the effects of leadership styles on its outcomes, the curriculum leadership skills that have empowered participants, and the effects of stimulations from external consultants.

Chapter 4 reports the first action cycle of the two-round redesigned case study in 2004. This report was based on teacher interviews on the effect of leadership styles, the role of the external consultants, the reflective nature of teacher engagement, team effects, and curriculum decision making. To the best of our knowledge, this is the first empirical investigation of these issues that have been raised in the international literature and is essential to understanding the interactions between leaders and followers in school contexts. The findings are positive and have shown the differences of directive and non-directive leadership styles on discourse and teacher experiences. A directive leadership style limited the opportunities of participation, whereas a non-directive style allowed more opportunities for teachers. The other issue concerns the institutionalization of a mechanism at schools that formalizes teacher participation in curriculum decision making. This is a form of distributed leadership in curriculum decision making at middle managerial level at schools in Hong Kong.

Chapter 5 is based on the second action cycle of the redesigned work in 2005. The design was repeated to ensure that a distributed form of leadership was enacted. This design was also organized to ensure a flattened leadership in one of the two curriculum development teams. The leader was an experienced teacher with a low hierarchical status at school. This condition determines whether leadership practices emerged in interactions in team meetings. The assertive and directive positional leader (panel head) on the Chinese team dominated the discourse in the meeting and exerted effects on opportunities for participation. The mathematics team enjoyed a relaxed atmosphere. Thus, team members were eager to participate and contribute to the discussion and had increased influence in decision making. Leadership practices emerged from team members in the mathematics curriculum development team with a positional leader who asserted less influence on interactions. The interactions also showed that teacher contribution was more distributed among team members in the mathematics curriculum development team, whereas teacher contribution in the Chinese curriculum development team was more focused or concentrated. An external consultant was assigned in the design to provide different perspectives and professional inputs into the discussion. The teachers who participated in both curriculum development teams told the interviewees that they learned how to differentiate among various instructional strategies, identify student needs, and plan and design instructional materials in their interactions with the team members in the redesigning task. This finding was aligned with other empirical investigations and shows that teacher participation empowered the individual professional capacity of teachers. Student interviews revealed that students were aware of the changing pedagogical strategies among teachers and that they were engaged and motivated in the trial lessons.

Chapter 6 is based on the videotaped meetings of the mathematics curriculum team in the second action cycle in 2005. This chapter has adopted a combination of data analysis methods. This chapter analyzed discourse functions on transcriptions of one planning meeting and two reflection meetings. A quantitative analysis of the amount of participation distribution was conducted in the three meetings, and the behaviors of the team members were analyzed based on visual images in three videotaped meetings. The approaches to data analysis were found in studies on distribution leadership. The purpose is to identify the leadership functions and reconstruct the patterns of leadership practices in teams and the emergent properties embedded in the interactions among members. An experienced teacher, but with a low status in the school hierarchy, was assigned to chair the team. Thus, the chair demonstrated in the meetings some leadership functions that were less directive. The leadership functions enacted were observed as follows:

1 Guiding exploration;
2 Re-orienting the direction of the discussions;

6 *Developing curriculum leadership*

3   Inviting contributions from all team members; and
4   Reflecting on personal experiences.

The analysis of the distribution of contributions and initiations showed that members without positional leadership functions were willing to contribute and initiate during meetings. The discourse was elaborated and stretched over different followers within the team meetings.

Chapter 7 reports on another analysis based on the interview data and discourse interactions in the meetings. The methods of analysis include quantitative analysis of the distribution of teacher participation and teacher initiation as well as an analysis of the leadership functions in interactions among members in the Chinese curriculum development team meetings. The results of the analysis highlight the effects of the directive and hierarchical leadership styles of the positional leader on limiting the distribution of teacher participation. The discourse analysis also showed that leadership style restricts the space for teachers to explore pedagogical themes and practices in the meetings. Interactional patterns tend to be uni-directional and discourse density concentrates on positional leaders.

Chapter 8 outlines the findings from a study in a primary school in Hong Kong in 2007. The design was based on the previous studies conducted by the author with the following features. First, the two teams were organized using a rotational leadership approach in two action cycles, which allow changes in leadership styles and their effects on interactions among members. The purpose was to observe and investigate the extent that the effects of changing positional leadership styles had on patterns of distribution and the emergence of leadership functions and practices. Second, all planning and reflection meetings of each team in two action cycles were studied and analyzed. This enabled the researchers to capture the holistic picture of all data and their meanings in this leadership project. Third, three data analysis methods were conducted for triangulation. The distribution of the participation time of each member in each round and in each team shows the contribution and distribution patterns of teacher participation. Social network analysis showed whether the distribution was focused or well-dispersed. Moreover, it indicated who took initiatives in orienting and re-orienting the discourses. This is a form of influence of individual members in the team meetings. Finally, the discourse analysis showed what leadership functions were enacted and how these leadership functions were distributed or located among team members (i.e., concentrated or dispersed or emergent or developing). Discourse analysis also demonstrated how leadership styles, directive or collaborative, had effects on the nature of participation. Thus, whether participation is restricted or elaborated is determined.

Chapter 9 is an attempt to apply activity theory in the analysis of the data available from the first school project in 2005. The data used were not the same as in other chapters. The key concepts from activity theory, such as artifacts and meditational effects, were used. Artifacts are understood in their physical entities and their conceptual properties. Consultants and leadership styles were utilized as the two artifacts used by the subjects in achieving their goals. These two artifacts asserted their mediational effects on the goals or tasks and shaped the interactions of the two teams. On the one hand, the directive consultants and the assertive positional leaders in the Chinese curriculum development teams created team interactions, which were uni-structural, power-coercive, and informative. On the other hand, the liberal and collaborative consultants and positional leaders created interactions among members, which were multi-directional, exploratory, re-educative, and socially interactive. The former is more restrictive and allows less space for teacher learning, whereas the latter is more elaborated and allows more space for teacher learning. The application of activity theory in the analysis has resulted in new perspectives in understanding the structural relationship between leaders and followers. The adoption of activity theory has also shown researchers how properties of leadership functions emerged in interactions in task-based contexts. The leadership functions discovered in the discourse analysis extend specifically to curriculum development skills, which combine leadership functions with the skills necessary in evolving curriculum development in school-based contexts.

Chapter 10 attempts to apply the key concepts of activity theory in data analysis. This study's attempt is exploratory, and the application needs more solid understanding of the theory. This chapter focuses on the use of Engestrom's expansive cycles of learning in his activity theory to uncover the layers of underlying meanings in the interactions among members in the curriculum development meetings. This was used to determine how new ideas are taken up and re-oriented by the mediation of artifacts, such as power and tensions in ideological preferences. The use of expansive learning cycles shows the tensions between the consultant and the teachers in determining the critical object of learning in lessons. The tension extends from the discussion and design meeting to the reflection meeting. The decision of the two parties is significant. The decision was a compromise, and both parties withdrew their original arguments and moved the decision to another object of learning of less controversy between the two parties. This was a typical Asian solution when conflicts arose to maintain social cohesiveness. The analysis showed that the solution did not aim to solve the original pedagogical problem by testing out the hypothesis. A decision would be made based on the evidence. The decision of the two parties was political and social at the expense of the pedagogical enhancement of teaching and learning in classrooms. The tensions between the consultant and the teachers stretched to the reflection meeting. The insistence of the teachers on their traditional conceptions about learning and objects of learning may be a result of the lack of a risk-taking attitude in curriculum development or to save face. The consultant could have suggested to the teachers that they try out the hypothesis and the real problems with the object of learning and base the evidence from practice. Both parties failed to adopt a more exploratory and experiential approach in their professional decision making.

This book is an attempt to uncover the structural and conceptual complexity in establishing a professional culture of building communities of curriculum leaders and leadership practices as an alternative model to the hierarchical conception of SCBD in Hong Kong, an Asian city that infuses Western thoughts with Eastern practices (Law & Li, 2013).

References

Law, E.H.F. (2014). In search of a diverse curriculum: Toward the making of a post-modern Hong Kong in the twenty-first century. In W. Pinar (Ed.), *International handbook of curriculum research* (pp. 217–226). New York: Routledge.

Law, E.H.F., & Li, C.Z. (Eds.). (2013). *Curriculum innovations in changing societies: Chinese perspectives from Hong Kong, Taiwan and Mainland China.* Rotterdam: Sense Publishers.

Law, E.H.F, & Nieveen, N. (Eds.). (2010). *Schools as curriculum agencies: Asian and European perspectives on school-base curriculum development.* Rotterham: Sense Publishers.

Skilbeck, M. (1984). *School based curriculum development.* London: Harper & Row.

2 Models of distributed leadership
Focus, development, and future

For the selection of key papers on the topic, this review adopted the systematic review approach used in Hallinger and Bryant (2013) along with a mixed-methods approach. First, we selected key scholars who published substantial works on this topic, "distributed leadership," with a focus on their recent publications. The key arguments of each scholar, including Christopher Day, Peter Gronn, Alma Harris, and Peter Spillane, are outlined. The reason we chose to adopt this mixed approach is the lack of new perspectives in the recent reviews of distributed leadership (Crawford, 2012; Tian, Risku, & Collin, 2016). We shall return to these key reviews in our discussion section.

Second, we selected the eight "core" international journals on leadership and educational leadership, including *Educational Administration Quarterly, Journal of Educational Administration, School Effectiveness and School Improvement, Educational Management Administration and Leadership, International Journal of Leadership in Education, International Journal of Educational Management, Leadership and Policy in Schools,* and *School Leadership and Management.* The justifications proposed in their selection are that the mean *h-index* of these eight journals remain at 45, and that these core journals "would provide a broad representation of moderately to highly selective, internationally relevant articles sharing theoretical and empirical knowledge on educational leadership and management" (Hallinger & Bryant, 2013, p. 4). Our selection focused on the period from 2007 and 2016, covering the last 10 years of the publications on distributed leadership. We deliberately selected the key publications in the last 10 years because, although some key theoretical foundations and empirical investigations based on the notion of "distributed leadership" have been conducted before 2007, there have been at least three reviews of the past literature on distributed leadership (Bennett, Wisc, Woods, & Harvey, 2003; Crawford, 2012; Tian et al., 2016) covering literature from 1996 to 2013 and four reviews of the past literature on educational leadership or school leadership (Day, Hopkins, Harris, & Ahtaridou, 2009; Hallinger and Chen, 2015; Szeto, Lee, & Hallinger, 2015). From these eight journals and for this period, we found 71 papers with the keywords "distributed," "distributed perspective," or "distributed leadership."

Third, in order to cover more papers published in international journals, we also checked the ERIC database on the same period from 2007 to 2016 and

10 *Developing curriculum leadership*

identified the papers published apart from the aforementioned eight core journals. This is a more logical reason despite the limitation resulting from the lack of direct access to publications in languages other than English. A total of 150 publications can be found in the ERIC database during this period. However, not all papers are relevant to primary and secondary education; therefore, studies in higher education and early childhood education are eliminated from this review, resulting in a total of 54 research papers.

According to Hallinger (2013b), reviews are rarely systematic. Hence, he derived a conceptual framework for systematic reviews in the future from his examination of the reviews found in the literature. His framework includes the following five items of information:

1 What are the central topics of interest, guiding questions, and goals?
2 What conceptual perspective guides the review's selection, evaluation, and interpretation of the studies?
3 What are the sources and types of data employed for the review?
4 How are data evaluated, analyzed, and synthesized in the review?
5 What are the major results, limitations, and implications of the review?

To simplify our presentation of the review, we deliberately restructured Hallinger's five types of information in our review by using the questions below.

1 What are the research questions and what are the theoretical underpinnings of the studies?
2 What research methodology and data collection methods are adopted? How are data analyzed?
3 What are the findings and implications on the general theories of distributed leadership specifically?

While we acknowledge the systematic framework of literature review proposed by Hallinger (2011), we embedded these three essential elements in our review below, rather than have separate sections on each.

Part A: Research papers published in journals (2007–2016)

Multiple usages of distributed leadership

Only a couple of papers have focused on the fundamental issues related to the conceptions of distributed leadership. Most empirical studies reviewed below adopted one or another aspect of distributed leadership proposed by Gronn and Spillane. This is a pragmatic and feasible approach in designing research studies. However, Mayrowetz (2008) reviewed the fundamental issues of "distributed leadership" and proposed four orientations in understanding the functions of distributed leadership. First, distributed leadership is to be understood as a series of processes of interactions among members of an institution in achieving tasks. These interactions involve people who may be positional leaders in the hierarchy and those who may be ordinary members of the institution. Depending on the leadership styles and the characters of the members, the interactions may allow the emergence of different types of outcomes, one of which may be "leadership." Therefore, what is important in this orientation is the amount of leadership functions and practices being distributed among members as well as the patterns of interactions that are shaped by the all members. In this orientation, leadership is taken as the consequence of the interactions – something that may have emerged in their negotiations. Leadership is not seen as the sole properties of the positional leaders but becomes a networked phenomenon of the institution. As a consequence, the unit of analysis shifts to the school or the institution and not the individuals. This orientation is based on distributed cognition theories and activity theories. Mayrowetz commented that few studies adopted the activity theory approach in their design and analysis (Mayrowetz, 2008).

The second usage of distributed leadership is for democracy, and involves members of the institution in its decision making processes. The third usage is for efficiency and effectiveness, specifically the process by which tasks are distributed among members (Robinson, 2008). The fourth usage is distributed leadership's agential dimension to enhance collective capacity building. In conclusion, leadership is conceptualized as the agential influences of formal leaders and their members. Leadership is not an exclusive property of the positional leaders; rather, it is distributed among the people. Indeed, according to some arguments, leadership that is widely distributed or dispersed enhances individual and collective capacities.

Involving multiple leaders as a form of distributed leadership

Out of 54 research papers reviewed, 34 empirically investigated one of Spillane's key conceptions about distributed leadership, namely, the "leader plus" aspect, which sees distributed leadership as a prescription on the part of the principals to "involve" (or stretch over) more positional leaders with pedagogical and other leadership functions in their schools. Some variations among this model have been presented. We call these leadership practices "principal-led distributed leadership practices."

The first cluster involves principal leadership functions that have been extended to include a co-principal (Bunnell, 2008), a leadership team led by the principal (Bush and Glover, 2012); (Abrahasen, Aas, & Hellekjaer, 2015; Larsen and Rieckhoff, 2014), multiple leaders among eight schools under one principal (Mifsud, 2015), multiple leadership networks (Park & Datnow, 2009), and shared leadership practices between a principal and a departmental chair (Klar, 2012; Storey, 2004; Tubin & Pinyan-Weiss, 2015). The titles of all these research papers carry the keyword "distributed leadership." This indicates that the term has been used and interpreted quite widely, covering various forms of leadership practices focused on principal leadership functions. However, all these papers featured literature reviews based on Spillane, Gronn, and Harris. Bush and

12 *Developing curriculum leadership*

Townsend (Townsend, 2015) claim to have used the hybrid model of leadership from Gronn, while others claimed to have used the "leader-plus" aspect of Spillane's model. Two other papers focused on the perceptions of the principals (three in one case and four in another case) concerning their notion of distributed leadership (Piot and Kelchtermans, 2015; Torrance, 2013) and how they worked to overcome cultural and structural barriers in building a leadership-dense organization.

All these papers adopted a mixed-method approach, which features a range of data collection methods, including questionnaires, narrative interviews, observations of meetings, shadowing, and analysis of interactions and leadership functions. One research from Malta used discourse analysis (Mifsud, 2015). The findings in these papers have shown the complexity of the interactions in terms of power and autonomy, indicating the tensions and conflicts in the distribution of leadership functions. None of these papers have used activity theory in their analysis or as a theoretical framework in guiding the investigations. Among these papers, a strong assumption exists concerning the role of principals in initiating, designing, and implementing a form of distributed leadership by extending the principal leadership to a co-principal, "stretching" over multiple leaders, or forming a senior leadership under the principal (Klar, Huggins, Hammons, & Buskey, 2016).

Leadership functions

One attempt among scholars is to establish what leadership is and, specifically, exactly what leadership functions are. The early work of MacBeath (2005) attempted to distinguish the nature of "distribution" based on its functions. Six types have been proposed, including formal, pragmatic, strategic, incremental, and opportunistic distributions. What is important to the development of the concept of distribution leadership seems to be the recognition of the developmental nature of leadership from a more restricted and focused pattern toward a more distributed pattern of leadership practices. MacBeath (2005) identified the three stages, from an emergent stage to a developed and mature stage of having leadership embedded in the institutional culture. Another contribution of MacBeath's early work on distributed leadership is his distinction of two dimensions in the conceptualization of leadership practices: structural and agential (MacBeath, 2005). However, the key question about "who distributes what" still remains. The other two research studies have given some evidence about the underlying assumption about distributed leadership in the minds of these scholars. Ritchie and Woods (2007) have followed the five dimensions of distribution in the questionnaire used by National College of School Leadership. They are "instruct," "consult," "delegate," "facilitate," and "neglect." These action verbs, however, explicitly indicate that the underlying assumption of leadership functions is about those leaders who can perform these functions, such as "instructing" and "delegating," to name but two. Another study by Mullick, Sharma, and Deppeler (2013) in Bangladesh also adopted a similar approach, in which the leadership functions are defined in terms of the capacities of those who are positional leaders. Their leadership functions include "determining directions," "supporting professional development," and "designing organization and supervising teaching." One must note that only positional leaders are expected to fulfill the responsibilities of realizing these roles. Both papers based their data collections on interviews with school leaders. The third paper more explicitly includes managerial responsibilities, such as "providing and selling a vision" and "handling disturbances" in the work redesign project to engage potential leaders in a series of training activities (Mayrowetz, 2008).

Clearly, the concept of "distributed leadership" implies the transfer of administrative and managerial skills and responsibilities to those who are identified as the potential positional leaders. The strategy is to expand the network of leadership functions and responsibilities to a wider group of personnel in the institutions (Blitz & Modeste, 2015; Firestone & Martinez, 2007). Meanwhile, another study (Lima, 2008) used a social network questionnaire approach to establish patterns of distribution of "influence" among school members.

Effects of distributed leadership

The research studies published during this period reported no conclusive findings on how distributed leadership activities directly affect student achievements (Lamby, 2013). This is in direct contrast with the findings reported by Leithwood and Mascall (2008), who stated that collective leadership explains a significant proportion of variation in student achievement across schools. Reservations have been expressed as to the democratic and ethical functions of distributed leadership; it has been speculated that distributed leadership is used as a managerial measure to alleviate the workload of the positional leaders (Hartley, 2010; Stoten, 2015; Woods & Roberts, 2016).

However, the effects on teachers, particularly on commitments and job security, have been found to be significant (Hulpia, Devos, & Keer, 2011; Ozdemir & Eemircioglue, 2015). The concept of "distributed leadership" has also been used in work redesign projects meant to cultivate professional learning communities in schools, such as those in the United States and Singapore, with the aims of empowering teachers, engaging teachers in pedagogical decision making processes, and enhancing leadership development (Hairon, Goh, & Lin, 2014; Melville, Jones, & Campbell, 2014; Yuen, Chen, & Ng, 2015). Suspicions have been raised in the Singaporean case study concerning the limitations of distributed leadership amidst a cultural context that favors hierarchical power and pragmatic values (Yuen et al., 2015). The limitation of distributed leadership in an Asian context has been found to be contrary to a similar case study on a more collective form of leadership context in Sweden, whereas some planned patterns of distributive leadership practices have been well received by the teachers (Lilijenberg, 2015).

Summary

The above-mentioned papers on distributed leadership, which have been published in the recent 10 years, reported that the definition of "distributed leadership" has been taken quite elusively to cover an extended leadership style of

14   *Developing curriculum leadership*

principals involving individuals in a form of collaborative partnership or engaging more individuals in leadership teams. This multiple approach to the usage of the terms has dominated the aforementioned publications. This trend has shown that the leadership style focused on individual positional leaders has moved toward a more shared pattern of leadership style among positional leaders and, in some cases, the involvement of informal members in the leadership teams in the institutions.

Another observation is the refinement of the notion of "leadership functions." However, the list of leadership functions seems to be biased toward the notion of a uni-directional "leader-follower" relationship, rather than a reciprocal one mediated by artifacts, and realized in contexts that both Gronn and Spillane are interested in. Finally, the attempts to establish a clear relationship between "distributed leadership" and its effects on student learning and achievement are still inconclusive, although there are some indications that these forms of distributed leadership practices are associated with student learning and achievement.

Part B: Key scholars on distributed leadership

Christopher Day

Day has not written substantially on the specific topic of "distributed leadership." First, we used the three articles that had his name and with direct references to the topic. The first two articles (Sammons, Davis, Day, & Gu, 2014, p. 4; Sammons, Gu, Day, & Ko, 2011, p. 2) used a mixed-methods approach starting with the quantitative surveys of 378 primary schools and 362 secondary schools in England, followed by 20 case studies reported in the third paper (Sammons et al., 2011, p. 97). Data analyses adopted confirmatory factor analysis and structural equation models. The first paper reported that school leadership has an indirect impact on student learning, while the second paper gave evidence that school leadership can influence school improvements and student learning. The latter paper further proposed that some patterns of distributed leadership are more effective than other patterns, while both leadership practices are both focused and distributed in the same school context. However, it has also been found that the levels of leadership distribution can vary from one school to another.

The last article is a review paper (Day & Sammons, 2013) on contemporary studies of school leadership. This specific paper has a section on the distributed type of leadership, which reports that the process by which leadership is distributed in school organizations can influence school improvement and student learning. It has also been reported that the distributed perspectives of leadership practices have their origins in the theories of "distributed cognition" and "activity theory," both of which highlight the constituting elements of leadership studies, such as contexts, agents (tools), and the interactions between subjects and objects in the achievements of their task goals (Day & Sammons, 2013, p. 35). Therefore, the focus of analysis should be on how leadership functions are socially distributed and "stretched" over the work of a number of individuals through the interaction of multiple leaders. This article emphasizes that distributed leadership is an emergent property of a group or network of individuals, in which group members pool their expertise. The article also points out the potential structural, cultural, and micro-political barriers to the implementation of distributed leadership or in constraining or facilitating the intensity of leadership distribution among members in a group or in a school. It has also been pointed out that a coordinated form of distributed leadership may be more effective on student learning compared with other forms.

Peter Gronn

Peter Gronn is one of the few scholars who extensively published original works on distributed leadership (DL) in the last 20 years. The following is an attempt to summarize his major concepts and proposed orientations in the study of leadership in general and distributed leadership practices in schools, in particular, based on his most recent publications.

Changing leadership orientations from positional to distributed leadership practices

First, Gronn reviewed works on leadership studies and found that most works and their orientations focused on a particular form of leadership that is based on positional leaders in hierarchically organized institutions (Gronn, 1999, 2010). The primary interest is on "single-handed leadership" (Gronn, 1999), which is a concentrated and focused type of leadership (Gronn, 2010). This type of study assumes a uni-directional form of relationship between positional leaders and their followers within the organizational structure (Gronn, 1999, p. 58). For Gronn, both transformative and charismatic leadership studies also have their assumptions based on a type of "solo" or "stand-alone" leaders and their positional effects on decision making processes and outcomes (Gronn, 2003a). He observed that this type of leadership and its assumptions are often challenged because of its rigidity in understanding the mutual and reciprocal relationship between positional leaders and their followers and because of its alienation from the practices in real contexts of the institutions that tend to be "interactional" and "collective" (Gronn, 2010). Gronn observed that there exists a trend in which leadership studies shifted from a focused type toward more distributed or dispersed type of leadership practices in institutions, such as schools (Gronn, 2003a), and from a hierarchical approach toward an egalitarian approach in terms of capacity building in institutions (Gronn, 2010).

Gronn's assertions are based on his understanding that these various forms of leadership practices, such as distributed, dispersed, or shared orientations, have their recognition of the constraints in the "leader-follower" versions of leadership practices and their effects on institutional performances. Lately, Gronn criticized the concept of "distributed leadership" and its connotations, arguing that distributed leadership neglects the likelihood that influential individuals work well

16 *Developing curriculum leadership*

"in parallel with the collectives" (Gronn, 2008, p. 152). Based on his field studies in Australian schools, Gronn proposed replacing "distributed leadership" with a "hybrid" view of leadership practices. Such a view encompasses both positional and distributed types of leadership practices in institutions.

Definitions of distributed leadership

Gronn extensively discussed various definitions of "leadership" in his publications. From his publications, we can say that his major preferences have not changed drastically. His quotation from Hosking and Morley (1991, pp. 239–261) succinctly summarizes his view about what leadership should be "a view of leadership as less the property of individuals and more as the contextualized outcome of interactive, rather than unidirectional causal processes" (Gronn, 2002b, p. 444). In other words, he does not see that leadership is "only confined to formal role incumbency, but is emergent work-related influence" (Gronn, 2002a). He further explains in his own words that he is "not in favour of the specific leadership of individual principals or teachers, but for a form of overall organizational leadership grounded in a recognition of distributed intelligence" (Gronn, 2001, p. 411). He specifically defines "leadership" as "a status ascribed to individual, an aggregation of separate individuals, sets of small numbers of individuals acting in concert or larger plural-member organizational units" (Gronn, 2002b). He conflates "leadership" with "influence" (Gronn, 2002b), specifically in "mutual reciprocal" interactions. He considers leadership as "a network of mutual dependent relationship" (Gronn, 2003a, p. 30).

To summarize, Gronn does not see "leadership" as the sole property of individuals or the privilege of positional leaders but as various forms of human relationship realized in workplaces. These forms are characterized by their degree of mutual dependency among members of the workplaces. He specifically conflates leadership with influence. In other words, individuals with or without formally appointed roles in leadership positions in the organizational structures of workplaces or institutions could assert various types of "influences" in the completion of tasks in dyads, groups, or teams.

From a distributed to a hybrid leadership

Gronn has written specifically about "distributed" leadership. As he considers "leadership" as various forms of "influences" ascribed to individuals and aggregates by members of the workplaces or institutions regardless of their formal and informal institutional status rather than instructions from positional leaders (leader-follower relationship), "distributed leadership" is defined as "the demonstrated or presumed structuring influence attributable to organization members acting in concert" (Gronn, 2002a, p. 679). In other words, "distributed leadership" is about patterns of how leadership practices are realized among members regardless of their formal positional roles in their workplaces or institutions. Gronn considers "distributed leadership" as follows: "community influence was dispersed amongst a number of influential groups rather than concentrated in one small elite and from time to time, was expressed directly and indirectly by elite and sub-elite power groups" (Gronn, 2003b, p. 275).

Distributed leadership has two forms: numerically multiple actions of individuals, groups, or units and concerted actions. Gronn views the second one as a conjoint agency that emphasizes the mutual interdependence and coordination (interpersonal reciprocal influential synergy) among members (Gronn, 2003a, p. 43).

Gronn identifies two properties in distributed leadership practices. The first property is the interdependence among members or among units or departments in a workplace or institution (Gronn, 2003b). The second property is coordination, which has three categories (Gronn, 2002b). Moreover, he proposes three forms of coordination among members. First, the nature of coordination emerges from the spontaneity of the needs embedded in the context of workplaces. Second, the further development of coordination in dyads or groups or teams continues to mature into a state, whereas coordination becomes "intuitive" and work patterns become internalized among members. Third, coordination further develops and work patterns become institutionalized (Gronn, 2003a).

He further argues that units of analysis should be about the relationship among members in a dynamic unit and the patterns of correlation across its elements (Gronn, 2009, p. 390).

However, his reservation about the future of distributed leadership remains heavily on the possible exclusion of personal influence from individual positional leaders in a workplace or institution. He argues that the continuum between concentrated leadership and distributed leadership should be replaced by the notion of a "hybrid leadership," which is inclusive of a wide range of leadership practices from heroic toward democratic leadership (Gronn, 2008, p. 152).

He has also co-authored journal papers that examined team-level leadership development and practices (Day, Gronn, & Salas, 2004). These studies, although situated in the contexts of medical professions in hospitals, have illustrated the basic arguments of Gronn in distributed leadership. The importance of these empirical studies on teams in our understanding of distributed leadership practice is the positive effects of formal leaders' communications styles and beliefs about leadership functions in team performance and team capacity building. Openness, expecting changes, and fallibility of leaders are essential in fostering conditions conducive to the emergence of leadership practices from team members. However, the team processes and outcomes are far from being simply a result of the deliberation of formally designed leaders as they are the result of collective leadership practices as mutual and reciprocal social influence in team interactions. The frequency and multiplicity of "influence" realized in the patterns of role sharing, networking, and consensus decision making account for team capacity building, team processes, and team outcomes. Sampling a sufficient number of teams is a key issue in future empirical studies (Day, Gronn, & Salas, 2004, p. 870).

Summary

Gronn argues that interest in distributed leadership is derived from the inadequacy of leadership models that focus on single leaders in workplaces and institutions.

18   *Developing curriculum leadership*

He observes that leadership practices are much more diverse in forms and in sources regardless of members' formal and informal roles in the hierarchy of the organization. If the leadership functions are dispersed or distributed, the work performance of the units or the organizations will be more effective (Gronn, 2008, p. 571). Gronn identifies two essential elements in distributed leadership, namely, mutual interdependence and forms of coordination. He further proposes two forms of distributed leadership based on these two elements: numerical action of separate units and concerted action among members in units and groups. However, he considers distributed leadership an inadequate model and proposes a hybrid form of leadership practices that includes both focused and distributed forms of leadership practices in workplaces and institutions.

Philip Hallinger

The publications of Philip Hallinger cover a wide range of topics within the domain of leadership studies and school management. Recently, his work has been extended to investigating the qualities and orientations of reviews of research publications in the field of school leadership and administration. However, he seems to be more interested in establishing the relationship between leadership and student learning. Our focus here is on his publications directly related to studies on distributed leadership.

On distributed leadership studies

Hallinger's publications on distributed leadership indicate that his definition of distributed leadership is a more encompassing one as it includes "shared" and "collective" leadership (Hallinger & Heck, 2009, 2010a). Leadership covers responsibilities in developing a vision for change among members in the community, in bringing about more involvements of community members in decision making (his understanding of distributed leadership), and in creating conditions that support teaching and learning (Heck & Hallinger, 2010). In other words, his understanding of leadership is based on various forms of leadership practices and their relationship with their actions and practices in the creation of structurally and socio-cultural processes for enhancement of student learning (Heck & Hallinger, 2010, p. 879).

His methods were quantitative and longitudinal. His investigations focused on teacher perceptions through surveys in large school cohorts (197 elementary schools in 2010 and 200 elementary schools in 2009) in the United States (Hallinger & Heck, 2009; Heck & Hallinger, 2010). Data analyses adopted multilevel latent change analysis and multilevel analysis on nested data.

The major findings show that changes in leadership distribution contributes to growth in student learning in reading and math. Moreover, distributed leadership affects schools' broader capacity for improvement (Hallinger & Heck, 2010c). His studies also attempted to investigate different models of relationship between leadership and student learning. The models of interaction include the "direct effects model," "mediated effects model," "reversed mediated effects model," and "reciprocal effects model" (Hallinger & Heck, 2010b). He found that distributed leadership "forged and sustained professional interactions among staff across programs and organizational units" (Lee, Hallinger, & Walker, 2012, p. 665). For Hallinger, leadership practices are also reciprocal processes (Heck & Hallinger, 2010, p. 879). However, the nature of the distribution of collaborative leadership varied across different schools (Hallinger & Heck, 2010b, p. 672).

On the critical analysis of reviews

Hallinger's recent contribution to leadership studies includes his critical analysis of research reviews on leadership in eight core international journals in the field (Hallinger & Bryant, 2013; Hallinger & Chen, 2015). Two major findings can be derived from these studies. The first finding involves the publications in Asia from 1995 to 2012. Most of these publications in the field of leadership and educational management came from East Asia, mainly from Hong Kong and Singapore, although most of these publications emerged in the last few years in these eight core international journals with high impact on the knowledge base of educational leadership and management (Hallinger & Chen, 2015; Szeto et al., 2015). The second finding is that "leadership for learning is both mediated and shaped by the school's academic capacity" (Hallinger, 2011). These studies also indicate that broadening the sources of leadership within the school is essential to school improvement, and what is important is that leadership practices are "mutual influence processes" (Hallinger, 2011, p. 136).

Although the increasing number of publications on leadership studies and school administration in Asia adopted mixed methods of quantitative and qualitative approaches in empirical studies, the knowledge base on leadership studies and educational administration based on empirical studies remained comparatively small in comparison with the total number of articles published in this period. Hallinger proposed a conceptual framework for the conduct of reviews in the literature. The framework includes thorough reviews on research topics, theory building and perspectives, sources of data collection, types of data analysis, and nature of results and contributions (Hallinger, 2013a).

Although Hallinger's analysis of the 40 reviews does not aim at distributed leadership, the findings and discussions about the articles have implications for our understanding of distributed leadership and its practices. First, the findings show that contextual factors do affect leadership practice and their inter-relationship is mutual rather than hierarchical (Hallinger, 2011). Second, the relationship between leadership and contexts is a process of mutual influence (Hallinger, 2013b).

In summary, Hallinger's contribution to distributed leadership is the analysis of longitudinal quantitative data based on a large number of elementary schools in the United States, and the findings show that changes in distributed leadership is positively related to the growth of student learning. Moreover, as indicated in his analysis of reviews in the past 52 years, leadership practices are mutually influential processes within the school context.

20 *Developing curriculum leadership*

Alma Harris

Harris did not conduct empirical studies on distributed leadership although she published papers on the topic. From time to time, she would review current literature and studies on the topic. In what follows, we present her four articles related to distributed leadership.

Harris observed that the trend of studying leadership has moved from a focused form of positional leadership to an interactive pattern of situated leadership practices in contexts (Harris, 2008). Leadership practices widely distributed among members in organizations have a positive influence on teacher effectiveness and student engagement (Harris, 2012). She expressed her concerns about the concept of distributed leadership, which has been used and understood quite loosely in research. The concept has been taken as the equivalent of shared leadership, participative leadership, and collaborative leadership. She observed that the concept of distributed leadership has been widely adopted and implemented in Western countries, such as the United States, the United Kingdom, the Netherlands, and the Scandinavian countries (Harris, 2012). She also discovered the dissemination of the concept in East Asia, such as in Hong Kong. She commented that the concept of distributed leadership has been used in opposition to the hierarchical model of leadership practice with positional leaders as the major sources of influence and power (Harris, 2012).

Harris argues that studies on leadership practices should focus on patterns of leadership distribution in the organization and on how these various patterns affect organizational improvement and student learning (Harris, 2010). In other words, the relationship between positional leaders and informal leaders is a focal point of concern. The question remains of how positional leaders with formal power and influence adopt a leadership approach to enable members to take up informal leadership roles and of how their power and influence should be shared. In this way, leadership practices are considered a constitutive part of the interactions in teams or in groups vertically or laterally formed with the specific leadership functions to be achieved (Harris, 2012, 2013, 2014).

James P. Spillane

James P. Spillane is one of the key scholars who have engaged actively in the study of leadership practices with a focus on adopting a distributed perspective in the last 15 years.

To Spillane, the majority of studies in the past 30 years has focused on the roles, structures, and effectiveness of positional leaders, such as principals or unit heads, in institutions including schools. Studies of this kind have not captured the essence of leadership, which is defined as "a social influence relationship or an influence interaction" (Spillane, 2005, p. 384; Spillane & Zuberi, 2009, p. 379) in an institution. He considers school leadership as activities that involve "identification, acquisition, allocation, and coordination" in the use of "social, material and cultural resources" to "establish the conditions for the possibility of teaching and learning" (Spillane, Halverson, & Diamond, 2004, p. 11).

He argues that one major aspect of work in leadership theory building that has been neglected is the consideration of leadership as practices that extend beyond "leaders" to cover "followers" and "contexts," particularly their "interdependence" (Spillane et al., 2004, p. 16). Therefore, he contends that "in theory building using a distributed perspective is the development of study operations grounded in empirical work with qualitative and quantitative, in real schools" (Spillane & Healey, 2010, p. 278). In other words, the focus should be on the development of conceptual frameworks that could be operationalized in real contexts with appropriate analytical tools and instruments.

Spillane's interest is in understanding the complexity of leadership practices from a distributed perspective and how they affect teaching and learning in schools. In other words, he considers leadership as practices that involve formally designated leaders and informal leaders who assert "social influences" in interactions in real contexts in schools (Coldren & Spillane, 2007). Spillane perceives leadership as a form of practice that can only be realized in interactions between actors (positional leaders and followers) and situations (contexts) through artifacts (conceptual tools and physical instruments) (Spillane et al., 2004, p. 9).

Theoretically, he has based his work on theories about "distributed cognition" and "socio-cultural activity theory" of Lave and Wenger (1991). These theories are complicated in their original forms. The following is my attempt to outline some key ideas that are relevant to our understanding of their usefulness in Spillane's research based on his own interpretation in his articles. Cognition is a mental activity in the realization of the purposes and goals of the interactions between actors and environments (Spillane et al., 2004, p. 9). Cognition is "distributed" in situations and is socially distributed through people in collective efforts to complete complex tasks (Spillane et al., 2004, p. 9). In these processes and interactions, "artifacts" play a mediational role in enabling, transforming, or constraining the realization of these social activities. These artifacts include language, symbolic instruments, theories of actions, and interpretive schema (Spillane, 2005 p. 384; Spillane et al., 2004, p. 10). Therefore, the unit of analysis lies in the situational interactions among actors in the realization of the purposes and in the enactment of tasks through the use of mediational artifacts (Spillane et al., 2004, p. 14). The focus is on the "reciprocal influence" in the negotiation processes (Spillane et al., 2004, p. 28). Spillane's recent work shows that the structural problems within the schools constrain the extent to which novice principals could implement a distributed perspective toward leadership practice within their school (Spillane, Harris, Jones, & Mertz, 2015, p. 1081).

Spillane's work not only contributes substantially to the theoretical discussions about leadership theories but also to the development, validation, and application of research instruments and research designs in the investigation of leadership practices from a distributed perspective, including the validation of social network survey in the study of "social influence interactions" (Pitts & Spillane, 2009, p. 16), the validation of Leadership Daily Practice Log in the collection of data showing the distribution of "social influence," and "advice seeking" in the interactions among actions in the completion of leadership tasks (Spillane & Zuberi, 2009). Other data collection methods include shadowing, interviews,

22 *Developing curriculum leadership*

and videotaped meetings. Field works have focused on collecting "thick descriptions" of the distributive patterns of leadership practices.

In summary, Spillane extends the traditional approach in the study of leadership from solely focusing on individuals in the institutional hierarchy to the study of leadership practices as forms of human distributed cognition situated in the collective efforts of completing leadership tasks. His work is substantially based on theories of shared cognition and socio-cultural activity theory. Spillane also contributes substantially to empirical field studies on how leadership in the form of "social influence" is realized in the interactions among actors in completing leadership tasks through the mediation of natural and designed artifacts. His work is pioneering in understanding how distributed leadership practices affect instructional improvements and the professional development of teachers in the school context.

Conclusion

The three major reviews (Bennett et al., 2003; Crawford, 2012; Tian et al., 2016) outline the major trends of leadership studies in the past 40 years, from investigations based on concentrated styles of leadership styles to leadership styles of shared, dispersed, and distributed patterns. Tian's review attempts to identify from the literature before 2012 the features of research publications to determine if some evidence exists that the definitions of "distributed leadership" have received some consensus. His observation shows no indication of a universally accepted or received definition of what "distributed leadership" is. Our review here further strengthens this observation. "Distributed leadership" is understood quite diversely. However, the reviewed empirical studies indicate that an expanded version of principal leadership styles from a single positional leader to a collective form of principal leadership has been popular in leadership practices. This condition can be understood as a form of "hybridity" in leadership practices. However, the multiple usages of "distributed leadership" in leadership practices have extended our understanding of leadership as a network of "influence" in contexts, and its effects are mediated by tension among power, control, and autonomy. Another trend in distributed leadership is that it is assumed to play an agential function in empowering and developing leadership among teachers, and in engaging teachers in decision making as a democratic form of organizational structure. A gap is identified among the empirical research studies reviewed so far, that is, how "influence" is negotiated in interactions among formal leaders and "followers," and how the properties of "leadership" emerging from the interactions are still missing substantive evidence in research studies.

Table 2.1 is a summary of the key features of distributed leadership.

Chapter 3 will outline the mechanisms and processes used in a series of redesign curriculum development projects in two primary schools in Hong Kong. Chapter 4 reports our first attempt to organize a curriculum leadership project and its effects on teacher learning. Chapter 5 focuses on the findings in the second action cycle of the project by illustrating the effects of directive and collaborative

Table 2.1 Summary of literature on distributed leadership

	Solo Leadership	*Distributed Leadership*
Leadership	Positional	Delegated, dispersed, inclusive
Influence	Concentrated	Formal leaders and informal with emergent leaders
Leadership style	Hierarchical, authority, distance	Flattened and collaborative
Distribution pattern	Concentrated and uni-directional	Reciprocal and mutually interactive; inter-dependence
Principal leadership	Directive and instructional	Democratic and participatory
Teachers	Followers and passive	Empowered, emergence of leadership properties
Discourse	Restricted	Elaborated with ownership
Student learning	Indirect effect	Indirect but certain forms are more effective
Individual capacity building	Secondary priority	Empowerment
Collective capacity building	Secondary priority	Change agent
Functions	Management and achievement	Change and innovations

Source: Created by author

leadership styles on teacher learning. Although improvements in student learning were observed, they did not appear to be the direct consequence of the leadership styles. Chapters 6 and 7 demonstrate the adoption of a discourse analysis and a quantitative approach to the distribution of participations in meetings. These two methods show us that specific leadership functions in curriculum development and how leadership properties in curriculum emerged or restricted these interactions. Chapter 7 reports another redesign study that used a rotational leadership approach in two action cycles to observe the changes in interactions among members. Collaborative leadership allows greater spaces in participation by members and leadership functions emerged and widely "distributed" among members. Chapter 8 follows the previous report in Chapter 6 but compares the findings on leadership styles and their effects on interactions and distribution patterns of leadership functions among members of the two curriculum development teams. Directive leadership restricts the emergence and distribution of leadership practices whereas collaborative leadership allows leadership functions and practices to be widely dispersed and distributed among members of the curriculum team. Chapter 9 adopts an activity theory approach in analyzing data on the previous redesign projects and shows how communication and leadership

24 *Developing curriculum leadership*

styles mediated the emergence of leadership properties. Discourse analysis on leadership practices among members revealed a list of leadership functions in curriculum development. Chapter 10 continues to adopt an activity theory perspective by using the theory of "expansive cycles" to show how the emergence of innovative ideas and professional discourse was mediated by the political and cultural priorities of the consultant on one side and the teachers on the other side. This piece of microscopic analysis shows us how "political and cultural ideological preferences" embedded in individuals or groups in the team may "mediate" the professional nature of the curriculum development activities. The consultant insisted that curriculum decisions should be based on professional and pedagogical considerations, whereas teachers preferred a pragmatic consideration in decision making. Chapter 11 uses the major themes derived from the literature review in this chapter as a framework of our conclusion, highlighting the major problems and the future of distributed leadership in educational practices in schools.

References

Abrahasen, H., Aas M., & Hellekjaer, G.O. (2015). How do principals make sense of school leadership in Norwegian reorganized leadership teams? *School Leadership and Management, 35*(1), 62–78.

Bennett, N., Wisc, C., Woods, P.A., & Harvey, J.A. (2003). *Distributed leadership: A review of literature (Full Report, National College for School Leadership)*. London: The Open University.

Blitz, M.H., & Modeste, M. (2015). The difference across distributed leadership practices by school position according to the Comprehensive Assessment of Leadership for Learning (CALL). *Leadership and Policy in Schools, 14,* 341–379.

Bunnell, T. (2008). The Yew Chung model of dual culture co-principalship: A unique form of distributed leadership. *International Journal of Leadership in Education, 11*(2), 191–210.

Bush, T., & Glover, D. (2012). Distributed leadership in action: leading high-performing leadership teams in English schools. *School Leadership & Management, 32*(1), 21–36.

Coldren, A.F., & Spillane, J.P. (2007). Making connections to teaching practice: The role of boundary practices in instructional leadership. *Educational Policy, 21*(2), 369–396.

Crawford, M. (2012). Solo and distributed leadership: Definition and dilemmas. *Educational Management Administration & Leadership, 40*(5), 610–620.

Day, C., Hopkins, D., Harris, A., & Ahtaridou, E. (2009). *The impact of school leadership on pupil outcomes: Final report*. Nottingham: University of Nottingham.

Day, C., & Sammons, P. (2013). *Successful leadership: A review of the international literature*. Reading: CfBT Education Trust.

Day, D.V., Gronn, P., & Salas, E. (2004). Leadership capacity in teams. *The Leadership Quarterly, 15*(6), 857–880.

Gronn, P. (1999). Substituting for leadership: The neglected role of the leadership couple. *The Leadership Quarterly, 10*(1), 41–62.

Gronn, P. (2001). Crossing the great divides: Problems of cultural diffusion for leadership in education. *International Journal of Leadership in Education, 4*(4), 401–414.

Gronn, P. (2002a). Distributed leadership. In K. Leithwood & P. Hallinger (Eds.), *Second international handbook of educational leadership and administration* (pp. 653–696). Dordrecht, NL: Kluwer Academic Publishers.

Gronn, P. (2002b). Distributed leadership as a unit of analysis. *The Leadership Quarterly, 13*(4), 423–451.

Gronn, P. (2003a). *The new work of educational leaders: Changing leadership practice in an era of school reform.* London: Paul Chapman.

Gronn, P. (2003b). Leadership: Who needs it? *School Leadership & Management, 23*(3), 267–291.

Gronn, P. (2008). The future of distributed leadership. *Journal of Educational Administration, 46*(2), 141–158.

Gronn, P. (2009). Leadership configurations. *Leadership, 5*(3), 381–394.

Gronn, P. (2010). Leadership: Its genealogy, configuration and trajectory. *Journal of Educational Administration and History, 42*(4), 405–435.

Hairon, S., Goh, J.W.P., & Lin, T.B. (2014). Distributed leadership to support PLCs in Asian pragmatic Singapore schools. *International Journal of Leadership in Education, 17*(3), 370–386.

Hallinger, P. (2011). Leadership for learning: Lessons from 40 years of empirical research. *Journal of Educational Administration, 49*(2), 125–142.

Hallinger, P. (2013a). A conceptual framework for systematic reviews of research in educational leadership and management. *Journal of Educational Administration, 51*(2), 126–149.

Hallinger, P. (2013b). Reviewing reviews of research in educational leadership: An empirical assessment. *Educational Administration Quarterly, 50*(4), 539–576.

Hallinger, P., & Bryant, D.A. (2013). Accelerating knowledge production on educational leadership and management in East Asia: A strategic analysis. *School Leadership & Management, 33*(3), 202–223.

Hallinger, P., & Chen, J. (2015). Review of research on educational leadership and management in Asia: A comparative analysis of research topics and methods, 1995–2012. *Educational Management Administration & Leadership, 43*(1), 5–27.

Hallinger, P., & Heck, R.H. (2010a). Collaborative leadership and effects on school improvement. *The Elementary School Journal, 111*(2), 226–252.

Hallinger, P., & Heck, R.H. (2010b). Collaborative leadership and school improvement: Understanding the impact on school capacity and student learning. *School Leadership & Management, 30*(2), 295–110.

Hallinger, P., & Heck, R.H. (2010c). Leadership for learning: Does collective leadership make a difference in school improvement? *Educational Management, Administration & Leadership, 38*(6), 654–678.

Harris, A. (2008). Distributed leadership: What we know? *Journal of Educational Administration, 46*(2), 172–188.

Harris, A. (2010). Distributed leadership: Evidence and implications. In T. Bush, L. Bell, & D. Middlewood (Eds.), *The principles of educational leadership & management* (2nd ed., pp. 55–69). London: Sage.

Harris, A. (2012). Distributed leadership: Implications for the role of the principal. *Journal of Management Development, 31*(1), 7–17.

Harris, A. (2013). Distributed leadership: Friend or foe? *Educational Management Administration & Leadership, 41*(5), 545–554.

Harris, A. (2014). *Distributed leadership matters: Perspectives, practicalities, and potential.* Thousand Oaks, CA: Corwin.

26 Developing curriculum leadership

Hartley, D. (2010). Paradigms: How far does research in distributed leadership "Stretch"? *Educational Management Administration & Leadership, 38*(3), 271–285.

Heck, R.H., & Hallinger, P. (2010). Testing a longitudinal model of distributed leadership effects on school improvement. *The Leadership Quarterly, 21*(5), 867–885.

Hosking, D.M., & Morley, I.E. (1991). *A social psychology of organizing: People, processes and contexts.* New York: Prentice Hall.

Hulpia, H., Devos, G., & Keer, H.V. (2011). The relation between school leadership from a distributed perspective and teachers' organizational commitment examining the source of the leadership function. *Educational Administration Quarterly, 47*(5), 728–771. doi: 10.1177/0013161X11402065.

Klar, H.W. (2012). Fostering distributed instructional leadership: A sociocultural perspective of leadership development in urban high schools. *Leadership and Policy in Schools, 11,* 365–390.

Klar, H.W., Huggins, K.S., Hammons, H.L., & Buskey, F.C. (2016). Fostering the capacity for distributed leadership: A post-heroic approach to leading school improvement. *International Journal of Leadership in Education, 19*(2), 111–137.

Lamby, J. (2013). Distributed leadership: The uses and abuses of power. *Educational Management Administration & Leadership, 41*(5), 581–597.

Larsen, C., & Rieckhoff, B.S. (2014). Distributed leadership: Principals describe shared roles in a PDS. *International Journal of Leadership in Education, 17*(3), 304–326.

Lave, J., & Wenger, E. (1991). *Situated learning: Legitimate peripheral participation.* New York: Cambridge University Press.

Lee, M., Hallinger, P., & Walker, A. (2012). A distributed perspective on instructional leadership in International Baccalaureate (IB) schools. *Educational Administration Quarterly, 48*(4), 664–698.

Leithwood, K., & Mascall, B. (2008). Collective leadership effects on student achievement. *Educational Administration Quarterly, 44*(4), 529–561.

Lilijenberg, M. (2015). Distributing leadership to establish developing and learning school organizations in the Swedish context. *Educational Management Administration & Leadership, 43*(1), 152–170.

Lima, J.A.D. (2008). Department networks and distributed leadership in schools. *School Leadership and Management, 28*(2), 159–187.

MacBeath, J. (2005). Leadership as distributed: a matter of practice. *School Leadership and Management, 25*(4), 349–366.

Mayrowetz, D. (2008). Making sense of distributed leadership: Exploring the multiple usages of the concept in the field. *Educational Administration Quarterly, 44*(3), 424–435.

Melville, W., Jones, D., & Campbell, T. (2014). Distributed leadership with the aim of 'recruiting': A departmental case study. *School Leadership & Management, 34*(3), 237–254.

Mifsud, D. (2015). Distributed leadership in a Maltese college: The voices of those among whom leadership is 'distributed' and who concurrently narrate themselves as leadership 'distributors'. *International Journal of Leadership in Education, 1*–27. doi: 10.1080/13603124.2015.1018335.

Mullick, J., Sharma, U., & Deppeler, J. (2013). School teachers' perception about distributed leadership practices for inclusive education in primary schools in Bangladesh. *School Leadership & Management, 33*(2), 151–168.

Ozdemir, M., & Eemircioglue, E. (2015). Distributed leadership and contract relations: Evidence from Turkish high schools. *Education Management Administration & Leadership*, 43(6), 918–938.

Park, V., & Datnow, A. (2009). Co-constructing distributed leadership: District and school connections in data-driven decision making. *School Leadership and Management*, 29(5), 477–494.

Piot, L., & Kelchtermans, G. (2015). The micropolitics of distributed leadership: Four case studies of school federations. *Educational Management Administration & Leadership*, 44(4), 632–649. doi: 10.1177/1741143214559224.

Pitts, V.M., & Spillane, J.P. (2009). Using social network methods to study school leadership. *International Journal of Research & Method in Education*, 32(2), 185–207.

Ritchie, R., & Woods, P.A. (2007). Degrees of distribution: Towards an understanding of variations in the nature of distributed leadership in schools. *School Leadership and Management*, 27(4), 363–381.

Robinson, V.M.J. (2008). Forging the links between distributed leadership and educational outcomes. *Journal of Educational Administration*, 46(2), 241–256.

Sammons, P., Davis, S., Day, C., & Gu, Q. (2014). Using mixed methods to investigate school improvement and the role of leadership: An example of a longitudinal study in England. *Journal of Educational Administration*, 52(5), 565–589.

Sammons, P., Gu, Q., Day, C., & Ko, J. (2011). Exploring the impact of school leadership on pupil outcomes: Results from a study of academically improved and effective schools in England. *International Journal of Educational Management*, 25(1), 83–101.

Spillane, J.P. (2005). Primary school leadership practice: How the subject matters. *School Leadership and Management*, 25(4), 383–397.

Spillane, J.P., Halverson, R., & Diamond, J.B. (2004). Towards a theory of leadership practice: A distributed perspective. *Journal of Curriculum Studies*, 36(1), 3–34.

Spillane, J.P., Harris, A., Jones, M., & Mertz, K. (2015). Opportunities and challenges for taking a distributed perspective: Novice school principals' emerging sense of their new position. *British Educational Research Journal*, 41(6), 1068–1085.

Spillane, J.P., & Healey, K. (2010). Conceptualizing school leadership and management from a distributed perspective. *The Elementary School Journal*, 111(2), 253–281.

Spillane, J.P., & Zuberi, A. (2009). Designing and piloting a leadership daily practice log using logs to study the practice of leadership. *Educational Administration Quarterly*, 45(3), 375–423.

Storey, A. (2004). The problem of distributed leadership in schools. *School Leadership & Management*, 24(3), 249–265.

Stoten, D.W. (2015). Distributing leadership in English Sixth Form Colleges: Liberation or another form of managerial control? *International Journal of Educational Management*, 29(5), 522–538.

Tian, M., Risku, M., & Collin, K. (2016). A meta-analysis of distributed leadership from 2002 to 2013: Theory development, empirical evidence and future research focus. *Education Management Administration Leadership*, 44(1), 146–164.

Torrance, D. (2013). Distributed leadership: Challenging five generally held assumptions. *School Leadership & Management*, 33(4), 354–372.

Townsend, A. (2015). Leading school networks: Hybrid leadership in action? *Educational Management Administration & Leadership*, 43(5), 719–737.

Tubin, D., & Pinyan-Weiss, M. (2015). Distributing positive leadership: The case of team counseling. *Educational Management Administration & Leadership*, *43*(4), 507–525.

Woods, P.A., & Roberts, A. (2016). Distributed leadership and social justice: Images and meanings from across the school landscape. *International Journal of Leadership in Education*, *19*(2), 138–156.

Yuen, J.H.P., Chen, D-T.V., & Ng, D. (2015). Distributed leadership through the lens of activity theory. *Educational Management Administration & Leadership*, *44*(5), 814–836. doi: 10.1177/1741143215570302.

3 Initiating, designing, and enacting curriculum innovations[1]

Procedures and processes

Background

The educational system of Hong Kong is among the few educational systems in the world that demonstrate a range of features characterizing efficient organizations. A 2010 study highlighted six factors that account for the success of an educational system. This chapter concentrates on the processes and the organizational features that "perpetuate innovative practices" at the school level (Law, 2015). This chapter based its report on a series of design-based studies led by the author in the last 10 years. Such studies aimed to uncover key organizational features that are likely to enhance opportunities that generate new and innovative ideas in pedagogical change at the school and classroom levels (Law, 2011; Law, Galton, & Wan, 2007; Law & Wan, 2006; Law, Wan, Galton, & Lee, 2010). The said studies present a background on key policy changes in engineering new pedagogical roles and identities for teachers in the last 30 years in Hong Kong.

Policy changes often consider the possibility that implementing policies while faithfully adhering to their intentions is unlikely. This situation occurred specifically in educational reforms in the 1960s when central curriculum agencies initiated and designed large-scale educational reforms. However, these policies encountered resistance from schoolteachers. Reflections on strategies led to the belief that change is a highly contextualized and situated social phenomenon, which is brought about by a network of agencies within the social context wherein change is initiated, developed, and institutionalized.

In 1982, the Llewellyn Report marked a new era in educational change in Hong Kong. In this report, a panel of foreign educational experts led by Llewellyn recommended that roles and identities of teachers must be changed to bring about changes and innovations to the traditional classroom practices of using a transmission model as a major pedagogical strategy (Llewellyn, 1982). As professionals, teachers must assume new responsibilities in making decisions about what the key learning objectives should be and how such objectives can be achieved in practice. Teacher participation in curriculum decision making and design has increased in recent years. Moreover, schools are now expected to play a major role in introducing changes to their traditional culture of being teaching communities, rather than communities of practices, which have the capacity to

30 *Developing curriculum leadership*

generate changes and innovations. Both institutions and individuals are expected to play a role in the change processes and provide mutual support. In case of non-alignment, their internal exclusiveness and conflicts are considered key variables in the successful implementation of changes and innovations.

One key research issue in this study is identifying conditions and processes that engage teachers in professional activities, which provide room wherein new ideas and proposals can be freely developed and determining processes can be applied. What can teachers learn and how can teacher leadership develop in the process of engaging in professional activities at the school-based level? These issues serve as the bases for discussion in the following sections.

Developing teacher curriculum leadership

Two major development projects with similar organization and educational principles were conducted over two periods (2004–2006 and 2007–2008) in two Hong Kong primary schools. These two projects were funded by the Quality Education Fund, which was established by the government in 1998 to support development initiatives and school-based innovations. The projects were designed according to the following contemporary educational principles in human learning.

- Development activities should be school-based, problem-oriented, and focused on pedagogical change and improvement.
- Teacher participants should be collaborative, and the model of power hierarchy, which is typical of Asian culture, should be mediated to an extent that social interactions allow active participation and individual contributions to the completion of the tasks.
- Interactions within teams should be open and reflective.
- Development activities should be organized in phases. The first phase is the planning and initial review of the current curriculum practice in classroom. The second phase is the design and application of concepts in the classrooms. The final phase is carried out by evaluating the actions and practices implemented.
- The development activities should be organized in ways that sustain motivation and momentum of change; these should be spirally and cyclically arranged to engineer and sustain a culture of change and lifelong learning.

The projects, called "Accelerating School-Based Curriculum Development," aimed to develop teacher leadership skills in curriculum planning, designing, and implementing innovations at the classroom level. Three subject-based curriculum development teams in each school were formed. The teams included three key school subjects in Hong Kong, namely, Chinese, English, and mathematics. Each team had around five to six teachers of different grades and experiences. The procedures and steps followed by each team formed a similar pattern that was modeled and modified after the key components in action research and

Engestrom's cycles of expansive learning (Engestrom, 2008). A simplified model is listed below.

Stage one: planning and reviewing

The team sat together and identified a key topic or an issue that the team generally found difficult to teach children. Then, the members shared their common practices and traditional pedagogical strategies in organizing and managing learning activities concerning the topic. Next, the team adopted an approach or strategy that was different from the traditional one. The purpose was to engage all members in a new or innovative alternative that influenced them to reconsider their own approaches and accept risk-taking actions to implement change.

Stage two: implementation and trial

The team designed appropriate strategies and developed a lesson plan to be used for the trial. The members also prepared teaching materials and learning activities that supported the achievements of the learning objectives in the lesson. In Hong Kong, each level has three to four classes of 30 students. Each member of the team was able to teach a class by using the same lesson plan. However, the project purposely arranged for each member to take turns in teaching a class. A time gap was set between the first and second classes and another between the second and third classes. The gaps allowed members to observe lessons and reflect on the approach used during each lesson. Thus, lesson plans were revised to suit the needs of the students according to the idea of each member.

Stage three: reflection

The team recorded all trial lessons and conducted a reflection meeting based on evidence from observations and video-recorded lessons. The purpose was to engage the team in a collective, reflective dialogue, which allowed the team to express diverse views according to commonly shared evidence among team members.

This method is considered essential if the cycle of planning, implementing, and reflecting is repeated with each team in another semester on another topic in the subject curriculum. This condition being so, the team could thus develop self-regulatory patterns of planning, implementing, and reflecting components. Further, established procedure and steps are assumed to generate innovative changes based on traditional patterns of teaching and learning at the classroom level.

Methods of data collection

Data collection methods were multi-targeted and aimed at different types of data for triangulation and crystallization. The methods can be cost-effective if the project could generate more international publications. Therefore, our design

32 *Developing curriculum leadership*

followed a comprehensive approach to cover as many useful data throughout the project as possible. The outline of the key methods at each stage of the procedure is presented below.

Stage one: planning and reviewing

1   Documenting the planning meetings by using a video recorder
2   Collecting lesson plans
3   Interviewing each member
4   Collecting written feedback from members
5   Collecting e-mail communications and feedback from external consultants

Stage two: implementation and trial

1   Recording all lessons by using a video recorder
2   Collecting all discussion notes
3   Interviewing each member
4   Interviewing groups of students
5   Collecting peer observation notes

Stage three: reflection

1   Collecting self-evaluation notes and checklists
2   Documenting the reflection meeting by using a video recorder
3   Interviewing both teachers who conducted the trial lessons and members who conducted the observations

Although the project engaged 13–15 teachers in each of the two schools, the project ultimately aimed to disseminate innovative ideas and practices among teachers of the two schools. Therefore, seminars were organized and presentations of findings were regularly arranged in staff meetings. Feedback was collected from the school community as well. This method sought to enhance the professional commitment of the teachers and professional capacity of the school community as a whole.

Findings

Data obtained from the projects are varied and numerous. In addition, we believe the data serve multiple purposes. At various stages of the project development, researchers employed different theoretical perspectives in understanding and reading the data. For example, the interview data were analyzed from a grounded perspective, whereas interactional data from meetings were analyzed with the use of a discourse approach complemented by additional theoretical perspectives from socio-cultural traditions. The list of findings discussed below do not adhere to a particular dimension in the study. However, the findings focus on the development of distributed leadership among teachers in curriculum development.

At the same time, all data, along with their meanings and implications, were not fully exhausted.

Leadership styles and expanding spaces for teacher learning

The teams in the two schools exhibited different types of interactions based on their leadership styles. The impact of leadership styles is significant because the effectiveness of school-based approach in fostering innovations is one of the positive effects on teacher development and learning. In this study, the two leadership styles do not necessarily have negative connotations from the perspective of the author.

Two types of leadership styles influence the interview data and the interactional patterns of the meetings. These effects led to the qualitatively different distributions of participation among members in the meetings and discussions. Further details on this matter shall be discussed later in the chapter.

The first type of leadership style is the authoritarian and directive style, which is considered typical of Asian societies. The panel chair of the Chinese language team was assertive and consistently reiterated his right to have access to the teaching materials used by other teachers. He gave clear instructions on what to do and how things should be done during the meetings. His language was directive. On the contrary, the panel chair of the mathematics team demonstrated a non-directive style without appearing to be power-coercive. She often adopted a tentative tone in her language and allowed the members more leeway during the discussions. These two contrasting leadership styles were triangulated with patterns of interactions in the meetings, particularly the distribution of communicative acts among members of the team with different positional powers in the social hierarchy of the school. For example, the number of communicative acts was counted against the positional powers of the members. In the authoritarian leadership style, members who were in a higher positional power had more communicative acts, had more time to speak, and made more assertions than those in the lower hierarchy. In comparison, in the open and non-directive leadership style, the number of communicative acts was more evenly distributed among members, and the members participated more actively regardless of their ranks and status.

The interactions among team members were analyzed to demonstrate the nature of the contributions and participations. For example, the number of initiations and responses among members comprised the essential elements in our analyses. Under a more assertive leadership style, initiations were restricted to a few members of the team who had more positional power and higher status. The non-directive style allowed more interactions among members, and initiations were more evenly distributed among all the members regardless of rank and status.

The impact of the two contrasting leadership styles on the distribution and the nature of participations in the interactions are significant to our argument on the effectiveness of using school-based curriculum development as an instrument for engineering changes in teacher professionalism. Constraints were identified in the interactions under the assertive and authoritarian leadership style (see Table 3.1). Participations were restricted, and initiations were limited

34 *Developing curriculum leadership*

Table 3.1 Characteristics of leadership styles and their impacts on team interactions

	Subject Team Chinese	*Subject Team Math*
Leadership style	Dominated	Distributed
Mediating factors	Assertive panel head	Less assertive panel head
	Didactic consultant	Facilitating consultant
Effects	Less team spirit	Stronger team spirit
	Resentment within team	Collaboration within team
Discourse style	Closed and informative	Open and exploratory
	Less interactive	More interactive
Participation style	Dominated by positional leadership	Multidirectional interactions
Teacher learning	Modeling and subservient	Engagement and decision making

Source: Law, E.H.F. (2014). Initiating change and innovations. In C. Marsh & C.K.L John (Eds.), *Asia's high performing education systems: The case of Hong Kong* (p. 200). New York: Routledge.

to a few members. Meanwhile, non-directive leadership style provided more opportunities for members to participate. This leadership style encouraged members to actively participate in negotiations and to shape final decisions. Thus, the entire process allowed members to be in charge of the discourse and to guide it to their preferred direction. In sum, the first type of participation is more quantitative, whereas the second type is more qualitative. Furthermore, the directive and authoritarian leadership style is close to the Asian model of social hierarchy, whereas the non-directive and participatory model is close to the traditional concept of a school-based curriculum development model (SBCD) (Skilbeck, 1984). The current study does not aim to identify which model is more effective in terms of achieving pedagogical changes in schools. However, the latter model provides teachers more space for decision making than the former one.

Developing teacher curriculum development skills

School-based models of improving teacher skills in the aspect of curriculum development have been proposed for some time. According to a portion of the 1982 Llewellyn Report in Hong Kong, teacher participation in curriculum development would generally enhance teacher professionalism. This idea was recommended against the background of a strong central curriculum agency that provided detailed guidelines for the school curriculum. Such guidelines leave little room for school and teacher autonomy, and prevent them from making decisions regarding curriculum adjustments and pedagogy to benefit individual students. Uniform learning outcomes and learning progression were expected. However, Hong Kong schools offer mixed-ability classes, and Hong Kong has implemented inclusive policies. Therefore, traditional curriculum models cannot accommodate different needs and learning outcomes of students having diverse backgrounds.

In our projects, we perceived various skills that teachers could have acquired while making curriculum decisions at various stages of our model. In the observations and in the interview data, we identified several situational and generic skills that were essential to becoming a leader in curriculum decision making. We argue that making curriculum decisions should be an essential skill for all teachers, particularly when their students have diverse abilities and backgrounds. This topic is in line with the Hong Kong educational policy and matches common understanding of general professional teacher capacity. The skills we identified in our projects in two schools in Hong Kong are presented below. Although they are not different from those used in another system, curriculum skills are greatly diffused among teachers of all grades and status in schools.

1   Teachers experiment with alternative approaches in planning and designing a learning unit. This risk-taking experience is likely to introduce new approaches to the traditional style, which is characterized by stability, in schools.
2   Teachers make decisions regarding new learning objectives aligned with educational reforms on lesson contents and alternative assessment methods. These objectives become part of the responsibilities and daily classroom skills of teachers.
3   In traditional curriculum models, all curriculum materials and progressions are standardized, with uniformity being the norm. During the projects, teachers were encouraged to adopt an alternative approach in designing and selecting curriculum contents to suit student needs. The task was not easy and required substantial experience from each team member.
4   Adjusting curriculum experiences according to the needs of the students is a tremendous responsibility for teachers of a class with more than 30 students. Unlike class sizes of around 20 or 25, which are common in other countries, a large class size prevents teachers from developing a more interactive teaching style.
5   In the projects, teachers adopt a more systematic model, which involves planning and reviewing, designing and implementing, and reflecting on practical experiences. Generating new ideas and alternatives as well as testing innovations are not innate to every teacher. This self-regulatory procedure of generating innovations and reflecting on actions enhances teachers' level of professionalism in general.

Situational and deep learning

One argument for school-based models for developing teacher professionalism is the practical and situational nature of the changes and innovations that are planned, reviewed, designed, and implemented directly by the teachers with pragmatic orientation in teams (Glazer, & Hannafin, 2006; ten Dam & Blom, 2006). The developmental nature of such experiences challenges and raises issues concerning traditional practices and beliefs, which are deeply rooted in actions and current practices. Traditional beliefs and practices do not necessarily have a

36 *Developing curriculum leadership*

negative effect on current reforms nor do they deserve to be ignored by practitioners. However, the current study is mainly concerned with introducing new ideas and innovative practices to classrooms, institutionalizing new ideas and practices within the current school infrastructure, and establishing a mechanism for generating innovative ideas within school boundaries.

One of the basic underlying principles of our projects is to establish cycles of learning and models of planning, implementing, and reflecting on changes and innovations in teams. Thus, teachers are engaged in a series of developmental but professional activities that result in changes and a new curriculum. The processes are intended to be creative; hence, teachers should no longer be mere curriculum users or consumers of ready-made or teacher-proof curriculum materials. Instead, the processes allow participants to negotiate a new learning unit, which is the outcome of the effort and collaboration of the teams. The new experiences were exploratory and have become part of real-life experiences of teachers on the team. In the interviews, the teachers indicated that they learned a great deal from the project and that their beliefs were challenged. New ideas that came about through actions and practices were incorporated with their beliefs, which in turn, guided participant actions. Reflective statements from teachers in the interviews, such as ". . . but now we adapted, revised, discussed, I think good, teach lively and not blindly" and ". . . teachers should abandon our traditional perspectives . . ." prove that their new experiences contrasted their traditional practices and beliefs. However, we have no further evidence that these new practices have long-term significance and impact on the future professional actions of these teachers.

Furthermore, the learning experience was exploratory and was, at times, a personal and professional experience wherein participating teachers discovered something new. Discovery is essential because the process may pave the way for new learning and allow teachers to cultivate a new professional identity and responsibility. In the traditional curriculum, uniformity in terms of learning objectives, progressions, and outcomes is expected and embedded. Teachers rarely adjust their educational strategies to suit diverse student needs. However, in a curriculum that emphasizes learning generic skills and competencies rather than the amount of knowledge gained, teachers instantly adjust their educational strategies to suit the social or psychological needs of students. Teacher statements during interviews, such as ". . . our classes used different methods and we thought it was impossible and would waste our time . . . however, we found that we could do different things in different ability classes . . ." show that the introduction of new teaching styles has significant impact on student learning. Indeed, teachers felt excitement upon experiencing new ways of seeing, feeling, and learning professional alternatives or decisions that were applied along with their effects on student learning. The overall experience was a reward for their attempts to revitalize classroom learning.

Discussion and future research

School-based curriculum development is a major change strategy conceptualized in the Western literature, particularly in Anglo-Saxon traditions. This endeavor has experiential bases in practice and in the cultural milieu of the school context in the 1970s. At that time, school-based curriculum development was conceptualized as a cluster of school-based initiatives led either by teachers or by school institutions, and were embedded in the democratic beliefs and powerful functions of the active participation of the practitioners in curriculum decision making relevant to enhancing student learning. Skilbeck's SBCD model was based on a pragmatic approach to adopt a problem-oriented strategy in teacher participation, which presumably enabled participants to focus on tasks relevant to student learning. His theoretical approach and practical SBCD model were modeled on an action research approach (McKernan, 2013). The model consisted of the following key steps: identifying key problems, designing solutions, testing feasibility and viability, and finally conducting a series of reflections for improvements in the next cycle of development work.

Although the model was considered basic, the proposal was considered a breakthrough in the conceptualization of how a school-based model can work in its early stage of development and dissemination. At that time, teachers and schools were still very much accustomed to the curriculum guidelines, which were mostly initiated and developed by central curriculum agencies in the 1960s. As a major change initiative in the late 90s, the adoption of SBCD in many Asian countries, such as Mainland China, Taiwan, South Korea, Singapore, and Hong Kong, has not deviated much from its original conception and its practical model originally generated by Skilbeck (1984). The problems involved in implementing a practical model were derived from participatory democratic tradition in Asian countries heavily influenced by cultures that respect seniority and hierarchy. In addition, the implementation raised fundamental issues about social theories of change and the various ways by which innovations could be initiated, generated, developed, accepted, and institutionalized in countries with very different cultural contexts (Kennedy, 2011).

Various studies have attempted to bring new information and experiences into our understanding of the nature of these issues. Such studies sought to establish several grounds in further developing a theoretical framework and a practical model in key East Asian countries with common cultural traditions amidst obvious diversity in language, population, and geographical locations (Lee, 2009). The following are key elements to the establishment and development of such common understanding on a culturally viable model of SBCD that can help generate, develop, design, and implement innovations and changes at the school level.

Leadership is a key consideration in curriculum development teams. Based on research data and experiences extracted from our design-based projects, rotational leadership – from positional leaders to teacher leaders as a form of distributed leadership – should be viable in Asian countries given the practical experience and administrative abilities of the leaders in the hierarchy. However, this form of leadership should be considered both the initial step in fostering team spirit and a preliminary step in developing a culture of generating changes. Much relies heavily on the second and the third steps to sustain the change in momentum. The first step is the development of an infrastructure and a pattern of procedures that

38   *Developing curriculum leadership*

facilitate discussions and allow testing of new ideas. Furthermore, this task is an important step in establishing a basic understanding of the framework of practice to be led by another participant, presumably by an experienced teacher without positional power. With a less dominant leadership style, this step facilitates a more open discourse and communication network.

In addition, people are encouraged to participate actively because of blurred leadership; thus, the distribution of participation in discussions and in decision making can be made possible. Therefore, a distributed form of leadership will emerge. Participant initiatives will occupy the discussions, and the adoption of a particular line of thought will be based on a rational model rather than a positional model if the team has a clear positional leader. Then, the third step of moving the leadership role to an inexperienced teacher in the team is most essential because through rounds of planning, generating new ideas, designing unit plans and lesson plans, application in classes, and conducting evaluations and reflection meetings, the inexperienced teacher will become familiar with the basic structure and organization of the innovation as well as the requirements and qualities of a leader who will facilitate discussions. Such "transformation" would encourage active participation among the members in the process of developing a new student curriculum. The completion of the cycle and its duty to the whole school community to cultivate a sense of change is essential; hence, it must be carefully planned and organized with the support of the school administration. Eventually, the cycled repetition of the same procedures and requirements could help establish an infrastructure of change and innovation in the school community. Moreover, each teacher should be expected to participate in the whole process at least twice a year.

The second component is the partnership with university faculties. Our research experience and data show that university faculties stimulate thinking and raise ideas and issues in the educational world with a global nature. School communities focus on practices, and in many cases, neglect attention to development activities in favor of good examination results. This adherence to test results is a response to parental pressures and public accountability to external reviews imposed as a quality assurance mechanism in many countries. Constant new inputs from various information sources and new ideas should become a sustainable feature of development action plans within the school infrastructure. These new ideas and inputs should then be part of the planning and reviewing stage of each cycle of the curriculum development actions. The goal is to ensure that innovation plans are closely aligned with best current practices and are supported by sound educational principles found in the literature in education and curriculum.

The third component is the institutionalization of good practices as well as an infrastructure and organization that work well with the school in generating pedagogical innovations with clear evidence of achievements in student learning and teacher learning. This component is the most essential step in completing the cycle of transforming the school culture into one that can generate novel ideas and practices by itself. Institutionalization means adopting new practices as a permanent and sustainable component of the organic whole of the school community. Designing such a component is not an easy task and requires incisive school leadership that is committed to changing the current traditional practices, thereby creating a new community culture. This new culture aims at generating innovations, designing actions to implement innovations, and evaluating and reflecting on evidence of innovative achievements.

Conclusion

This chapter outlined key features of a series of design-based research studies in our attempt to uncover key issues in adopting a school-based approach in developing innovative practices in schools in Hong Kong. The original model was based on a participatory democratic tradition, which placed value on the rights of every teacher in making decisions. However, such a model encountered resistance when implemented in East Asian countries that value teacher seniority and status. Based on research, this chapter provided evidence that a form of rotational leadership in which positional leaders and potential teacher leaders take part in a series of cyclical actions (including planning and reviewing the current practices, designing and applying innovations, and finally evaluating and reflecting on effectiveness of the innovations) is preferable to a leadership model based either on Western democratic traditions or on Eastern hierarchical traditions. Overall, our research experience shows that a combination of both is likely to bring changes to the school community, and that the proposed rotational leadership and infrastructure of a cyclical model can provide schools and their communities with a model of sustainable change.

Note

1 Another version of this chapter has appeared in Marsh, C., & Lee, J.C.K. (Eds.). (2014). *Asia's high performing education systems: The case of Hong Kong* (pp. 195–206). New York: Routledge.

References

Dam, G.T., & Blom, S. (2006). Learning through participation: The potential of school-based teacher education for developing a professional identity. *Teaching and Teacher Education, 22*(6), 647–660.

Engestrom, Y. (2008). *From teams to knots: Activity-theoretical studies of collaboration and learning at work.* Cambridge: Cambridge University Press.

Glazer, E.M., & Hannafin, M.J. (2006). The collaborative apprenticeship model: Situated professional development within school settings. *Teaching and Teacher Education, 22*(2), 179–193.

Kennedy, K. (2011). Transformational issues in curriculum reform: Perspectives from Hong Kong. *Journal of Textbook Research, 4*(1), 87–113.

Law, E.H.F. (2011). Exploring the role of leadership in facilitating teacher learning in Hong Kong. *School Leadership & Management, 31*(4), 393–410.

40   *Developing curriculum leadership*

Law, E.H.F. (2015). In search of a diverse curriculum in the making of a postmodernist Hong Kong in the 21st century. In W. Pinar (Ed.), *International handbook of curriculum research* (pp. 217–226). New York: Routledge.

Law, E.H.F., Galton, M., & Wan, S.W.Y. (2007). Developing curriculum leadership in schools: Hong Kong perspectives. *Asia-Pacific Journal of Teacher Education, 35*(2), 143–159.

Law, E.H.F., & Wan, S.W.Y. (2006). Developing curriculum leadership in a primary school: A Hong Kong case study. *Curriculum and Teaching, 21*(2), 61–90.

Law, E.H.F., Wan, S.W.Y., Galton, M., & Lee, J.C.K. (2010). Managing school-based curriculum innovations: A Hong Kong case study. *Curriculum Journal, 21*(3), 313–332.

Lee, J.C.K. (2009). The landscape of curriculum studies in Hong Kong from 1980–2008: A review. *Educational Research Journal, 24*(1), 95–133.

Llewellyn, J. (1982). *A perspective on education in Hong Kong.* Hong Kong: Government Printer.

McKernan, J. (2013). *Curriculum action research: A handbook of methods and resources for the reflective practitioner.* Kindle Edition. New York: Routledge.

Skilbeck, M. (1984). *School based curriculum development.* London: Harper & Row.

Section 2

Case studies of curriculum leadership development teams

4 Developing curriculum leadership in a primary school[1]

Context of curriculum change in Hong Kong

The call for involving school teachers in curriculum development as part of a decentralizing process has a long history in the highly centralized system of education in Hong Kong (Board of Education, 1997; Curriculum Development Council, 2001; Education Commission, 2000; Law, 2003; Llewellyn, 1982). Until 2002, the degree of teacher participation as well as the roles and the types of teacher decision making in curriculum planning and design activities outlined in various policy documents have been vague. Hence, much of the decision has been left to the deliberation of the heads of schools, the heads of subject departments, or to the personal initiatives and commitments of the teachers in many cases; however, teacher participation has generally received a certain form of consensus among policy makers and school educators (Law & Galton, 2004; Lee & Dimmock, 1999).

The year 2002 was considered a turning point. That year, the government took the policy initiative of "institutionalizing" curriculum decision making processes as one of the core professional activities within the school-based curriculum development. In relation to this, a senior post with key responsibilities of planning, reviewing, designing, and evaluating curriculum decisions and practices has been established for over 800 primary schools; however, the actual interplay between the curriculum coordinator and various situational factors varies from school to school (Education Department, 2002). The project reported in this paper is part of the curriculum initiatives of the curriculum coordinator who attended a training course commissioned by the government and taught by the first author of this paper.

Curriculum leadership: an international perspective

For many years, scholars have debated the forms and contents of developing the professional knowledge and skills of teachers. The traditional forms of training teachers started in the university faculties and colleges of education. This course-based pattern has received less criticism for the pre-service education of teachers. However, after the centralized curriculum projects failed to have an impact on classroom teachers and the overall teaching culture in the 1970s, the location where the training should be conducted had been intensely discussed.

44 *Case studies: a team approach*

This phenomenon became particularly evident when training took the typical pattern of offering workshops for classroom teachers facilitated by an expert, during which they learned new skills or information that they were expected to implement in their classroom or school. This approach did not produce the desired results because such courses tended to be too theoretical and unrelated to classroom practice. Moreover, these courses had nearly no reference to the needs of a school and its teachers. Therefore, new methods and approaches are needed (Darling-Hammond & McLaughlin, 1995; Sparks, 1994).

In the past years, teacher development has undergone decentralization from central agencies to the periphery, through which schools became the focal point of the professional development of teachers (Bell & Gilbert, 1994; Skilbeck, 1984). This shift, which now included schools as partners in the training of teachers, especially in professionally developing schoolteachers to meet the needs of the contemporary educational and curriculum reforms, has been accompanied by the theoretical argument that curriculum development is impossible without teacher development. This line of argument has evolved such that teachers should assume the role of being researchers to develop their professional abilities and embark on an inquiry- or evidence-based profession (Stenhouse, 1975). Therefore, the professional development of teachers has taken a different perspective, from a model in which teachers presumably assume a passive and inferior position underlying the processes of their university-based training programs and development activities, toward another model in which teachers are expected to assume an active role in action-based activities in various phases of developmental stages. These stages are characterized by their features of being self-critical and reflective in nature within the new tradition of restructuring schools (Carr & Kemmis, 1986; Day, 1993; Elliott, 1991; Fullan, 1993; Schon, 1983). This concept of teacher development within a school-based curriculum development environment has developed further in recent years. As often argued, teachers should assume an even more central and leading role in making curriculum decisions in schools, i.e., curriculum leadership. Curriculum leadership is a loose term that characterizes the above-mentioned changing conception of the role of teachers in curriculum decision making and its practical implications, encompassing a wide range of decision making processes and activities held in schools and classrooms (Loucks-Horsley, 1996). The following quote from a group of Australian curriculum scholars describes the current thinking of many researchers in this new tradition.

> From our perspective, curriculum leadership is a shared phenomenon at a teaching/learning site, and acknowledges the teacher as a curriculum maker, located within a context charged with possibilities for engagement.
>
> (Macpherson & Brooker, 1999, p. 1)

In essence, this concept could be equated with the concept of the changing role of teachers from curriculum users relying heavily on the production of teacher-proof textbooks to autonomous curriculum developers taking initiatives in reviewing, planning, and designing curriculum practices. This re-conceptualization of "leadership" and engaging teachers in the center of school-based curriculum decision making processes is contrary to the conventional perspectives of confining the leadership actions and activities only to those who are charged with official leadership positions within the school hierarchy.

Traditionally, both local and international studies on leadership in the field of education are confined to the investigation of positional roles of key personnel in the organizational structures of the schools, such as school heads, deputy heads, and heads of subject departments; at the same time, previous studies have explored the various ways through which these leaders are able to set the directions for the organizations and exercise influence on colleague and student learning (Fullan, 2002; Glatthorn, 2000; Hitt & Tucker, 2015; Lee & Dimmock, 1999; Leithwood, Louis, Anderson, & Wahlstrom, 2004; Leung, 2002; MacBeath, 1998; Marsh, 1997; Orphanos & Orr, 2014; Telford, 1996). The word "leaders" has been used nearly interchangeably as an equivalent terminology with administrators and personnel who are given formally designated positions in the school structures. Therefore, they are logically expected to play various types of leadership functions, such as transactional or transformational roles, in the management of the schools. However, these studies and development programs on role-based leadership have neglected the essential role of the teachers in making curriculum decisions in relation to teaching and learning within a learning-centered community. In addition, they have implicitly subjugated teachers to an inferior role in curriculum decision making processes. Specifically, teachers are being treated either as mere implementers of the official curriculum guidelines in a centralized model of curriculum decision making in some countries or as mere enactors or followers of the decisions of the school principal and heads of subject departments in a pseudo-decentralized system of curriculum responsibility. In many empirical studies, the high expectations of the "superhero images of leadership do not work," and the effects of the head teacher are usually indirect and minimal (Evers & Lakomski, 1996; Hallinger & Heck, 1996; Sergiovanni, 2001, p. 55).

British scholars on leadership studies have shared a similar view with their Australian counterparts wherein "re-conceptualizing" curriculum leadership is a necessary step to take the studies a step further.

> Leadership is reconceptualized as a set of behaviors and practices that are undertaken collectively. It is suggested that leadership for school improvement is not as a role or function assigned to those only with leadership responsibilities but as a dynamic between individuals within an organization. In this sense, leadership encompasses a broad group of people that contribute to the school's distinctive culture and community.
>
> (Harris, 2003, p. 75)

The broad and inclusive understanding of curriculum leadership as a form of "distributed leadership," which has been outlined briefly in the previous paragraphs, has received recognition from a number of researchers in many developed countries including Australia, the United States, and England. These countries aim

46   *Case studies: a team approach*

to place the teachers in the centrality of curriculum decision making processes in schools in recent years. These studies have also demonstrated that every teacher must take responsibility for providing curriculum leadership (Australian Education Union, 2004; Frost & Durrant, 2002; Macpherson, Aspland, Brooker, & Elliott, 1999; Ovens, 1999; Wallace, Nesbit, & Miller, 1999).

The development project and its preliminary findings reported in this paper followed this new tradition and predicated its theoretical assumptions upon a professional definition of curriculum leadership. In particular, teacher participation is regarded as consisting of necessary processes of enhancing the transformational experiences for the professional development of teachers and enhancement of student learning. The key characteristics of an effective leadership development program are provided below. These characteristics form the design principles and approaches of the current project, and echo the concept of learning-centered leadership within the school-based curriculum development tradition (Harris, 2003, p. 75; Henderson and Hawthorne, 1995; MacBeath & Moos, 2004).

- The development activities should be school-based and problem-solving in nature, with a focus on enhancing student learning.
- The development activities should be collaborative and the model of power hierarchy should be mediated to an extent that social interaction would emerge; each member should assume an equal but full professional status in curriculum decision making processes in the learning-centered community.
- The social interaction in the development activities should be open and reflective in nature.
- The development activities should be formulated and organized in an inquiry mode of planning, implementing, and reflecting upon actions that should be subjected to critical scrutiny.
- The development activities should be continuous and should form spiral and cyclical models of operation to engineer and sustain a culture of change and lifelong learning.

Curriculum leadership development project

Goals and aims

The project entitled "Accelerating School-based Curriculum Development" began in September 2004 and received financial support from the Hong Kong Quality Education Fund for two years. The overall aim of the project is to develop the leadership skills and capacities of teachers in reviewing, planning, designing, implementing, and evaluating curriculum innovations within a school-based curriculum development tradition. The goals of the project are as follows:

- To develop the abilities and skills of teachers in strategic planning and development as well as in using evaluation for school improvement;
- To enhance the effectiveness of school self-evaluation in the school; and
- To develop a quality culture for school self-evaluation for school improvement.

The project is also a response to the call for teachers to receive new professional development opportunities that will engage them in problem solving, evaluating, considering new ideas, and collaboratively developing school goals (Darling-Hammond & McLaughlin, 1995). As mentioned in the original proposal for funding, this project is a response to the initiative of the government to embark on two new quality assurance mechanisms to monitor the provision of education in Hong Kong: school self-evaluation and external school review conducted by a panel of professionals and inspectors appointed by the Education and Manpower Bureau in 2003.

In general, the development activities in the project include training of a selected group of teachers to achieve two primary aims. The first aim is to provide professional leadership and support for teachers and enable them to introduce pedagogical innovations in the school to ultimately cultivate among all teachers a quality and professional culture(s) of a learning community within the school context. The second aim is to develop performance indicators for each school subject for self-evaluation. The current report will focus on the activities and preliminary findings in the first year of the project in its first action cycle of developing teacher leadership in curriculum theory and practice in the period from September 2004 to December 2004. For this purpose, providing a brief account of the school context and its parameters, in which the project has been operated, at this early stage is necessary.

School aims and recent challenges

The school, established in 1975, belongs to a religious missionary in Hong Kong. The total number of teachers is 42, among which eight teachers have a master's degree in education and other school subjects. The school has around 700 primary students from the local Shatin community. To respond to the challenges brought about by the decreasing number of children in the district area, and the demand from the curriculum reforms endorsed by the government in 2001, the school authority has been purposely mounting a number of curriculum innovations to gain good reputation among parents in the community, and to prepare for the external school review. Specifically, the school head initiated a number of changes in recent years and provided strong leadership in administration and other aspects of improvement policies and measures. These measures include partnership schemes with the Education and Manpower Bureau, peer observation of teaching, teacher appraisal scheme, collaborative lesson preparations, school self-evaluation exercises, and application for external funding for development projects, such as the one reported in this paper.

Design and organization of the development activities

Development work has been planned in accordance with the underlying principles derived from the above discussion of the constituent theories and traditions in the theoretical and empirical studies of school-based development models of curriculum leadership activities. Workshops on key professional curriculum knowledge and skills, such as how to plan a school-based innovation activity and how to

48   *Case studies: a team approach*

conduct an analysis of strengths, weaknesses, opportunities, and threats (SWOT) to identify strengths and weaknesses for potential innovations, were organized for participating teachers. These activities aimed at preparing the participating teachers professionally in particular and all school teachers in general to understand what was going on with their colleagues in school. Strategically, involving all teachers in the school in these activities could disseminate knowledge about the intentions, the procedures, and the possible outcomes of the planned curriculum innovations. This approach would also establish the foundation for the second action cycle of development work. This strategy aimed at creating a social interaction model of dissemination (Kelly, 1999, p. 110). A part of the SWOT analysis conducted by the curriculum development team of Chinese language teachers is discussed in Table 4.1 to illustrate the kind of discussions created in the reviewing and planning stages of the curriculum development.

Table 4.1 SWOT analysis in school

Factors	Strengths	Weaknesses	Opportunities	Threats
Pupils	Active and expressive	Hugh difference in achievements	Putonghua is popular among students	Negative language learning environments
Teachers	Positive professional attitude Reflective teachers	Ineffective learning Lack subject knowledge depth	A few teachers with strong qualifications Plenty of professional development workshops Government funding available	Too much administrative work
Resource	Books are plenty for borrowing	Library is on seventh floor and inconvenient	Plenty of software	Threat to close the school
School Policy	Subject teachers must have appropriate subject qualifications	NIL	External resources	One specialist in curriculum
Parents	Have confidence in school	Working class background	Parental support available	Parents are not residents of Hong Kong
Society			Chinese language learning environment	

Source: Law, E.H.F. et al. (2006). Developing curriculum leadership in an elementary school: A Hong Kong case study. *Curriculum and Teaching, 21*(2), 61–90.

Curriculum leadership in a primary school 49

In the first action cycle of the development work, teachers from three core school subjects (Chinese language, English language, and mathematics) were chosen because these subjects occupied a majority of the curriculum time in the school and involved more school teachers. Three subject-based curriculum development teams were formed to review, plan, implement, and reflect upon curriculum practices. Teamwork has become a regular phenomenon of the school culture thereafter.

Selection of seed teachers and the curriculum development teams

The combination of members of each team differed in terms of years of experience and seniority in the occupational hierarchy. However, the ultimate goal was to create a conducive, social, and humanistic environment for developing collaboration and team spirit among the participating teachers. The Chinese and mathematics subject-based curriculum development teams consisted of their subject department heads with curriculum responsibilities in the innovation school, and two other participating teachers who had less practical experience but were recommended because of their commitment and enthusiasm. The English subject-based curriculum development team was not joined by its panel head deliberately to create a social group environment without any influence of human hierarchy among colleagues. The above deliberation aimed at establishing a positive working environment for its members with as few potentially negative and constraining factors as possible in the first action cycle of the development work. Therefore, the selection principles were strategically deliberated to highlight self-motivation, integrity, responsibility, and commitment among participants.

Each team had to follow a simplified three-stage model of conducting action research: (a) in the planning stage, the aim for the team is to identify an innovation goal; (b) in the implementing stage, the aim is to put the plan in action in classroom teaching; and (c) in the reflection stage, the team reviews the actions and decides on further innovations (Table 4.3). The key function of the three stages of teacher actions is to emphasize the importance of engaging teachers in a series of curriculum development activities such as reviewing the current curriculum practices, determining actions for experimentation, and reflecting on experiences for improvement and further deliberation (Elliott, 1991). In the project, teachers worked in teams for dual functions. On the one hand, discussion and collaboration of this nature would strengthen team spirit and create opportunities for solving pedagogical problems collectively. On the other hand, interactions would encourage teachers of various experiences and backgrounds to genuinely share their professional experiences and insights among themselves and to create professional conversations among them (Britt, Irwin, & Ritchie, 2001, p. 50). The data collected will unfold stories of greater complication and will shed light on the necessary conditions for the successful implementation of development work for curriculum leadership within the school.

Each stage was task-oriented. At the planning stage, each team conducted a survey in accordance with the SWOT framework to deepen their reflective understanding of the current school practices and their shortcomings. Accordingly,

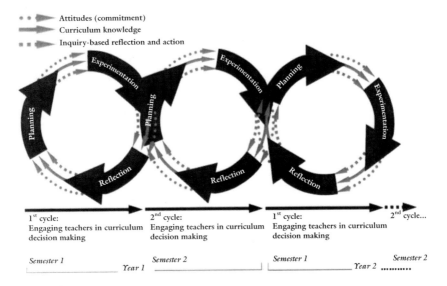

Figure 4.1 Re-conceptualizing school-based models of developing teacher curriculum leadership for lifelong education

Source: Law, E.H.F., Galton, M., & Wan, S.W.Y. (2010). Distributed curriculum leadership in action: A Hong Kong case study. *Educational Management Administration & Leadership, 38,* 286. Figure 4.1.

they were able to identify a key innovation that they wanted to introduce into their own practice. The result of the SWOT survey was further discussed with a teacher-educator who played the role of a subject consultant in the project. The purpose of having a subject consultant was to ensure that certain expert advice was offered in the process of designing the innovation for implementation, as well as to provide alternative pedagogical practices for each team. The experiences and views of the consultants were expected to stimulate reflection and encourage deep thinking in learning processes evident in the professional dialogues among members of each team. Then, each team worked out a lesson plan for the innovation collaboratively and then implemented this plan in their classroom teaching.

At the implementation stage, each team had different patterns of practice, although peer and consultant observation was a common feature of all team activities. The Chinese team chose the most inexperienced member to try the innovation. The target of the innovation was to develop the reading comprehension skills of two primary children. Each team member in the English group tried out the innovation plan in each class. The target of the innovation was for teachers to adopt a task-based approach in teaching children a process model of writing essays. Meanwhile, the mathematics team adopted a different approach of including all members in the implementation of the innovation. The target of the innovation was to strengthen students' understanding of concepts of "percent" and "percentage."

Table 4.2 Reconceptualizing school-based models of developing teacher curriculum leadership

Stage	Purposes	Developmental Activities
Initiating and Reviewing Stage	To review current practices and decide a theme of innovative practices by consensus	Team meetings, consulting experts, collecting information on effective practices
Experimentation	To trial the proposed innovative practices and collect feedback	Design materials, try out in classroom practices, adopting reliable approaches to data collection
Reflection	To reflect on practices and identify gaps for improvements in next rounds of experimentation	Team meetings, reviewing videotaped practices, identifying strengths and weaknesses for improvement and enhancement

The final stage of the first action cycle of the development work concluded with a reflection seminar. This seminar aimed at consolidating teacher learning from the entire process of planning, designing, implementing activities, and moving toward identifying a new goal of innovation in the second stage. Table 4.2 summarizes the teacher activities in the three stages of work in the first action cycle.

Method

Methods of data collection at different stages in the first action cycle of the project development were purposely varied to suit the changing focus of each stage of development work. At the planning stage, all teacher activities were videotaped. These videotaped activities include the five three-hour action planning meetings, two SWOT analysis meetings, the presentation of SWOT results in the school conference, and three collaborative lesson preparation meetings. Two representatives from each curriculum team were interviewed in a large group. External consultants were invited to provide written comments on the lesson plans.

At the implementation stage, seven teachers tried out their plans of innovation. Data were collected from the teaching aids used and 20 videotaped lessons. Nine observation checklists were collected from peers. At the reflection stage, seven teachers completed their self-evaluation forms. Data collection also included one videotaped post-observation conference, in which consultants were invited to participate so that they can share views and exchange comments, as along with 12 written reflections by participating teachers. Two kinds of teacher interviews

52 *Case studies: a team approach*

were arranged. Group interviews aimed at providing teachers with a platform for further discussion on pedagogical issues. Individual interviews aimed at eliciting feelings, views, and objects of learning from participating teachers.

Student interviews were also conducted to triangulate data from participants' different perspectives of the same project experience. A sample of students who were taught by the participating teachers was interviewed. Each subject-based curriculum development team had two interview groups. In these groups, students of low and high ability were selected together with students who tended to be quiet and reserved in class. The purpose of this arrangement was to create an interactive interview environment and to lower the formality of the interview. Accordingly, more authentic recollection of experiences from these students would be obtained.

An entire-school survey was also designed and conducted to determine the extent to which the non-participating teachers in the school were aware of the aims, objectives, and progress of the project. This survey had a dual purpose: to measure the knowledge of the non-participating teachers to plan dissemination strategies in the second cycle of the project in the second semester, and to identify potential teachers who expressed willingness and showed interests in the innovation project (see Table 4.3).

Strategically, the project aims to disseminate the professional experience of planning, reviewing, designing, and evaluating curriculum innovations to the teachers who have not yet participated in the first action cycle of the development work. This process is carried out to prepare the second cycle of the innovation work in this project by identifying teachers who are willing to join the project and experiment with some innovative practice in their subjects and classroom teaching. Twenty-six teachers who had not participated in the first action cycle of the development project were invited to complete a survey aiming to collect information on the extent to which they heard, understood, or were aware of the purposes of the work progress of the project.

Table 4.3 Data collection at each stage in the first action cycle of each subject-based curriculum development team

Categories of Data Sources	Initiating and Reviewing Stage	Experimentation Stage	Reflection Stage
Visual images Documentary Analysis Field work	Videotaping all meetings; Mind maps and evaluation instruments; Interviews of teachers, students, and experts	Videotaping all try-out lessons; Lesson plans; Observation notes and evaluation rubrics	Videotaping all reflection meetings; Reflective journals by teachers and students; Transcriptions of field observation

Findings and analysis

The collected data were organized to shed light upon the key characteristics of a school-based effective leadership development model discussed in the previous sections. The characteristics or preconditions of effective teacher learning, which should be understood in the contexts of restructuring schools as learning communities and empowering teachers as transformative agents collectively, should feature various aspects, including leadership style, professional and reflective conversations, educational discourse, team spirit and collaboration, professional commitment, and decision making opportunities (Retallick, 1999, p. 482; Sugrue, 2002, p. 317).

Leadership style

In the three stages of planning, implementation, and reflection of the innovations, the data exhibit diverse patterns of curriculum leadership on a continuum from directive and authoritarian to non-directive and participatory. Different styles have different types of influence and impact on the process and directions of the curriculum innovations. However, directive and authoritarian styles run contrary to the fundamental principles of school-based curriculum development, which value teacher participation and professional autonomy as the two essential conditions for teacher leadership development. We shall return to this point in our discussion section.

On the mathematics team, the panel head demonstrated a non-directive style without evidence of being power-coercive. This situation may be due to the fact that the panel head in the school has a lower grade than that of the other two panel heads in the same team. However, the discussion was open without any clear goal of innovation. The panel head often adopted a tentative mood in her language. For example, the panel head stated, "Could we (teachers) contribute more to setting questions for children?" (literal translation from videotaped SWOT meeting on September 27, 2004; reading at 18:30).

The panel chair of the Chinese language team was careful in the SWOT analysis when he learned that the discussion would be videotaped. In the middle of the discussion, he asked the research assistant to stop videotaping for a few minutes to allow him to express something possibly sensitive to the public. However, he was able to provide a certain form of leadership on the procedure of conducting analysis and to clarify its purposes.

Panel Head: Theoretically, we should discuss the strengths and weaknesses, and then identify the areas of concerns for improvement actions. We should not follow our instinctive feeling but we should discuss first, and then aim at the weaknesses as our priority. We could then discuss which year groups should start the implementation, and on how we could proceed step by step to improve the weaknesses. This way should be our thinking framework.

> (Literal translation from videotaped SWOT meeting on September 27, 2004; reading from 00:00 to 4:30)

54   *Case studies: a team approach*

In the focused group interview, the panel head showed his positional power by asserting his right to have access to the teaching and learning materials prepared by the teachers.

Meanwhile, the panel chair of the English language team was not involved in the subject-based curriculum team because she was the positional leader of the entire project and had the leadership responsibility over the entire school curriculum development work. Therefore, one of the team members was assigned to chair this team. The teachers worked together but little dialogue was observed. In addition, the teachers had no intention of engaging in conversations similar to those of the Chinese team, who clearly showed division of labor. As shown on the tape, the teachers on the English-language team had no intention of collaborating and working together to produce the SWOT analysis. Hence, the style of leadership was notably weak.

Role of consultants

The role performance of the consultants varied according to their own personalities and styles. The consultant for the Chinese team came from a local institute of education. He showed a dominating and didactic style in working with the Chinese team. In the three-hour collaborative lesson preparation meeting, he occupied the majority of the time by "talking down" to the teachers. His tone was authoritarian. For example, he "taught" the participating teachers that the focus of language learning should be according to the primary levels. Specifically, the focus should be on teaching "the Chinese characters and the combinations of characters" in the junior primary, on applying the language items in the middle primary, and on learning the themes of texts in the senior primary. He commented that the teachers should not use three learning sessions to teach individual words but should use only one session on text reading strategies.

In the collaborative lesson preparation meeting, the consultant for the Chinese team said, "You have to concentrate in the process of thinking to be able to succeed" (literal translation from the videotaped collaboration lesson preparation meeting on September 30, 2004; reading at 11:43).

The style of the consultant for the English team was also didactic. She tended to talk down to teachers about language learning and occupied the majority of the meeting time. The topics in her monologue included personal experience of learning and studying as well as general problems with teachers. She did not focus the discussion on the innovation and plan of actions.

In comparison, the consultant for the mathematics team tended to be more open, participatory, inquisitive, exploratory, and liberal. He adopted a nondirective style in his consultation meeting with the team, asked for opinions, and extended the dialogue from the perspectives of the participating teachers to the future proposal. He even asked, "What do you suggest to do for the other classes?" (literal translation from the videotaped collaborative lesson preparation meeting on December 8, 2004; reading at 36:39).

Curriculum leadership in a primary school   55

Professional conversations: reflective and action-oriented

One key feature of the professional development of teachers is the importance of engaging inexperienced and experienced teachers in reflective conversations about pedagogical issues (Britt, Irwin, & Ritchie, 2001). The processes should be stimulating to enhance deep learning among the teachers involved (Biggs, 1991; Schon, 1989). In all planning, implementation, and reflection stages of the first action cycle, the data show that the participating teachers were engaged in professional dialogues and conversations on practical issues about teaching and learning.

The SWOT activities in the planning stage created situations in which members of each subject-based curriculum development team used their observations and past experiences to identify the strengths and weaknesses of the teaching and learning environments. For example, the focus of the discussion of the Chinese team was on how the teachers could design a curriculum to accommodate the challenges imposed by the motivational problems of students. The team suggested the solution of building connections between school learning and daily life experiences of the students. The discussion topics focused on design issues of extending the life experience of students. Different views on the abilities of students were also negotiated between different parties.

Teacher 2:   If we follow the official syllabus, then we cannot teach children to write sentences until primary three and four. However, our primary two children have proven that they were able to construct sentences meaningfully.

Panel Head: I think we can teach junior primary regarding constructing paragraphs. We do not have to follow exactly the official curriculum.
>   (Evidence from the videotaped focused group meeting on
>   December 21, 2004; reading from 9:55 to 11:00)

SWOT analysis meetings and presentations in the entire school conference provided the English team with good opportunities to identify problems with the teaching and learning situations in the English language. According to the overall SWOT feedback written by the teachers, they benefited from the discussion that mirrored the problem-solving approach to the pedagogical issues in language teaching and learning. Some of the written comments and feedback by the participating teachers are presented below, especially when asked what they had learned in the first cycle.

Teacher 1:   I learned how to use the SWOT analysis as well as how to plan and organize a unit of learning.

Teacher 4:   I learned how to use the SWOT analysis in analyzing the weaknesses and strengths of the school and the English language teaching.
>   (Reflections by the participating teachers, as written on the
>   reflection sheets they wrote on September 27, 2004)

56 *Case studies: a team approach*

The combined interview, under the chairmanship of the project leader, was another opportunity to engage teachers in working together and to reflect on what they did in the SWOT exercises. This interview aimed to consolidate the reflective thinking of the teachers and to emphasize the importance of problem-solving approaches in planning what to teach and how to teach satisfactorily. A few excerpts from the interview are provided below.

Chinese team:

Teacher 1: In our first try-out, primary two pupils could not draw (pictures) satisfactorily on their own. Thus, they were unable to complete the task. Accordingly, we should use the compositions created by the senior primary pupils to let them learn the narrative form of an article.

(Literal translation from the written record of the combined interview on October 25, 2004)

English team:

Teacher 1: After the SWOT analysis, we decided to conduct a task-based learning unit plan to focus our teaching on grammar to the pupils more effectively through the process of writing.

(Literal translation from the written record of the combined interview on October 25, 2004)

Mathematics team:

Teacher: We identified that the learning problem of the pupils lies in their problem-solving skills. Thus, our action plan focuses on this aspect. We would like to learn more about action research to help us track what we are doing.

(Literal translation from the written record of the combined interview on October 25, 2004)

A post-observation conference was organized with the participation of the consultants. This conference aimed to provide opportunities for focused discussions among the practitioners, consultants, and panel heads. Accordingly, reflective dialogues among team members of the school could be cultivated. The conservational topics of the conference among members of the Chinese team included the following considerations: students' needs at different stages of their development in planning a curriculum, language learning needs of students, and identification of future goals of curriculum experimentation.

Some selected written teacher reflections are discussed below to illustrate the features of reflective discourse from the survey conducted on January 4, 2005, after they had finished the first action cycle of the innovation. When the three teams were asked about what they had learned in the first action cycle, the Chinese team said they had learned to understand their own teaching methods and problems as well as the learning characteristics of the children. The mathematics team said they had understood that different teachers implemented differently, and thus, the impact was varied. The team found the consultant useful in integrating theory and practice. When the three teams were asked about what they wanted to learn in the second action cycle, the Chinese team said they wanted to learn how to use various types of teaching strategies to teach senior primary children, and how to organize interactive learning activities. The teachers also said they wanted to learn how to enhance the creativity of their students. The English team wanted to learn how to evaluate teaching effectiveness and how to conduct action research to improve teaching. The mathematics team wanted to learn how to lead group discussion and how to enhance the problem-solving ability of students.

The above descriptions have shown that teachers had been actively engaged in various types of professional activities. These activities aimed at encouraging reflective thinking approaches with a view to solving pedagogical problems. This condition is necessary for advancing the professionalism among teachers and teacher leaders (Day, 1993).

Educational terminologies in discourse

The participating teachers in various meetings in the three different stages demonstrated frequent uses of the educational terminologies. These terminologies were the key concepts in the current curriculum reforms. The use of jargon also indicated that the key reform concepts had become part of the consciousness of these teachers to a certain extent or, at the very least, they had acquired an active language repertoire in the professional conversations of these teachers. The jargon includes research methodology used to collect data and evidence of student learning:

> We designed some questionnaires and we have plenty of questionnaires.
> (Literal translation from the videotaped collaborative lesson preparation meeting of the Chinese team on October 9, 2004; reading at 10:00)

In the reflection stage, the project leader did three focused group interviews with the three teams, aiming to elicit more data on how participating teachers reflect on their experience of trying out their innovations. In the verbal discourse of the teachers on the Chinese team, they demonstrated the frequent use of educational jargon such as "action plan" and "creativity" (Literal translation from the videotaped group interview on December 21, 2004; reading at 17:00).

In some cases, the focus of an extended discourse was about action research, such as the issue of identifying problems with pedagogy and student learning,

58 *Case studies: a team approach*

as well as the proposed solutions. An excerpt from the group interview with the Chinese team is presented below.

Teacher 1: According to the evaluation of student learning last year, the problem with reading habits is comparatively small, but the problem with the lack of initiative is significant. Therefore, our theme for this year revolves around motivating the reading habit among pupils.

(Literal translation from the videotaped group interview with the Chinese team on December 21, 2004; reading at 00:03)

In the SWOT analysis, the discussion focused on the use of appropriate pedagogical strategies to cater to individual differences. Teachers indicated that they had little experience with using "action research." They were also designing a curriculum plan for the mathematics subject for the first time. However, they had some experience of planning a creative lesson (literal translation from the videotaped SWOT meeting on September 27, 2004; reading at 1:31).

For the English team, a teacher said, "We used SWOT to sharpen our understanding, apply more systematic approaches, and be more focused on our work" (literal translation from the videotaped group interview on January 21, 2005; reading from 00:00 to 15:00).

For the mathematics team, the following dialogue demonstrates the use of current educational terms in the discussion.

Teacher 1: We do not know the exact aims of the lesson. We thought of it as a lesson study that aims to find a theme to investigate. We hope that the pupils would learn better and more effectively. We wonder if we achieved the aims of the project.

(Reading at 01:55)

Teacher 3: How do you feel now?

Teacher 1: We aimed at using student-centered approaches. Thus, we think we could help pupils learn how to solve problems. They could also learn some life skills.

Teacher 2: Indeed, the focus and the theme were unclear to us. We took it as a lesson study. We wonder whether what we did was the aim of the project. In the project, we focused on problem solving and the application work for pupils. Whether this approach is what the project aimed is still unknown to us.

(Reading at 02:46)
(Literal translation from the videotaped group interview on January 21, 2005; reading from 1:55 to 2:46)

In response to the questions about what they had learned in the first action cycle and what they expected to learn in the second action cycle, the teachers used

Curriculum leadership in a primary school 59

terminologies such as "shared mission," "SWOT analysis," "interactive learning strategies," "teaching effectiveness," "action research," and "collective lesson preparation."

Team spirit and collaboration

Building team spirit and collaboration is one of the key development areas for teacher leadership. Teams were formed and opportunities for team building were created in all the three stages of the first action cycle. However, the patterns of collaboration on each team varied.

The Chinese team demonstrated a stronger sense of division of labor, and each teacher had a clear role to play in the SWOT discussion. In particular, one played the role of being the secretary, one served as the leader, one was the typist, and the other had various duties in the group. The English team seemed to show some level of unease with videotaping. When they conducted the SWOT analysis, they lined up face to face with the computers. They did not bother on communicating and discussing with each other. The mathematics team also did not show much collaboration spirit.

Teacher 1: We used different methods in our discussion about deciding a theme . . . we were looking for a method we feel comfortable with, in other words, we consider others' perspectives and methods, and then you learned how to use diverse methods and alternatives to solve problems.

(Literal translation from the videotaped group interview on January 21, 2005)

Other examples to illustrate the team spirit came from the written reflections by the teachers on the Chinese and the mathematics teams after the first action cycle of the innovation on January 3, 2005.

Chinese Teacher 1: We learned from the consultant that the participating teachers should share a common mission, which helps efficient implementation. Participating teachers should be from the same year group. In this way, teachers could offer mutual support to each other.

Chinese Teacher 2: We deepened the understanding of our pedagogical approaches and the ways to improve them. We learned from the consultant about the current curriculum reforms, and the specific features of the children at each year group."

Mathematics Teacher 1: The teachers from the same year group focused their discussion on the same topic and shared ideas, and we learned much from this activity. The same learning topic, the same teaching method, but the interpretation

60   *Case studies: a team approach*

by different teachers was totally different. The effects on student learning were different, and therefore I learned more pedagogical alternatives to teach the same topic in future."

Mathematics Teacher 2:   Collaborative lesson preparation as well as curriculum design and improvement are useful activities to enhance teaching effectiveness. In addition, the consultants helped to integrate theory and practice.

Professional attitude and curriculum decision making

Teacher commitment to student learning is essential and should be part of the professional development of these teachers. Professional attitude also includes the willingness of the teacher to take risks in trying new initiatives in achieving effective learning in schools.

The English team showed that they wanted to experiment with a new task-based learning approach to teach English language to enhance the creativity of students. The mathematics team shared their experience of participating in a few professional development activities. Their discussion on the collaborative lesson preparation focused on pedagogical issues such as individual differences and the selection of appropriate learning topics from the textbooks.

Consultant: How do we understand the issues by designing a lesson plan?

Teacher 1:   Because I do not understand much . . . let's focus on teaching and learning, and let us try it out and let us experience it, and therefore we can help our pupils to enhance their learning . . . about high-level thinking. I do not have any experience of action research, therefore I do not know much about SWOT. How we can do it?

Teacher 2:   We can choose different topics such as percentage or calculating circumference. Problem solving is problem solving, but what do we give them to learn?

(Literal translation from the videotaped collaborative lesson preparation meeting on September 30, 20014; reading at 8:02)

In the implementation stage, the teachers on the English team employed multimedia resources to support teaching and learning in addition to the interactive games and group work as the adopted major teaching approaches. Teachers were also willing to design learning materials and became less dependent on textbooks and syllabi.

Teacher 1:   We have planned many activities, urgently, difficult to pass the resources to another class for teaching. We normally use group work. Teacher A and I teach more classes, have more groups; if one more teacher shares the work, teachers give more attention to pupils, we can monitor pupil progress. We have to be a photographer as well,

Curriculum leadership in a primary school   61

it will distract our work, our work will be less focused. Now pupils' reactions are very good; they are committed. . . . We want to teach them verb tenses; they are interested. The activities on grammar are interesting.

Teacher 2:   We used activities to teach preposition. My class worked smoothly. The schedule in the first week was tight, but no problem in the class. Their PowerPoint work was unpredictable, excellent.

(Literal translation from the videotaped group interview on January 21, 2005; reading from 00:00 to 15:00)

One argument for school-based curriculum development is to allow teachers to exercise their judgment in making curriculum decisions. The opportunities for teachers to make such decisions are considered a key development component in the innovation project. At various stages of its development, teachers were given freedom and autonomy to make judgments and decisions on curriculum.

For example, in collaborative lesson preparation meetings on the Chinese language team, the teachers decided not to stick to the original plan of integrating reading with picture-drawing activities. This method is derived from Bruner's theoretical assumption about the benefits to student learning when children are engaged in transforming one representation of experience to another, such as from symbolic representation (language) to iconic representation (pictures and images) (Bruner, 1960, 1966). The teachers abandoned the original plan of using picture-drawing activities because they found children were unable to draw pictures effectively. Instead, they opted to use "storytelling" strategies or symbolic representations in verbal form. This team also conducted evidence-based judgment when they used the questionnaire data from the parents to show how they had considered what focus of learning should be in teaching reading.

The teachers on the Chinese team attempted to adapt the curriculum with the experience from the project.

Teacher 1:   Can we adopt a similar approach in other classes or other year groups?

Teacher 2:   Problems with learning materials could occur. In the beginning, we thought about teaching pupils how to write descriptive accounts of an experience of going to the beach or shopping in a supermarket . . . We may not be able to find suitable materials. Then we invited senior primary pupils to write about their experience, and we used them as learning materials for the junior primary pupils. This worked well.

Teacher 3:   If we use this in senior primary pupils, we have to adjust, especially there could be more varieties in characters, about their personalities, feelings. These are much complicated already and belong to high level. Events could also be interwoven to create a strong sense of suspense and the plot could be complicated for senior primary pupils. They could manage this.

(Literal translation from the videotaped group interview (part one) on December 21, 2004; reading at 14:10)

62 Case studies: a team approach

On the selection of materials, teachers would consider some underlying principles about the needs and abilities of pupils, forms of presentations, and levels of cognitive demands. The following is an excerpt from the same group interview as presented above.

Teacher 1: [It is] difficult to develop learning materials, extremely difficult . . . because they have to align with the learning goals of the chapter, but you cannot have a new one because of the comprehension ability of the pupils, which means my teaching is not smooth. If the text types are different, it is difficult to find some graphs or pictures, and the text must be narratives, and it must be about a visit. . . ."
(Literal translation from the videotaped group interview (part one) on December 21, 2004; reading at 14:10)

The teachers on the mathematics team also showed their search for appropriate methods in the selection of teaching approaches.

Teacher 1: We conducted a test and found that the performance of the current pupils was far better than that of the previous groups. In other words, classes of different abilities showed that the pupils clearly understand the concepts [about percentage].
Teacher 2: The method was useful to the pupils. We spent much time on discussion and revised the teaching plan several times.
(Literal translation from the videotaped group interview on January 21, 2005; reading at 5:56)

Teacher 1 . . . Like this time, we think, we found the ability of analysis, for example, this time, their problem-solving ability is low; this means their ability to sort out application questions. This time, we may have different methods. The effects are different; possibly the results in post-tests are higher. This means our solutions and methods proposed for the problems we identified in the SWOT are appropriate.
(Literal translation from the videotaped group interview on January 21, 2005; reading from 16:30 to 17:00)

In the collaborative lesson preparation meetings, the English team engaged in a series of curriculum development activities: determining learning objectives, selecting learning activities and teaching strategies, and assessment modes.

Student interview

A group of selected students from the classes wherein innovations were implemented by the participating teachers was interviewed to elicit more data about the implementation of the innovations for triangulation purposes. Mixed-group interview techniques were used. In other words, each interview group had six students: one active, one quiet, two with high achievement, and two with low achievement in their academic subjects. This technique aimed to ensure that a wider representation of the student backgrounds was available in the interviews. As a result, views and reactions from different student groups in the innovation classes could be obtained.

The students from the Chinese class expressed some confusion when the teacher changed her teaching style and patterns.

Student 1: We did more work than we normally do.
Student 2: We enjoyed the lessons more.
Teacher 1: Do you feel you have learned something or anything?
Student 2: I am not sure.
(Literal translation from the videotaped group interview with primary two students on January 5, 2005; reading from 00:30 to 15:00)

In general, the students were positive about the innovation. They said they were happier and that they learned the communication skills and problem-solving skills in the innovation lesson.

The primary five students taught by the English teachers told the research assistant that their English teachers were more lenient, relaxed, and allowed them to express in classes when the innovation was implemented. However, their feelings about the innovation were mixed. The primary six students felt the teachers allowed them to explore and had given them freedom. They thought that the innovation encouraged students to learn communication skills and the ability to express in public. Allowing them to express had given them confidence in public speech.

Discussion

A large number of places and spaces for teacher leadership development were created at the planning, implementation, and reflection stages of the first action cycle of the project. The experiences collected in the first action cycle of the project are rich and enlightening. Specifically, they provide researchers and school educators with some ideas about the preconditions for making teacher curriculum leadership a viable concept to be adopted by schools across cultures and contexts. The following discussion shall be organized around the major themes of arguments for a "distributed" style of teacher leadership. In other words, teacher participation in curriculum decision making should become central and activities in teaching and learning sites should be shared.

Which type of leadership is more effective?

The leadership styles in the three curriculum development teams were diverse. However, panel heads from the Chinese and mathematics teams were given positional powers to exercise influences and assert directions. The power and its

64   *Case studies: a team approach*

execution by the mathematics panel head was mediated by her own perceived lower professional and academic status among members of the team. She also tended to allow team members to share the power of making curriculum decisions. Meanwhile, a more directive style of leadership was observed from the Chinese panel head, who asserted a strong role and personality in decision making processes and the ultimate goal of experimentation. The English team proceeded without a role-based leader, and the innovation work of this team seemed open to more criticism. Therefore, whether a role-based leadership concept was less effective remained unclear. More substantive data among leadership styles and their effects could be possibly revealed in the second action cycle. The reason is that these subject-based curriculum development teams have more opportunities to work collaboratively on future planned innovations on teaching and learning.

However, the evidence shows that the participating teachers actively assumed the role of being curriculum developers in a non-directive style of leadership group (the mathematics team); meanwhile, the participating teachers on a more directive curriculum team tend to be less participatory and assertive (Glickman, 2002). Therefore, a more open and non-directive style of positional leadership called "procedural leadership" would be conducive to the emergence of active teacher leadership actions and activities that are re-conceptualized on the basis of a participatory model of curriculum leadership. The latter concept of teacher leadership is called "participatory curriculum leadership." However, the emergence of the leadership styles in this project was a function of a combination of situational variables such as personality, status, power, perception, self-esteem, and school ethos, rather than a deliberative planned innovation by the designated curriculum leader of this project. In other words, the proposal that one form of leadership should be adopted at the expense of other alternatives should receive caution (Harris, 2004, p. 19). Thus, schools and teachers should be encouraged to take a more eclectic approach to allow the emergence of numerous teacher curriculum leadership patterns, either participatory or procedural (Leithwood & Riehl, 2003).

What are the contributions of partnership with university faculties?

Educators have argued that partnership with university faculties should give benefits to the schools concerned (Gordon, 2004; Sandholtz, 2002). From the data, the participatory styles and the perceived roles of the three consultants from the university faculties were mediated by their personalities and self-perception of their roles in the curriculum development process. The first two had stronger and more assertive views, whereas the third one tended to assume a more facilitating and reflective position in providing academic and professional advice and support. The former two consultants could be good examples of providing "top-down leadership" in the ways they perceived appropriate. However, the third one was a good example of how playing a facilitative leadership role in a more subtle and professional way allowed for diverse practices and experimentations to flourish. The latter form of partnership with university faculties should provide more spaces for a participatory model of curriculum leadership.

Is professional development evident?

Teacher participation in curriculum decision making processes such as the ways the project has organized and arranged for the teachers significantly allowed teachers to engage in reflective and professional conversations in ways that were goal- and action-oriented. The participating teachers explicitly expressed that they had learned the professional skills and knowledge essential and necessary for anyone involved in making serious curriculum decisions about student learning. These decisions mainly involve decisions on learning objectives, principles of selecting contents of learning, the pedagogical strategies being adjusted to student variations in motivation and ability, as well as collection of evidence about student learning. The participating teachers had actively used the most contemporary educational terminologies in their professional conversations in solving their identified pedagogical difficulties. These professional conservations have demonstrated that the participating teachers were involved in a relational type of intellectual discourse, thus demonstrating more sophisticated and higher-order-thinking learning outcomes (Biggs, 1991; Blasé & Blasé, 1999, p. 367).

Are teamwork and collaboration strengthened?

Each team worked together, but whether the collaboration has been conducive to teacher participation and learning remains unclear. This could be a feature of the beginning of some collaboration among teachers who have not been given much opportunity to work in teams. Notably, the data collected were only from the first action cycle wherein teams have only begun to start working. Achieving a sense of teamwork is considered a time-consuming and labor-intensive endeavor by many teachers. In the project, the Chinese group behaved similar to a team with some division of labor and clear role play. Meanwhile, the mathematics team had a less hierarchical power structure among members and demonstrated another form of genuine collaboration. The English team had a very loose and open style of collaboration.

Institutionalization of structures for curriculum decision making

The second action cycle of the project was planned such that it was based on the experiences in the first action cycle. Key structures of the leadership development model will be retained, such as subject-based curriculum development teamwork, action research-oriented planning and design, professional nature of reflective discourses and shared power of social interaction among members of each team, as well as a more professional input from external consultants. Entire school seminars must also be conducted to share among all teachers the fruits and pains of teacher participation in curriculum decision making processes. These key structures

66 *Case studies: a team approach*

will provide professional autonomy for every member in the school; they will also cultivate a sense of lifelong learning within a learner-centered community (Blasé & Blasé, 2000; Harris & Lambert, 2003; Miles, Ekholm, & Vandenberghe, 1987).

Conclusion

Leadership studies in education have focused mainly on a positional and hierarchical basis to an extent that teachers in schools are considered mere peripheral components in making pedagogical decisions. Recent studies on curriculum leadership have shifted from a model of organizational leadership to a model that has been trying to recapture the essence of the professional role of teachers in making curriculum decisions within the tradition of school-based curriculum development. Teacher leadership in curriculum decision making in schools is a new phenomenon in both international and local literature, and its practice has been in its embryonic stage. How this concept and practice could be institutionalized within the infrastructure of the current school ethos needs substantial theoretical and experimental work.

The report of the first action cycle of a curriculum leadership development project in Hong Kong demonstrated the complexity of two key structures. One is the establishment of curriculum development teams and processes. The other one is the three-stage model of teacher planning, implementation, and reflection of curriculum practice that the case school has created in response to the challenges from the community. These structures and processes have yet to find their home within the traditions and the cultures of the school in the study. However, the experience has proven that engaging teachers in curriculum decision making processes enhances the development of professional knowledge and skills among teachers in general. However, two important issues should be explored and investigated in both theoretical and empirical studies. One issue concerns the process by which the concept of teacher leadership in curriculum decision making could be put into practice more effectively in schools. The other issue concerns how the structures and processes could be institutionalized in schools on a wider scale. These issues could be resolved through collaboration between researchers on university faculties and the teachers in schools. The goal of developing teacher leadership in curriculum decision making should receive policy priority; its successful achievement also needs resource and professional support from government and other stakeholders in the education enterprise (Hulpia, Devos, & Van Keer, 2011).

Note

1 Another version of this chapter has appeared in Law, E.H.F., & Wan, S.W.Y. (2006). Developing curriculum leadership in an elementary school: A Hong Kong case study. *Curriculum and Teaching, 21*(2), 61–90.

References

Australian Education Union. (2004). *Educational leadership and teaching for the twenty first century: Project discussion paper.* Retrieved from http://www.aeufed eral.org.au/Debates/elat21pap.pdf

Bell, B., & Gilbert, J. (1994). Teacher development as professional, personal, and social development. *Teaching & Teacher Education, 10*(5), 483–497.

Biggs, J. (1991). *Teaching for learning: The view from cognitive psychology.* Hawthorn, VIC: Australian Council for Educational Research.

Blasé, J., & Blasé, J. (1999). Principals' instructional leadership and teacher development: Teachers' perspectives. *Educational Administration Quarterly, 35*(3), 349–378.

Blase, J., & Blase, J. (2000). Effective instructional leadership: Teachers' perspectives on how principals promote teaching and learning in schools. *Journal of Educational Administration, 38*(2), 130–141.

Board of Education. (1997). *Report on review of 9-year compulsory education.* Hong Kong: Board of Education.

Britt, M.S., Irwin, K.C., & Ritchie, G. (2001). Professional conversations and professional growth. *Journal of Mathematics Teacher Education, 4*(1), 29–53.

Bruner, J.S. (1960). *The process of education.* Cambridge, MA: Harvard University Press.

Bruner, J.S. (1966). *Toward a theory of instruction.* Cambridge, MA: Belknap Press of Harvard University.

Carr, W., & Kemmis, S. (1986). *Becoming critical: Education, knowledge and action research.* London: Falmer.

Curriculum Development Council. (2001). *Learning to learn : Life-long learning and whole-person development.* Hong Kong: Curriculum Development Council.

Darling-Hammond, L., & McLaughlin, M.W. (1995). Policies that support professional development in an era of reform. *Phi Delta Kappan, 76*(8), 597–604.

Day, C. (1993). Reflection: A necessary but not sufficient condition for professional development. *British Educational Research Journal, 19*(1), 83–93.

Education Commission. (2000). *Learning for life, learning through life: Reform proposals for the education system in Hong Kong.* Hong Kong Special Administrative Region of The People's Republic of China: Education Commission.

Education Department. (2002). *Provision of an additional teacher post for leading curriculum development in primary schools for five years* (Administration Circular No. 13/2002). Hong Kong: Education Department.

Elliott, J. (1991). *Action research for educational change.* Buckingham: Open University Press.

Evers, C.W., & Lakomski, G. (1996). *Exploring educational administration.* Oxford: Elsevier.

Frost, D., & Durrant, J. (2002). *Teacher-led development work: Guidance and support.* London: David Fulton.

Fullan, M. (1993). *Change forces: Probing the depths of educational reform.* London: Falmer.

Fullan, M. (2002). Principals as leaders in a culture of change. *Educational Leadership, 59*(8), 16–21.

Glatthorn, A.A. (2000). *Principal as curriculum leader.* Thousand Oaks, CA: Corwin Press.

Glickman, C.D. (2002). *Leadership for learning.* Alexandria, VA: Association for Supervision and Curriculum Development.

Gordon, S.P. (2004). *Professional development for school improvement: Empowering learning communities.* Boston: Allyn & Bacon.

Hallinger, P., & Heck, R.H. (1996). Reassessing the principal's role in school effectiveness: A review of empirical research, 1980–1995. *Education Administration Quarterly*, February, 5–44.

68　*Case studies: a team approach*

Harris, A. (2003). Teacher leadership and school improvement. In A. Harris, C. Day, D. Hopkins, M. Hadfield, A. Hargreaves, & C. Chapman (Eds.), *Effective leadership for school improvement* (pp. 72–83). London: Routledge/Falmer.

Harris, A. (2004). Distributed leadership and school improvement: Leading or misleading? *Educational Management Administration & Leadership, 32*(4), 11–24.

Harris, A., & Lambert, L. (2003). *Building leadership capacity for school improvement.* Milton Keynes: Open University Press.

Henderson, J.G., & Hawthorne, R.D. (1995). *Transformative curriculum leadership.* New York: Teachers College Press.

Hitt, D.H., & Tucker, P.D. (2015). Systematic review of key leader practices found to influence student achievement: A unified framework. *Review of Educational Research,* 86(2), 531–569. doi: 10.3102/0034654315614911.

Hulpia, H., Devos, G., & Van Keer, H. (2011). The relation between school leadership from a distributed perspective and teachers' organizational commitment examining the source of the leadership function. *Educational Administration Quarterly, 47*(5), 728–771.

Kelly, A.V. (1999). *The curriculum: Theory and practice* (4th ed.). London: Sage.

Law, E. (2003). In search of a quality curriculum for the 21st century in Hong Kong. In W. Pinar (Ed.), *International handbook of curriculum research* (pp. 271–283). Mahwah, NJ: Lawrence Erlbaum.

Law, E., & Galton, M. (2004). Impact of a school based curriculum project on teachers and students: A Hong Kong case study. *Curriculum Perspectives, 24*(3), 43–58.

Lee, J.C.K., & Dimmock, C. (1999). Curriculum leadership and management in secondary schools: A Hong Kong case study. *School Leadership & Management, 19*(4), 455–481.

Leithwood, K.A., Louis, K.S., Anderson, S., & Wahlstrom, K. (2004). *Review of research: How leadership influence student learning.* New York: The Wallace Foundation. Retrieved from http://www.wallacefoundation.org

Leithwood, K.A., & Riehl, C. (2003). *What we know about successful school leadership.* Nottingham: National College for School Leadership.

Leung, K.W. (2002). *Exploring curriculum leadership: A case study of school-based curriculum development in a local primary school* (Unpublished dissertation in partial fulfillment of the requirements of Master of Education, University of Hong Kong.)

Llewellyn, J. (1982). *A perspective on education in Hong Kong: Report by a visiting panel.* Hong Kong: Government Printer.

Loucks-Horsley, S. (1996). Professional development for science education. In R.W. Bybee (Ed.), *National standards and the science curriculum (BSCS)* (pp. 83–90). Dubuque: Kendall/Hunt.

MacBeath, J. (1998). *Effective school leadership: Responding to change.* London: Paul Chapman.

MacBeath, J., & Moos, L. (2004). *Democratic learning: The challenge to school effectiveness.* London/New York : Routledge/Falmer.

Macpherson, I., Aspland, T., Brooker, R., & Elliott, B. (1999). *Places and spaces for teachers in curriculum leadership.* Deakin West, ACT: Australian Curriculum Studies Association.

Macpherson, I., & Brooker, R. (1999). Introducing places and spaces for teachers in curriculum leadership. In I. Macpherson, T. Aspland, R. Brooker, & B. Elliott (Eds.), *Places and spaces for teachers in curriculum leadership* (pp. 1–20). Deakin West, ACT: Australian Curriculum Studies Association.

Marsh, C.J. (1997). *Key concepts for understanding curriculum*. London: Falmer.

Miles, M., Ekholm, M., & Vandenberghe, R. (1987). *Lasting school improvement: Exploring the process of institutionalization*. Leuven: ACCO.

Orphanos, S., & Orr, M.T. (2014). Learning leadership matters: The influence of innovative school leadership preparation on teachers' experiences and outcomes. *Educational Management Administration & Leadership, 42*(5), 680–700.

Ovens, P. (1999). Can teachers be developed? *Journal of In-Service Education, 25*(2), 275–305.

Retallick, J. (1999). Teacher learning in New South Wales schools: Facilitating and inhibiting conditions. *Journal of In-Service Education, 25*(3), 473–496.

Sandholtz, J.H. (2002). Inservice training or professional development: Contrasting opportunities in a school/university partnership. *Teaching and Teacher Education, 18*(7), 815–830.

Schon, D.A. (1983). *The reflective practitioner*. London: Temple Smith.

Schon, D.A. (1989). Quotations. A symposium on Schon's concept of reflective practice: Critiques, commentaries, illustrations. *Journal of Curriculum and Supervision, 5*(1), 6–9.

Sergiovanni, T.J. (2001). *Leadership: What's in it for school?* New York: Routledge/Falmer.

Skilbeck, M. (1984). *School based curriculum development*. London: Harper & Row.

Sparks, D. (1994). A paradigm shift in staff development. *Journal of Staff Development, 15*(4), 26–29.

Stenhouse, L. (1975). *An introduction to curriculum research and development*. London: Heinemann.

Sugrue, C. (2002). Irish teachers' experience of professional learning: Implications for policy and practice. *Journal of In-Service Education, 28*(2), 311–338.

Telford, H. (1996). *Transforming schools through collaborative leadership*. London: Falmer.

Wallace, J.D., Nesbit, C.R., & Miller, A.C.S. (1999). Six leadership models for professional development in science and mathematics. *Journal of Science Teacher Education, 10*(4), 247–268.

5 Impact of school-based curriculum innovations on teachers and students

Context of change

Decentralization of curriculum decision making has been one of the key debates in the broad discussions of change strategies to enhance school improvement, teacher development, and student learning for the past several decades (Fullan, 2001; Hopkins, 2001; Skilbeck, 1984). The need for decentralization is a result of the failure of using the central agencies in designing and planning new curriculums for implementation in schools. Decentralization is also a response to the call for a more democratic participation of professional teachers in school and curriculum decision making processes in the 1960s and 1970s in such developed countries as the United States and Australia (e.g., Australian Education Union, 2004). Decentralization means moving decisions, such as what to teach more relevantly, how to teach more effectively, and how to assess more accurately closer to where learning occurs. This concept aims to meet the diverse needs of students in mixed-ability classrooms as a result of the introduction of compulsory education for all in the 1970s. Therefore, decentralization also means changing the traditional roles of teachers from mere curriculum users to curriculum developers; in other words, in this new paradigm, teachers assume more responsibilities in making curriculum decisions for enhanced student learning (Harris, 2003a; Marsh, 1997; Ovens, 1999; Stenhouse, 1975; Wallace, Nesbit, & Miller, 1999). This movement of involving and engaging teachers in a wider range of curriculum responsibilities has been considered formally by the Llewellyn report in 1982. This shift has also been examined systematically by various education reports on the Hong Kong situation. However, the pattern and the level of involvement and commitment by teachers have yet to be well defined and elaborated, along with the empirical data about what works and what does not work in the Hong Kong context (Law & Galton, 2004). The establishment of a curriculum coordinator at a senior level in the primary schools in 2002 demonstrated the determination of the government to invest in needed resources. However, the efficiency and effects of this initiative on teacher development and student learning remain largely unexplored empirically.

The current project adopts a different approach about teacher involvement, which is understood as a shared phenomenon and responsibility to be realized collectively in school settings (*The Ten School Leadership Propositions*, retrieved on

October 3, 2005). Therefore, curriculum decision making is not the sole responsibility of a few key personnel appointed by the school hierarchy but a process (or a phenomenon) to be shared equally among all teachers in the school (Ball & Cohen, 1996; Elliott, 1991; Harris, 2003b; McLaughlin & Talbert, 2001; Shulman & Sherin, 2004). Every teacher should be responsible and must have the ability to make their own curriculum decisions for students in their respective classrooms. By accepting this responsibility, participation creates opportunities for school improvement, teacher development, and enhancement of student learning (Hiebert, Gallimore, & Stigler, 2003).

Curriculum leadership development project

The project, entitled "Accelerating School-based Curriculum Development," began in September 2004 and is financially supported by the Hong Kong Quality Education Fund. The goals of this project, as stated in the proposal, include the following:

- To develop the abilities and skills of teachers in strategic planning and development as well as in using evaluation for school improvement;
- To enhance the effectiveness of school self-evaluation in the school; and
- To develop a quality culture for school self-evaluation leading to school improvement (Shatin Tsung Tsin School, 2003).

Curriculum development teams

Three curriculum development teams were formed according to three key subjects, namely, Chinese language, English language, and mathematics. These subjects comprise over half of curriculum time in the Hong Kong primary schools. The selection of team leaders was deliberately manipulated. The team leaders were "chosen" based on their observed commitment and professional attitudes toward curriculum reforms and innovations. In the first action cycle of the innovation project during the first semester, the subject panel heads were chosen as they assumed hierarchical power. Their selection was also expected to alleviate certain political tensions against the introduction of a new structure in the working lives of the teachers within the infrastructure of the school. In the second action cycle held in the second semester, these team leaders were changed and other participating colleagues were "persuaded" to take turns in leading the team.

The two arrangements had two advantages. First, the subject-based approach in the formation of a curriculum development team is intended to control the subject content of the interactions among members in teamwork activities; hence, the positive effects of the shared subject identity and working experiences among team members could be maximized (MacBeath, 2004; Schon, 1983). The second approach aimed to eliminate the potential negative influence of any hierarchical structure and power relationship among team members to create a conducive teamwork environment for the emergence of professional dialogues

72   *Case studies: a team approach*

among members; accordingly, a culture of shared and distributed curriculum leadership among team members can be fostered and nurtured (Black & Atkin, 1996; Carr & Kemmis, 1986; Putnam & Borko, 2000). The latter advantage can provide teachers with the confidence to initiate and lead activities in pedagogical changes in schools. The two factors are deemed essential because they allow the development of a common but open educational language; they also strengthen the shared but democratic identity among a group of professional teachers, enabling them to focus on collectively solving an identified pedagogical issue (Day, 1993).

Planning, experimentation, and reflection model of change

The innovation pattern adopted the planning, experimentation, and reflection (PER) model (Table 5.1). Using this model, the team reviewed, planned, and designed a lesson or a unit of learning during the collaborative meetings. Then, the team assigned teachers to trial the planned innovation lesson. Finally, the team conducted a reflection meeting.

This model of change is used in the first action cycle and is repeated in the second action cycle in a spirally continuous structure (Figure 5.1) (Law & Wan, 2005). This organization has several advantages. First, opportunities for collaboration and teamwork are created. Second, changes in pedagogy based on the teaching subject are identified. Third, a problem-solving and critical approach is adopted. Fourth, the change becomes an open venture; thus, rather than a group of definitive subjects that are merely imposed from external agents to the professional deliberation at school sites, knowledge is considered a matter of possibility

Table 5.1 Reconceptualizing school-based models of developing teacher curriculum leadership

Stage	Purposes	Developmental Activities
Initiating and Reviewing Stage	To review current practices and decide a theme of innovative practices by consensus	Team meetings, consulting experts, collecting information on effective practices
Experimentation	To try out the proposed innovative practices and collect feedback	Design materials, try out in classroom practices, adopting reliable approaches to data collection
Reflection	To reflect on practices and identify gaps for improvements in next rounds of experimentation	Team meetings, reviewing videotaped practices, identifying strengths and weaknesses for improvement and enhancement

School-based curriculum innovations 73

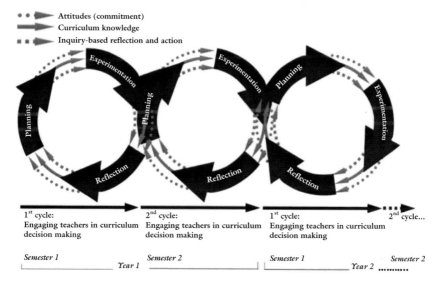

Figure 5.1 Re-conceptualizing school-based models of developing teacher curriculum leadership for lifelong education

Source: Law, E.H.F., Galton, M., & Wan, S.W.Y. (2010). Distributed curriculum leadership in action: A Hong Kong case study. *Educational Management Administration & Leadership*, 38, 286. Figure 5.1.

and is opened for challenges. The key elements of the development process in this model are teacher engagement in systematic inquiry and classroom experimentation (Frost & Durrant, 2002, 2003; Harris, 2004; Macpherson & Brooker, 1999; Macpherson, Aspland, Brooker, & Elliott, 1999).

Focus of innovation

Each curriculum development team was free to choose between two directions of change. Each team selected a teaching topic and then decided on whether to use the same pedagogical approach for all trial lessons or to adopt a different pedagogical approach in each trial lesson. For example, the mathematics team chose the topic "fraction" to organize their learning activities. This team experimented on two pedagogical approaches: one using peer questioning and computer technology to support learning, and another initially using a few hands-on tasks for the students and then moving to studies of abstract concepts. The creation of internal variations on pedagogical approaches to teaching and learning aimed to create opportunities for contrast and comparison in both of the discussions in planning and reflection meetings. In addition, the realization of these pedagogical approaches in the trial lessons provided teachers with concrete experiences to be discussed and analyzed (Ball, 1996; Birman, Desimone, Garet, Porter, & Yoon, 2002; King & Newmann, 2000). Therefore,

74 *Case studies: a team approach*

curriculum reforms and change would not remain as certain abstract language or concept in policy documents, but would become authentic experiences that are closer to the real lives of most of the teachers (Garet, Porter, Desimone, Birman, & Yoon, 2001).

Methodology and data collection

A mixed-methods approach was adopted to collect a wider range of direct experiences with the innovation and to understand the effects of the innovation from various perspectives of the project participants (Teddlie & Tashakkori, 2003). The key participating teachers and groups of students were interviewed. The planning and reflection meetings, along with all trial lessons, were videotaped. All teachers and students were interviewed by the project leader in April (i.e., before the trial lessons) and in July (i.e., after the trial lessons for students and after the reflection meeting for the teachers). This chapter reports the findings from the structured interviews conducted before the trial lessons and after the reflection meeting of the mathematics and Chinese-language curriculum development teams. The data from the videotaped meetings and lessons are also presented for triangulation and further illumination.

Structured interviews before the trial lessons and after the reflection meetings were conducted to elicit views and data from both the participating teachers on the team as well as the students who experienced the trial lessons. Given the time constraint, only the key teachers, such as the team leader, the panel head, and the trial teachers on the team, were interviewed individually to ensure privacy and confidentiality. Questions were also adjusted to match their roles in the team. Four participating teachers on the team were interviewed. The questions for the teachers focused on the following aspects of their experiences about the innovation:

- Their understanding of the project objectives, processes, and outcomes;
- Their experiences and observations about the trial lessons they implemented or observed; and
- Their evaluations of the innovations.

Student interviews were organized differently. Two selected groups of students who had experienced the trial lessons were interviewed before and after each lesson. A total of two groups of 12 students were interviewed. Each group comprised six students. Each group of students consisted of two noisy, two quiet, one high achiever, and one underachiever student. The selection aimed at creating an informal environment. In this way, the students could more freely express their experiences of the innovation lessons. The questions included their reactions toward the learning processes of the trial teachers and what learning outcomes they felt they had acquired. They were also asked to compare explicitly their feelings toward the trial teachers before and after the trial lessons they conducted.

Findings and analyses

The organization of the data and findings adopts a more naturalistic approach. A few emerging themes from the data form the major categories of the topic headings below. However, for convenience, two perspectives from teachers and students are used to provide a macrostructure of the findings.

Did distributed leadership work?

In the project, the leadership style was deliberately manipulated. The style was changed from the traditional conception of leadership based on the hierarchical structure of the school using panel or subject department heads (as in the first action cycle of the innovation project during the first semester), to a conception of leadership that is instrumental and administrative. In this way, more genuine, professional, and open-ended dialogues occurred in team interactions on pedagogical issues. Teacher leadership in school-based curriculum development would also be developed in the second action cycle during the second semester. In such a situation, the power relationship between followers and leaders becomes blurred. The teacher interviews showed a certain progress in this area and indicated the positive effects of this manipulation.

The team leaders of the mathematics and Chinese teams assumed the role of facilitators performing the following tasks: liaison work with the external consultant, coordinating meetings, searching for discussion materials, motivating colleagues to participate, preparing PowerPoint presentations as learning materials to support teaching, and collecting documents as part of administrative duties.

> I am a so-and-so leader, how to contact the consultant, organize meeting, concerned about whether I can motivate colleagues to attend meetings . . . whether we can compromise, but colleagues collaborated well . . . more easily than I expected. . . .
> (Interview with Teacher F from the mathematics team; literal translation no. 13)

These team leaders were also conscious about the changing style of leadership and expressed their agreement with the new style of appointing chairs for the curriculum development teams.

> Once we sat down together, we did not have the idea about who was the leader, panel head, or try-out teachers. Our roles were loose; we felt relaxed because we were not try-out teachers. The panel head and I talked quite freely, not aware of our formal roles. We enjoyed our conversations.
> (Interview with Teacher F from the mathematics team; literal translation no. 8)

76 *Case studies: a team approach*

Teacher F, the mathematics team leader, described her role as follows:

> This time I was an observer. Last time I was the try-out teacher. Because now you are an observer, you watched and saw more how the try-out teachers handled teaching. Are they correct or is there room for improvement? This is learning.
>
> (Interview with Teacher F from the mathematics team; literal translation no. 5)

The perceptions of the team leaders matched those of the other members who worked with them in the second action cycle of the project. The Chinese team members described their observations as follows:

> Teacher A is responsible for coordination . . . She had a lesson plan and package . . . tells us what the problems are . . . tells us what to attend to. . . .
> She could not tell us what is the idea about the project but supports us in the planning lesson . . . learning materials.
>
> (Interview with Teacher B from the Chinese team; literal translation no. 44)

> [She] guides us in the meeting . . . In fact the PowerPoint and the module idea were her ideas . . . She used them before and this time they adapted them for use in each class. . . .
>
> (Interview with Teacher C from the Chinese team; literal translation no. 45)

> She is quick and efficient. . . [often] talks to members. . . .
>
> (Interview with Teacher C from the Chinese team; literal translation no. 45)

The curriculum development team members acknowledge that their team leaders served as a supporter and facilitator of the curriculum-making process, rather than traditional leaders who assumed a more directive role. However, evidence showed that the leader of the mathematics team was more effective than that of the Chinese team. One of the trial teachers from the mathematics team expressed her observations as follows:

> She leads us to think . . . She thinks of many issues . . . leads us to ask the consultant . . . and gives us a summary . . . what to attend to . . . a good supporter . . . support us to design a curriculum . . . but her leadership role is not strong. . . . I feel we are equal, share work. Everyone can be a team leader . . . The leader helps collect information . . . chair meetings.
>
> (Interview with Teacher H from the mathematics team; literal translation no. 21)

School-based curriculum innovations 77

This observation was triangulated with the videotaped meetings of both teams. The team leader of the mathematics group tended to be more articulate and willing to pose questions to the meetings. In comparison, the leader of the Chinese team was less willing to lead discussions. We then considered the roles played by the traditional leaders of both teams and determined how they compared with these team leaders.

The panel heads of the Chinese and mathematics subject departments were not given any prominent role in this round of the innovation. However, the two panel heads asserted varying degrees of influence on the curriculum-making processes. The panel head of the mathematics team was more resilient and reserved in asserting herself. By contrast, the Chinese panel head still dominated the direction and contents of the professional discourses in most of the planning and reflection meetings. He was unwilling to surrender his traditional status in the school hierarchy, asserting influence in the deliberation of the innovation.

> I am the coordinator and facilitator . . . and locate where the focus is . . . what to do in different levels . . . where the problems are . . . where to do a bit more. . . .
>
> (Interview with Teacher E from the Chinese team;
> literal translation no. 22)

> I reminded the teacher not to criticize the ancient people from our modern perspectives; we should appreciate from their own value system. I would suggest a class should download materials by themselves, not the teacher.
>
> (Interview with Teacher E from the Chinese team;
> literal translation no. 22)

Judging from his use of language that implies control and demand, the Chinese panel head assumed a dominant role in the curriculum decision making processes and deliberately downgraded the role of the team leader. He recognized the team leader as solely a liaison person with the external consultant and a facilitator tasked to discuss design issues with the other members. His sense of power was also asserted in the videotaped planning and reflection meetings. Specifically, he severely criticized the linkages between the studies of a historically tragic figure who committed suicide and the modern way of viewing the value of life. Meanwhile, the trial teachers wanted to experiment with the students in the trial lesson. The Chinese panel head also assumed a leadership role in making decisions about subject content.

> [My role is] to provide knowledge background for the topic.
>
> (Interview with Teacher E from the Chinese team;
> literal translation no. 22)

> There is a division between panel and consultant: panel [head] is responsible for content; consultant for pedagogy. . . .
>
> (Interview with Teacher E from the Chinese team;
> literal translation no. 22)

78 *Case studies: a team approach*

The reactions of members to the leadership styles of the two traditional panel heads differed. The members of the Chinese team developed a sense of negative feeling toward the overt assertiveness in the leadership of their panel head.

> He was busy . . . or he gave us pressure because we based our teaching on our pupils . . . but he insisted on subject content. . . . [He was] quite serious about content . . . but we based on pupil ability to design . . . and this is a great difference. . . .
> (Interview with Teacher C from the Chinese team;
> literal translation no. 45)

The Chinese team members would have preferred having their discussions without their panel head, although they acknowledged his positional power in the line of accountability.

The members of the two other development teams recognized the facilitative role deliberately played by their former panel heads. They also had a stronger sense of team spirit being developed among the members.

> I felt the panel head was not a panel head anymore. I felt she was a member of the team . . . we share work . . . we are equal . . . we all can solve problems . . . She gives us views and ideas when we [lack them].
> (Interview with Teacher H from the mathematics team;
> literal translation no. 21)

One member of the mathematics team even felt she was acting on behalf of the curriculum development team to put the plan into action.

> I felt that [I was] acting out the collective decisions . . . I am an actor . . . I am implementing our ideas and decisions.
> (Interview with Teacher H from the mathematics team;
> literal translation no. 26)

This feeling of a shared community was also found on the Chinese team. The members generally felt the working spirit was collaborative. They did not feel directed in a way distant to their expectation and willingness. One even felt he was implementing the collective decisions of the team.

> I think we work together and methods and roles are similar; just coordinating, we look at what we have, talked about features of each class to help each teacher, give some ideas, to construct something.
> (Interview with Teacher B from the Chinese team;
> literal translation no. 42)

> [I was] like an implementer . . . others want me to teach this thing . . . then I could adjust accordingly to my class features . . . to revise the lesson plan.
> (Interview with Teacher B from the Chinese team;
> literal translation no. 43)

The decision making processes highlighted underwent some form of change – from a style of leadership that was assertive and dominant because of the ascribed status of the leaders, to a form of leadership that was much more collaborative and allowed room for personal professional expression. The members still appreciated the profound knowledge of the panel head. However, they also expressed the desire to venture and explore areas of alternatives beyond the traditions.

In the videotaped meetings and reflections of both teams, the interactions illustrated the effects of the social dimension of the interaction between members of the teams. Maintaining social cohesion among members of the team was essential because this process enhanced teamwork and spirit. This long-term process was crucial for each member of the team. Therefore, teachers tended to be less critical and reflective, and comments were mild in tone. Even the panel head and the team leader played rather secondary roles in terms of leadership in professional domains. However, once the leadership in professional matters was initiated by the consultant from outside the school context, the dialogues and interactions became more focused on pedagogical efficiency and the conceptual clarity of the learning target. The role of the consultant offers professional and academic leadership in action to the teachers in the team. This point will be revisited in much detail in the section discussing the role of the consultant.

In general, the adoption of distributed leadership by the mathematics curriculum development team encouraged the emergence of a community of professional learners. This approach focuses on formulating a task aimed at achieving pedagogical innovation in action within classroom settings. Meanwhile, professional leadership was less salient on the Chinese team because of the leadership styles of both the consultant and the dominating influence of the traditional leadership in the curriculum decision making processes. Changing roles result in changing perceptions about traditional practices; thus, beliefs and practices have room for change. The deliberation of a leadership style based on the collective responsibility of each individual member in curriculum decision making enhances personal and professional learning in a public manner. Therefore, teachers are prepared to assume leadership roles of various domains in the school-based curriculum development in a collective fashion. This finding is also true for a team whose collaboration and professional leadership has been mediated by the traditional form of power and influence of the panel head and the didactic style of the consultant.

Table 5.2 summarizes the different leadership patterns and their mediating effects on the key players in each team.

What are the contributions of the consultant to the implementation of the curriculum innovation?

The formation of the curriculum development team and the organization of the various types of support, such as professional support, are essential to the successful implementation of the curriculum change. Some of the key considerations are as follows: how professional input could be solicited from outside the school

80   *Case studies: a team approach*

Table 5.2 Leadership styles and effects

	Chinese Team	*Mathematics Team*
Leadership style	Distributed	Distributed
Mediating factors	Dominated by assertive panel head; Didactic consultant	Less assertive panel head; Facilitating consultant
Effects	Less team spirit; Developing resentment within the team	Stronger team spirit; Developing collaborative pattern
Discourse style	Closed and informative; Less interactive; Less expressive	Open and exploratory; More interactive; Full of stories; Expressive
Participation style	Less interactive; Less active	More interactive; Active
Teacher learning	Less effective professionally	More effective professionally

Source: Law, E.H.F., Galton, M., & Wan, S.W.Y. (2010). Distributed curriculum leadership in action: A Hong Kong case study. *Education Management Administration and Leadership, 38*(3), 286–303.

and how this type of input could be effectively integrated with the needs of the school-based reforms and the professional needs of the teachers (Borko, 2004; Fullan & Quinn, 2015). Partnership with the university faculties in education has been one of the key factors in the successful implementation of educational reforms (Brabeck, Walsh, & Latta, 2003; Sherrill, 1999, p. 57). This success is even more evident when the style of collaboration fits well with the professional needs of the school-based innovation, and when it is taken in a developmental perspective rather than in an ad hoc and unsustainable manner.

At the same time, the current project emphasized the need to initiate collaboration with professionals from university faculties. Each subject team has been assigned an expert in the field to provide professional support and advice on pedagogical innovations. The appointed experts worked with the curriculum development teams, joined the collaborative lesson preparation meetings, observed trial lessons, attended the reflection meetings, and provided advice and feedback on the focus of the pedagogical innovations. The functions and practices involved in having an appropriate consultant from outside the school to work with the school-based curriculum development teams or projects have not been well documented in many school improvement or curriculum development project reports. Close-up evidence of several relevant issues has also been unexplored, including how the functions of external consultants have been realized in practice and how their effectiveness in some cases could have been mediated by other micro-political factors within each development team and the professional styles of the consultants themselves.

The consultants appointed for the two curriculum development teams worked with each of the teams in the first action cycle during the first semester. They also developed a certain form of understanding among themselves. Members of both teams found the consultants helpful, and appreciated their professional inputs in

School-based curriculum innovations 81

the discussions before and after the trial lessons. The consultants led the team members to think about the pedagogical issues and to explore possible alternatives for the future.

> We unconsciously use didactic methods . . . because it is the quickest, looks more effective, but this time Mr. Wong told us that we do not know how to use some questions to stimulate thinking. This makes me feel I should not only ask yes or no questions, so simple and factual questions; we learned this in training but once we walked into classrooms we forget.
> (Interview with Teacher G from the mathematics team;
> literal translation no. 32)

> Before [the] meeting he led us to think . . . weaknesses of the pupils . . . give instructions on lesson plans . . . after observation give views . . . and lead us what we could do in future . . . he is knowledgeable about the curriculum. . . .
> (Interview with Teacher A from the Chinese team;
> literal translation no. 22)

> Cut text . . . how to read books . . . what happened in Shanghai . . . suggest pupils buy a book of Tang poems and recite one each week . . . the pupils will know many poems. . . .
> (Interview with Teacher A from the Chinese team;
> literal translation no. 22)

However, the effectiveness of the two consultants on the curriculum deliberation of the two teams differed in a number of dimensions of activities. Each case is presented separately below with a few common frameworks, such as the emerging models of collaboration and models of personality or professional style.

The consultant for the mathematics team used a confrontational model. He presented his views directly contrary to those of the team members. Whether he was conscious about this application requires further investigation. Conflicting views were recorded as shown in the interview excerpt below.

> He does not understand us yet . . . Like we want a lesson to teach pupils about festivals in China . . . but he thought a lesson is not enough . . . he possibly wanted us to use a whole module . . . We had only one meeting . . . last meeting, we had some initial idea about the topic for the try-out lesson . . . and how to develop . . . design instructional plan successful . . . We are busy, very busy. . . .
> (Interview with Teacher A from the Chinese team;
> literal translation no. 5)

The conflicting views might have been handled smoothly by the team leader in the planning meeting or in the discussion to arrive at a consensus. Unfortunately, this approach failed to solve the problem. Consequently, the conflicts remained, and each teacher used their own views in the trial lesson.

82 *Case studies: a team approach*

> We had many mistakes because we were not well prepared . . . we had no consensus . . . the consultant suddenly arrived . . . we did not have the guidelines but suddenly Phoebe gave us many guidelines; we need time to digest; we did not follow the guideline . . . we could have only one lesson . . . we also had some internal arguments . . . the consultant then gave some suggestions . . . asked us to give him the plan by email; he was suggesting we need not think by ourselves but can use website materials developed by other schools. Many schools are doing the same thing with different topics; we could download them and teach them in our classes. We did not have any conclusion and we followed that up later.
>
> (Interview with Teacher C from the Chinese team;
> literal translation no. 58)

The style of the consultant's professional input as well as his relationship with the team have been salient and explicit in the videotaped planning and reflection meetings. The videotaped planning meeting showed some agreement with the teacher observations about the consultant as well as the relationship between the teachers and the curriculum development team. The consultant gave much professional input on pedagogical principles and practices in relation to the Chinese curriculum in the planning meeting. A similar observation was found in the reflection meetings after the trial lessons. He tended to dominate the discourse and closed the discussion, rather than being open to more alternatives and seeking possibilities from the perspectives of the participating teachers. The observations given by the teachers were also congruent with the discussion contents in the planning meeting. These observations indicated that the focus of the meeting was not on the instructional design or the innovative aspect of the trial lessons, but on general issues with curriculum and teaching in the primary schools in Hong Kong. In the reflection meeting, the teachers had little reflection on the trial lessons and the comments were solely from the observations of the consultant. Therefore, the reflection meeting failed to create opportunities through which the teachers could share experiences and seek improvements from their practical experiences of trying out the innovation.

The contribution of the consultant sometimes moved far beyond our imagination. The consultant not only served as a mentor for some members but also served as a mediator between colleagues in the school in case of embarrassments such as peer observation. The following two quotations from the teacher interviews demonstrate the socio-political functions of the consultant in the implementation of a curriculum innovation.

> We colleagues did the peer observation, but because we were colleagues, we tend to be lenient and more accommodating . . . but Mr. Wong is an outsider, he does not have our tradition. He is able to observe many problems that we are so used to.
>
> (Interview with Teacher G from the mathematics team;
> literal translation no. 32)

Mr. Wong gave us many good ideas . . . his role is a mentor, not a higher authority. He is thinking with you; his attitude is good.

(Interview with Teacher G from the mathematics team;
literal translation no. 35)

In the case of the panel head, the contribution of the consultant led him to reflect deeply about his own traditional practice in classroom teaching. The panel head also indicated having gained deep learning from his participation in the curriculum decision making process.

To look at the same topic and how to teach from a different angle, learned very much . . . particularly learned from Mr. Wong, the consultant, discovered that what we thought and practiced may not be correct . . . using different angles would see different things . . . discovered what pupils think is different from what we think they know in mind.

(Interview with Teacher I from the mathematics team;
literal translation no. 42)

The videotapes of the planning and reflection meetings were used to triangulate the various roles played by the consultant in the different stages of the innovation project. First of all, he acted as a facilitator to lead discussions; then, he initiated topics for discussions of pedagogical significance in both the planning and reflection meetings. Some of the topics used by the consultant to stimulate professional reflection among the team members in the videotaped meetings are presented below.

In the planning meetings:

- He emphasized the conceptual issues of teaching the concept of "fraction." He also suggested that the meeting should focus on how the concept of fraction could be taught with clarity and accuracy. He reiterated that the problem was not the shortage of methods for teachers but lay in whether the methods used were closely related with learning the target concepts in mathematics.
- He used communication skills, such as clarification, probing, asking for explanations and concrete examples, and seeking alternatives. He also challenged the traditional practices of the team members.

In the reflection meeting:

- He determined the conceptual problems for the younger learners in the trial learning sessions and achieved this when a generic issue with fraction was contextualized with the use of paper, shapes, and folding as main elements in learning the concept.
- He moved the focus of the discussion from the inability of the students to the inability of the teachers to clarify the various key properties of the concept of fraction for their students.
- He also argued that the transition from one activity to another should be linked up strongly to conceptual terms; otherwise, the students would be unable to appreciate the values and linkages between activities.

84 Case studies: a team approach

Following is a literal transcription of a series of leading and probing inputs the consultant had posed to the meeting to stimulate reflections among members. Such inputs indeed readdressed the learning issue with students.

> The teacher did give two examples to pupils . . . one using square and one circle . . . Pupils are still unable to conceptualize the issue or generalize the principles . . . from one example, (restricting to the use of square and circle only) and then move to something general . . . The pupils may not understand how this task is related to the second task or the task of coloring . . . The problem is with transition . . . how to give more background information to support learning . . . It is the flow or the transition from one task to the second task which matters.

Meanwhile, the contribution of the consultant to the mathematics curriculum development team is twofold: offering professional and academic inputs concerning pedagogical issues on the topic that the teachers wanted to explore, and leading the team to reflect upon personal pedagogical experiences and practices. He not only facilitated discussions openly and professionally, he also helped achieve the following: allowing expressions of views; highlighting key pedagogical concerns, such as linkages between learning activities and learning sessions; stretching the understanding of members of the underlying issues with deep learning; and moving the focus of the discussion from students' inability to a reconsideration of the appropriateness of the selection of pedagogical strategies in relation to the achievement of the content knowledge by students. He practically demonstrated a form of professional leadership to the team.

In summary, we obtain two contrasting models of professional inputs from the two consultants with similar backgrounds. The characteristics demonstrated by the consultant to the Chinese team show a restricted model of professionality, whereas those by the consultant to the mathematics team demonstrate an extended model of professionality (Holye, 1969). Table 5.3 summarizes the characteristics and potential effects of these models on curriculum deliberation.

Table 5.3 Models of professionalism and effects

	Models of Professionality	
Domains of contributions	Restricted	Extended
Input	Personal instructional experience	Instructional alternatives
Role	Informative	Exploratory
Discourse style	Closed	Open
Collaboration	One-way; Didactic	Negotiable
Social cohesion	Diffused	Converged
Leadership	Ascribed; Power-coercive	Re-educative; Social interactive

Source: Law, E.H.F., Galton, M., & Wan, S.W.Y. (2010). Distributed curriculum leadership in action: A Hong Kong case study. *Education Management Administration and Leadership, 38*(3), 286–303.

How did the members of the curriculum development team perceive or experience the innovation?

Participating members of the curriculum development teams often viewed the innovation from their own perspectives. Accordingly, internal potential tensions were created between what was intended and how that curriculum intention was interpreted in action. Such tensions may present obstacles for the achievement of the original aim of the project. However, this potential tension may be negotiated among different parties by participating in the curriculum deliberation, and may apparently become part of the essential learning experience for each party (MacDonald & Rudduck, 1971). Therefore, awareness of the importance of the innovation activities to the pedagogical needs of the students and to the professional development of teachers themselves is essential for the professional development of each teacher on the curriculum development teams. Sharing this awareness among the majority of the members who have been working together would be even more rewarding for each member. The shared awareness or the enhancement of this shared awareness is one of the key conditions of the successful implementation of curriculum reforms. This objective is also a major function of forming curriculum development teams as a structural approach to respond systematically to the curriculum changes in policy and society.

Understanding the aim

The majority of the members of the two teams have shared a common understanding of the broad issues related to the aim of achieving innovation. They also have similar views on the prescribed contributions of the innovations to the three aspects of school improvement initiatives, namely, pedagogical innovations, teacher professional improvement, and student learning enhancement.

> I think analyzing the weaknesses of each level and each subject . . . then think of solving the problems . . . and see whether the implementation is effective . . . and then improve [on it].
>
> (Interview with Teacher A from the Chinese team;
> literal translation no. 10)

> Traditionally, we lectured and then asked pupils to work on a task . . . but this time . . . we used a task asking the pupils to have some hands-on experiences about division first, how to divide things . . . We started with some concrete tasks and then moved to abstract concepts . . . then consolidation . . . one step after the other to teach . . . One group of teachers used talk, and the other group like mine used concrete experience first and lead the pupils to abstraction . . . The first method was less effective than the latter method of starting with concrete experience.
>
> (Interview with Teacher H from the mathematics team;
> literal translation no. 22)

86 *Case studies: a team approach*

Notably, the views of teachers about the innovation had changed as reflected in their interviews before and after the trial lessons. One trial teacher expressed some uncertainty about the innovation before the trial lesson, but articulated clearly the objectives of the innovation project after the trial lessons.

> I am not experienced, and have no experience of working for the project. . . .
> I am not certain what the project is expecting of us.
>> (Interview with Teacher G from the mathematics team;
>> literal translation no. 28)

> I think using additional resources can help teachers work with outside professionals, [thus] improving teaching and ensuring staff development.
>> (Interview with Teacher G from the mathematics team;
>> literal translation no. 31)

> Less uncertainty.
>> (Interview with Teacher G from the mathematics team;
>> literal translation no. 34)

The other trial teacher had fewer problems with the aim of the project. Her understandings recorded before and after matched each other.

> Using a problem solving approach . . . we work collaboratively to solve it for pupils.
>> (Interview with Teacher H from the mathematics team;
>> literal translation no. 15)

> Using the power of collectiveness with the help of the consultant . . . help us to see problems clearly . . . effective lesson preparation.
>> (Interview with Teacher H from the mathematics team;
>> literal translation no. 19)

In summary, members of the curriculum development teams developed their understanding of the aims of the curriculum reforms. The paradigm shifted from teacher-centered pedagogical approaches to student activities that aim at stimulation, acquisition of procedural skills and knowledge, as well as hand-on experiences with the mathematical problem posed by the trial teachers to the team. Members were more aware of these aims and their meaning in practical terms, and were able to express these aims in language openly. The readiness of the teachers to open their private experiential knowledge to the public is also one of the key professional development strategies. Being ready and comfortable to be observed and to be openly criticized and discussed in public takes time.

Experiencing the innovation

Team members also played different roles. In fact, some roles of the teachers were deliberately changed to create more flexibility and room for professional dialogues

School-based curriculum innovations   87

as well as to allow extension of personal experience in making curriculum decisions. These deliberations had some effect on the trial teachers and on those who experienced changes in their roles in the innovation process. To illustrate the importance of experiencing the innovation in a new perspective from the professional development of the participating teachers, we deliberately used the interview data from the Chinese team to gain a more in-depth understanding of the issues in question. Although the team experienced a restricted model of professionality under the influences of the two key members, namely, the hierarchical leader and the didactic consultant, the experiences of the members seemed to be enriching. Participation in this case served well as a catalyst for thinking and reflecting around the practice of teacher professionality (Rayner & Gunter, 2005, p. 157).

Chan was a panel head and assumed a fairly superior status. This observation was supported by his style of presentation in his interview and the perceptions of his role described in the interviews with the other team members. This finding was well recorded in the previous section on leadership change. Given that his current role had become less prominent and that less influence was asserted over the contents and directions of the pedagogical change, his significantly detailed description of the changes in the trial lessons reflected this. Table 5.4 summarizes his observation of the pedagogical differences and their effects on trial learning.

Chan made the following comment on the performance of the trial lessons:

> Allow pupils to take initiative to investigate from different perspectives; better than from the teachers' own perspectives; we can think of many alternatives in processes.
> (Interview with Teacher E from the Chinese team;
> literal translation no. 23)

Teacher C, the support teacher for the Chinese team, gave a slightly more detailed observation. She commented plainly on the change of her personal feeling about the innovation.

Table 5.4 A unit plan in curriculum

Theme	Chinese culture and customs		
Focus	Dragon boat festival and the story of poet Wat Yuen		
Class	Student needs	Pedagogical strategies	Effects
A/B	Able; Strong in language	Self-searching materials; Group discussions; Presentation; Critical thinking skills; Discussion; Design; Peer assessment	Analytical skills; Reading skills
C/D	Weak; Less motivated	Materials downloaded by teachers; Role play; Forms and meanings of celebration	Performing skills; Creativity

88   Case studies: a team approach

I had the first cycle experience . . . then I am the clearer this time . . . now my space for teaching is bigger . . . on module teaching and use of resources.

We had a bigger room . . . We can design topics and methods according to the class level . . . and each class could be very different.

Room and flexibility on instructional design.

We could use the same package to teach in the following years.

Now I [have] a clearer concept about the project . . . the first time we are worried to make mistakes . . . so more restrictions by ourselves . . . but this time was different . . . with the past experience our thinking becomes more extended.

(Interview with Teacher C from the Chinese team;
literal translation no. 60)

The two other trial teachers provided detailed descriptions of their experiences of the innovation content, process, and events of the trial lessons. The first one was experienced but inactive, while the second one was inexperienced but committed. Both had not participated in the first action cycle of the project. The following is an outline of the experience given by Teacher D, the first trial teacher.

He described traditional methods as practices that were dominated by teacher talk leading toward the deterioration of student self-learning ability, whereas the current curriculum reforms aimed at motivating students to initiate learning by themselves. He even admitted that some students were more capable of searching learning materials, and that the role of the teachers should lead and direct student learning (interview with Teacher D from the Chinese team: literal translation nos. 48 and 49). The trial lesson was successful and students were excited and stimulated by the activities (interview with Teacher D from the Chinese team; literal translation no. 53). He described his teaching approach in this trial lesson as liberal, aimed at encouraging student discussion against the traditional conception of the festival, and created more interactions between the teacher and the students. He discovered after the trial lesson that the teachers were able to teach students deeper meanings of the festival and the suicide of poet Wat. The details of the activities in the trial lesson are presented in the following excerpt:

One discussion . . . afterwards they report . . . teachers conclude . . . give praise to the good ones; not satisfactory ones, we supplement . . . not to criticize them . . . the second discussion about poet Wat's funeral. . . [I] asked them about methods to commemorate his death . . . they suggested paintings, stamps . . . pupils led and teachers assisted and allowed pupils to develop . . . beginning starts with their imagination . . . allow pupils to imagine wildly . . . and then teachers point and narrow their ideas, and then [provide] a summary.

(Interview with Teacher D from the Chinese team;
literal translation no. 55)

He described the students in the trial lesson as energetic, engaged, enthusiastic, and possessed a fair amount of division of labor among members in each group (interview with Teacher D from the Chinese team; literal translation no. 56). Compared with his present teaching, he recognized this previous teaching style as being more focused on students' correct answers, lacking student discussions, and not encouraging students to search for materials independently. The videotaped lesson showed that the students were active and willing to participate in class discussions and activities, although the performance of some seemed to lag behind the other more able students.

Teacher B, the second trial teacher, was an inexperienced but committed teacher. His understanding of the innovation was to use different methods to teach different types of students with different abilities and characters. Able students should be given more opportunities to conduct a presentation because they are more able in language, whereas weak students should be given more activities on action-related activities such as role plays. He described his methods in the trial lesson as having more tasks in the beginning providing students with opportunities to imagine, explore, draw concept maps, and conduct reports. In the latter part of the lesson, he focused on drawing conclusions, organizing a more holistic picture about various learning elements for students. He was honest about not using a concept map or role play strategies and that he would rather rely on texts in books in normal lessons. His answer to the question surrounding why he chose role play and concept mapping is provided below.

> I noticed that pupils from Class 5R became bored when their teacher distributed materials to them. They would also be bored if I would do the same. Thus, I allowed them to write and draw freely as well as to engage in different roles. In that way, they would have something to discuss. I asked them to act like a negotiator and persuade poet Wat not to commit suicide. I allowed them to understand the value of life. This topic has many elements apart from Chinese cultures.
>
> (Interview with Teacher B from the Chinese team;
> literal translation no. 35)

Teacher B appeared to be affected by the practice of his colleagues on the team. He did not want his teaching to be regarded as traditional because such method was often associated with something old-fashioned and ineffective. In the videotaped lesson, he was nervous and hesitant in the beginning but recovered well toward the middle and end of the lesson. His students were actively engaged and their overall performance was good based on his perspective. This observation matched those of the students, as they described in the interview.

Teacher A, the team leader of the Chinese team, also provided many details about the trial lessons and student learning. We deliberately chose her comment on the success of the pedagogical strategies of her team for different classes. Her comment summarizes her overall perception and experience of the trial lessons.

> We did well because we felt satisfied . . . Our classes used different methods and we thought it was impossible and wasted our time . . . but found we could do different things in different ability classes . . . More able classes [must do]

more reading and searching for information . . . Weak classes [must do] more teacher storytelling and short films . . . different classes, different teaching methods . . . More able classes [that are] strong in reading can do more presentation . . . For example class C has strengths in performing in public . . . and they used drama in learning to express themselves; [it's] very good.

(Interview with Teacher A from the Chinese team; literal translation no. 7)

Different experiences were recorded in the interview data and different participating teachers had different foci of experiences judging from their descriptions of their personal experiences and the events of the trial lessons observed in the videotaped lessons. The effects of the social cohesion played a role in moving members of the team forward when they saw the progress of the other teams in the innovation. Some members also expressed reflectively in the interview their willingness to experiment with changes in their normal lessons. The detailed description of the innovation processes given by the panel head is strikingly clear. If his leadership style matches the needs of his members and colleagues and is accepted by the team, then his social influence in the team will become even more significant.

The descriptions outlined above demonstrate two points: the importance of the shared understanding of an innovation project, and the dynamic nature of the interactions between the participating teachers and the object of innovation to be mediated by a multiplicity of factors. In other words, the richness of the experiences of the Chinese team members overrides the limitations imposed by the restricted models of professionality as a result of the two key players in the curriculum deliberation processes.

What did the participating teachers learn in making curriculum decisions?

One of the benefits that can be gained by teachers encouraged to participate in curriculum decision making is that teachers develop professionally when they are given opportunities to make pedagogical decisions. The process of decision making of this nature demands the active use of observations about student needs, selection of suitable teaching strategies and learning activities, and use of methods to obtain evidence of learning on the part of the teachers. This claim about teacher development in school-based curriculum development settings has been strongly advocated despite the necessary conditions to support teacher engagement in curriculum decision making. However, different kinds of participation lead to different kinds of experience and different professional skills accordingly, given that member teachers on the teams played different roles. Therefore, the social relationships created among members of each team allows or controls learning opportunities. Such relationships can also possibly shape the awareness of team members of the innovation being implemented.

Acquiring professional skills

The team members participated in the entire process of curriculum deliberation that leads to the implementation of the trial lessons. They also participated in the reflection meetings. The members of the two teams indicated their learning (interview with Teacher G from the mathematics team; literal translation nos. 27 and 38). The detailed descriptions of Teacher A, the team leader of the Chinese team, were illustrative of the kind of learning experiences specific to planning, review, design, implementation, and evaluation of the school curriculum in action. Therefore, we used her experiences to discuss the kind of professional skills required to participate in making curriculum decisions. Her descriptions will vividly demonstrate the kind of decisions that participation has created for her and that has become part of her consciousness. This experience is the most valuable for each teacher because experience of this kind leads to the possibility of change in beliefs and practices. The descriptions are organized under the nature of curriculum decisions in the planning and implementation processes to illustrate clearly the underlying meanings of the decisions and experiences in relation to leadership development in curriculum.

(1) Teachers experimented with various approaches and explored alternatives in curriculum planning.

We planned and designed teaching approaches. We found this method did not work and we found another method. . . . We also invited the senior pupils to help the lower pupils, drawing pictures . . . writing some narratives for demonstration . . . senior pupils can teach lower pupils . . . and we like peer observation. We learned something from others . . . we discussed together and we benefited . . . we also had some satisfaction . . . we found 2A class pupils very efficient . . . very smart . . . very organized way to present . . . really some comparison.

> (Interview with Teacher A from the Chinese team;
> literal translation no. 3)

(2) Teachers made decisions about the contents of learning.

[This means in the] normal curriculum, teaching is tight. This time we taught Chinese cultures and pupils must learn . . . textbooks have little to say . . . We did not teach a chapter and replaced it with cultural studies . . . very good experience.

> (Interview with Teacher A from the Chinese team;
> literal translation no. 9)

(3) Teachers identified student needs through various methods.

Pupils did not understand festivals, but this is about daily life, therefore we decided to teach them [about it].

> (Interview with Teacher A from the Chinese team;
> literal translation no. 14)

92   *Case studies: a team approach*

By observation in our normal lessons . . . worksheets . . . asking them. . . [there's] not enough in textbooks. . . .

> (Interview with Teacher A from the Chinese team;
> literal translation no. 14)

(4) Teachers adjusted their pedagogical strategies according to the students' needs.

Very tight schedule . . . because many additions and many revisions . . . we had to hurry and teach the lesson before the festival . . . not interesting if after the festival.

In fact we had many problems . . . possibly their understanding is weak . . . after reading the materials is still not sure . . . or because of the reading materials . . . not much interest in reading outside materials . . . they do not read any cultural materials.

> (Interview with Teacher A from the Chinese team;
> literal translation no. 14)

(5) Teachers differentiated instructions to meet individual differences.

. . . worksheets . . . more able classes are deeper . . . weak classes . . . after revisions are less difficult . . . about finding resources . . . 5R is able and they had no problem with reading materials . . . but other classes are less interested in reading . . . and then we decided teachers tell them . . . and change to using drama.

I taught 5R and B . . . I tried 5S first . . . no videotaping . . . after try-out then revised in classes A, C, D . . . my computer was slow . . . can't show music and videos! . . . smart next time . . . must bring a powerful one up . . . we overestimated the ability of 5T D . . . they took time to read . . . but their creativity is good . . . we could give this more to them.

> (Interview with Teacher A from the Chinese team;
> literal translation no. 14)

(6) Teachers reflected on their practical experiences.

[Aside] from the naughtiness of 5U after observation by the consultant . . . their nature is like that . . . very committed . . . Others are good, very creative, in particular persuading Mr. Wat not to commit suicide . . . very good activities.

We were greedy, talk about origins of the festival, customs, and some creative activities . . . each class has some revisions and some differences . . . For example Class C we wanted to bring out the issue with suicide and its values . . . for 5U we watched some poems from Mr. Wat . . . relating strongly to creativity.

First, they could talk about the origins, many stories, designing many activities . . . besides talking they assessed their peer presentation . . . whether it worked . . . whether causing environmental issues . . . how are these related to the festival of Mr. Poet Wat . . . train them to think critically. . . .

(Interview with Teacher A from the Chinese team; literal translation no. 14)

Teacher A, the team leader of the Chinese team, had been collecting experiences in the entire process in ways she had described in the interview. These experiences are relevant to the professional development of teacher leaders in curriculum because they empower teachers to become leaders in leading curriculum change and innovations in school-based settings.

The details and the nature of the experiences that each member contributed in the interviews varied. Therefore, the kind of learning and professional development of each participating teacher in the same curriculum decision making process also differed. Some teachers experienced more significant impact than others. Other members, such as Teacher A from the Chinese team, were able to conceptualize the entire process of curriculum planning, while the rest of the members remained having a less sophisticated level of professional understanding. However, all members have benefited one way or another from their participation.

Deep learning

Deep learning refers to a type of learning that has an impact on personal beliefs and traditional practices a person has been widely used to; as a result, the person becomes much addicted to them, resulting in inflexibility and rigidity even when encountering hard evidence of inadequacy and inappropriateness (Biggs, 1989). The design of the innovation aimed to allow teachers to think about the alternative pedagogical strategies for teaching a topic, apart from the methods they were extensively used to. This design is advantageous because teachers now have to abandon the traditional practice. They also have to think of a new approach or move away from their frame of practice. This deduction was echoed by the team leader of the mathematics team:

Because you are using different methods . . . you have to abandon the traditional methods of teaching this topic . . . thinking of a new method . . . This is not an easy task . . . then we think of using IT for learning.

(Interview with Teacher F from the mathematics team; literal translation no. 10)

The experience of the panel head presented below shows a deeper level of learning.

[We] treated each topic in greater detail analytically, used to be inattentive to details, but now I think of the design, each sentence, how pupils react, and what potential can each activity develop in pupils. Extending the curriculum, allowing pupils to observe from different perspectives, past were restrictive, but now more activities to develop learning diversity, more creative.

(Interview with Teacher I from the mathematics team; literal translation no. 41)

94 *Case studies: a team approach*

Deep learning was also experienced by other members. As the first trial teacher stated:

> [In] the beginning we do not know where the problem is . . . thought that was the problem . . . but after discussion with the consultant . . . we discovered that was not the problem . . . Indeed we did not understand where the problem is . . . we should learn not to look at the issue from the surface.
>
> (Interview with Teacher H from the mathematics team; literal translation no. 18)

The second trial teacher had the same feeling, as reflected from her comment:

> Using multiple angles to think about teaching . . . my teaching methods are traditional. I have been teaching mathematics at this level for some time; my methods are fine. Then I continue, but after the co-planning, I am thinking if there are other methods to teach these topics – are pupils really understanding percentage?
>
> (Interview with Teacher G from the mathematics team; literal translation no. 29)

The change in attitude and beliefs experienced by the panel head who had over 20 years of teaching experience in schools was notable in her comment:

> The curriculum is here, but depends on what approaches we adopt to teach; secondly, teachers should abandon our traditional perspectives, like me teaching for 20 years. . . . I have my own practices, but after this year, I will adopt a new approach, discovering different approaches or some are beyond my imagination . . . after collaborative lesson preparation, and professional ideas from our consultant, we really change, next year we shall change. . . .
>
> (Interview with Teacher I from the mathematics team; literal translation no. 44)

The panel head added the following statement:

> I think to change our traditional culture, some difference, before we used to teach according to textbooks and guidelines, but now we adapted, revised, discussed. I think good, teach lively and not blindly.
>
> (Interview with Teacher I from the mathematics team; literal translation no. 39)

Overall, changes were recorded in the domains of pedagogical beliefs (how to teach more effectively), perceived inadequacy (the need to change practice), and the recognition of the directions of change among all key members of the mathematics curriculum development team.

For the members of the Chinese curriculum development team, the degree of learning expressed in the interviews differs from member to member. In this part,

School-based curriculum innovations 95

we discuss the trial teachers one by one first. Teacher A, the team leader of the Chinese team, focused on pedagogical changes in her interview. The following pedagogical practices tried out in the lessons were new to her: the use of extension work for consolidating student learning after lesson, the allocation of sufficient discussion time in lessons, the alternative way of motivating students by emphasizing verbal activities rather than sticking to text-based learning, and the class differences on ability and learning styles. Although these preferences were pedagogical in nature and did not introduce any change in her beliefs, the implications of her recognition of their values can lead to the potential change of her traditional practices.

Teacher E, the panel head for the Chinese team, was careful when asked about what he had learned in the innovation project. His answers were plainly referring to "we" rather than showing his own learning. However, he admitted that, as part of the "we" he was talking about, he did discover that students learned more efficiently if teachers designed learning activities with care. Furthermore, he discovered the important of teaching with care through the innovation project.

> Each reflection meeting becomes a discovery. I discovered that the ability of students to learn depends on our design and instructions.
> (Interview with Teacher E from the Chinese team;
> literal translation no. 25)

The two other trial teachers had deep feelings about what occurred in their trial lessons. Teacher B described the learning activities in much detail and intended to adopt these new ideas to his teaching of the other subject, Putonghua (Mandarin). As he stated,

> I learned how to use different teaching methods as I worked with other colleagues. As I observed, different classes can be applied with different methods. I can use this in the coming term, like I teach Putonghua, teach all classes in one level, I will use this method . . . like we observed classes, 5R class is good at verbal presentation, easy to express themselves, 5T and 5U's organization is weak. My method of teaching Chinese and Putonghua will be based on these class differences. For example, given that Class 5R has good presentation skills, I will strengthen their presentation ability. Meanwhile, I will improve and supplement the learning of classes 5T and 5U.
> (Interview with Teacher B from the Chinese team;
> literal translation no. 31)

Teacher B is an inexperienced teacher in the school, and this was his first time participating in the innovation project. Being observed in the trial lesson is new and agonizing for him. However, he showed progress in getting used to being observed and being able to concentrate on teaching in the trial lesson. He also touched lightly on the power of social learning in his statement:

> [I felt] the pressure of being observed initially because four of my colleagues were observing me. Later on, I no longer noticed how many of my colleagues

96 *Case studies: a team approach*

were watching me. As we sat for reflection, my colleagues pointed out my weaknesses and strengths, which I could not have found out by myself.

> (Interview with Teacher B from the Chinese team;
> literal translation no. 42)

Teacher D is experienced but inactive. However, he believed his expression showed that the learning activities and teaching strategies had an effect on him:

> Some effects and some new ideas were provided, like learning the principles of teaching students, increasing the confidence of the teachers, and using methods with deeper impact.
>
> (Interview with Teacher D from the Chinese team;
> literal translation no. 52)

> We used more words to allow students to read more. We used more sounds allowing students to listen more. Discussion helped deepen their understanding of the topic before they actually reported it.
>
> (Interview with Teacher D from the Chinese team;
> literal translation no. 52)

Furthermore, Teacher D indicated his eagerness to learn how to use various pedagogical approaches to create opportunities for deep learning.

The evidence from the interviews of the two teams indicates the experiences of most of the members of the team were strikingly contrary to their traditional frame of practices and understandings. However, their emotional reactions tend to differ from member to member. These contrasting experiences imposed a significant challenge to their traditional practices. These habits were couched in the language of beliefs and values that they were commonly used to.

Discovering student learning power

Surprises bring breakthroughs to the traditional frame of mind of most teachers. Accordingly, innovations tend to challenge deep-rooted beliefs and practices of the school community and its members, inviting teachers to participate in a series of activities, such as engaging them in action planning, instructional design, and collaborative work with colleagues, with the aim of moving them into an area of experience that runs contrary to their routine practices. In this way, their frame of conventional practices is "disturbed," and thus, a state of mental confusion that demands problem-solving skills and processes can be created.

The participating teachers on the mathematics team were impressed by student learning. They also discovered that students could learn better than what they had been expecting. They had underestimated the potential power of learning among students.

School-based curriculum innovations 97

Our success lies in knowing the process. Accordingly, students think beyond the learning task more creatively. I also feel that they think flexibly and are quick to respond differently.

> (Interview with Teacher H from the mathematics team;
> literal translation no. 23)

When the students received their task on fractions, they produced some interesting graphical patterns. In fact, they went beyond what we had expected and went beyond our prescriptions. Whether they were correct was unclear. The trial teacher was flexible and had told the students to think again at home, because the teacher could not think of any comments for the students.

> (Mathematics Team: Teacher F interview,
> literal translation no. 2)

Teachers should appreciate the power of learning from the student perspective. They should also acknowledge the necessity of considering the needs of students in planning a curriculum.

Similar records of discovery were also found on the Chinese curriculum development team. Teacher A, the team leader of the Chinese team who had also participated in the trial lesson, described her experience of discovering more and new information about the students she thought she knew. For example, she learned about how her students could develop their creativity given time and opportunities for more engaging activities organized by her.

> We did well because we felt satisfied . . . our classes used different methods and we thought it was impossible and wasted our time . . . but found we could do different things in different ability classes . . . More able classes [must do] more reading and searching for information . . . Weak classes [must do] more teacher storytelling and short films . . . different classes [used] different teaching methods . . . More able classes [that are] strong in reading can do more presentations . . . For example, class C has strengths in performing in public . . . and they used drama in learning to express themselves is very good. . . .
> (Interview with Teacher A from the Chinese team;
> literal translation no. 7)

Notably, the student performance had brought her a new understanding of her students, an understanding beyond her expectation.

> We were able to identify and improve the weaknesses of the students. After four trial lessons, I think we achieved our goal because they were able to tell us the origin of the festival and its customs. We also aimed to develop their creativity, and thus, we gave them various activities. We then allowed them to use worksheets in lessons and oral presentation. The results were far better than we expected of them; they turned out to be very creative.
> (Interview with Teacher A from the Chinese team;
> literal translation no. 11)

98   *Case studies: a team approach*

Teacher A seemed certain that what the team had planned worked very effectively on this occasion. She was also assured about the new pedagogical directions of the current curriculum reforms. The following description illustrates her assurance:

> Designing activities in groups collaboratively and presenting in public are important. Group discussion is also important. The vocabulary of the students is limited. However, they remembered how to express opinions and accept opinions of others. They also learned how to persuade and convince other people to accept their views. They learned how to constructively criticize other people and gained student communication skills. These skills could not be learned from books but would be experienced if opportunities would be provided by teachers.
>
> (Interview with Teacher A from the Chinese team;
> literal translation no. 16)

Chan, the panel head, had to admit that the students showed creativity given opportunities. Teacher B, the inexperienced trial teacher, was impressed by the learning activities as well as their impact on student learning.

> Possibly we had many types of activities . . . they were very engaged . . . specially the activity on negotiator . . . pupils concentrated very much . . . pupils listened to how to persuade poet Wat . . . there was also role play . . . look at how you are his father to persuade him . . . you as her mother how to persuade him . . . they were very engaged.
>
> (Interview with Teacher B from the Chinese team;
> literal translation no. 39)

Recognizing that students can learn and can learn even better given opportunities appropriately organized and given learning processes carefully designed by the teachers is important. This is because educational achievement is attributed to an external factor that is totally manipulated and controlled by the teachers. Such a factor is also external to the innate ability and the socio-economic backgrounds of the students. This recognition challenges the traditional views that socio-economic factors and natural capabilities are vital in the education of the children. Therefore, this recognition places the responsibility back onto the teachers. What they do about learning and how they do teaching are serious concerns for the teachers themselves.

As mentioned earlier, teacher learning is an essential component in the argument for school-based curriculum development and the liberal conceptualization of teacher leadership in school improvement movements. Participation demands substantial professional skills and knowledge on what and how to make curriculum decisions most suitable for student learning. Participation also requires substantial skills of communication in professional dialogues, and assumes taking a learner role in negotiation of meaning in professional and academic domains of experience and knowledge. Traditional beliefs, practices, and teacher authority should give way to a culture of an authentic learner community among teachers, a collaborative and team spirit-oriented environment, and due recognition of students' needs (DuFour, 2004; Hord, 2008; Stoll, Bolam, McMahon, Wallace, & Thomas, 2006). These practices have long-term impacts on teacher development, school improvement, and student learning (Doppelt, Schunn, Silk, Mehalik, Reynolds, & Ward, 2009; Snow-Gerono, 2005; Vescio, Ross, & Adams, 2008).

What are the concerns of the participating teachers?

The experiences of the two teams differed. The Chinese team had more administrative and organizational issues, whereas their mathematics counterparts were more concerned about time. Therefore, we provide some details found in the interviews with the Chinese team first and then move the discussion to the mathematics team.

Efficiency is a key factor in nearly all innovation projects, especially when innovation objectives, contents, and processes are new to the teachers and the school. Efficiency refers to the time used to complete tasks and the usefulness of the innovation perceived by the participating teachers. Most of the members of this team were impatient with the organization of the first few meetings on collaborative planning and found it inadequate. They felt that more preparation would be necessary to lead to better outcomes for the innovation. Teacher D, the experienced trial teacher, stated the following description:

> We had many mistakes because we were not well prepared . . . we had no consensus . . . the consultant suddenly arrived . . . we did not have the guidelines but suddenly Phoebe gave us many guidelines; we need time to digest; we did not follow the guideline . . . we could have only one lesson . . . we also had some internal arguments . . . The consultant then gave some suggestions . . . asked us to give him the plan by email; he was suggesting we need not think by ourselves but can use website materials developed by other schools; many schools are doing the same thing with different topics. We could download them and teach them in our classes; we did not have any conclusion and we followed that up later.
>
> (Interview with Teacher C from the Chinese team;
> literal translation no. 58)

> We must have more meetings and experienced teachers should share their experience. We are new to this set-up. As a result, we mostly experienced technical issues and problems.
>
> (Interview with Teacher D from the Chinese team;
> literal translation no. 53)

Teacher B, the inexperienced trial teacher, shared similar feelings about the organization of the first planning meeting.

> We could have been given more time to prepare. We should work collaboratively and observe the teaching of each member. We had little time and short

100   *Case studies: a team approach*

discussions. We were unsure of how different our methods were because we only talked about this issue orally and did not observe how each of us conducted the lesson. We could only choose one or two methods, which is a difficult task. Working at the end of the semester would have been better because we could have more time by then.

(Interview with Teacher B from the Chinese team;
literal translation no. 28)

Organization issues could be solved administratively. However, Teacher C indicated in her interview above the conflicting views about the direction of the innovation recorded in the interviews. Teacher A, the team leader of the Chinese team, had also recorded the disagreement between the consultant and the panel head in her interview.

We needed time to sit down and discuss as well as design materials such as PowerPoint and worksheets. We needed people to help in performing those tasks but there were only few on the team. We used different teaching methods in different classes. The guidelines and how to use them were unclear to ask. We discussed our problem with the tutor but did not achieve consensus. We ran out of time and our panel head even had different opinions. Disagreements came between the consultant and the panel head because they also had contrasting opinions. Our objectives were unclear so we worked separately by ourselves in the end.

(Interview with Teacher A from the Chinese team;
literal translation no. 4)

Another key issue in the implementation of school-based innovation is determining how to solve conflicting views professionally without damaging the long-term relationship among members and the consultant, as well as without severing the genuine implementation of the innovation. The disagreement from within perceived by the members possibly had some impact on the feelings of the members and on how the innovation was planned and conceived.

This cycle was a bit confusing. We had to use different methods in teaching the same topic and then we had to improve them. The panel head said we cannot apply those methods in one lesson, which was confusing. Then, we found other teams were doing well with the pattern but we had yet to find a direction. We felt the time pressure considering that we had to start in a week. As a result, each of us followed our own methods and used creative means such as PowerPoint and group discussion, and introduced creative topics. I personally hope to develop the creative thinking of students, but achieving this objective would require extensive work.

(Interview with Teacher C from the Chinese team;
literal translation no. 57)

School-based curriculum innovations 101

The above description shows an additional interesting effect of how social pressure or social cohesion works on the minds and actions of people (social re-educative models of dissemination). This team learned how other teams were working possibly with some progress, and thus, they felt that any problems with the innovation project and its aims should not occur. They acknowledged that problems would probably arise from them and not from the project design. The team had to push the arguments aside and move on with the innovation.

New members required more coaching to ensure their participation was useful and beneficial to their professional development. The inexperienced teacher commented fairly negatively about the support he had received. Apparently, his conception of teaching was still traditionally shaped by the conventional practices he had been widely used to, as observed from his interview data. He felt learning activities were a waste of students' time.

> I did not feel and see any support. I worked on my own. I do not know who the support teachers were.
>
> (Interview with Teacher B from the Chinese team;
> literal translation no. 37)

> Each year, we have to teach certain chapters in a given time frame. We have to use all four books without skipping any chapter. This year is different because we have more reading activities for students. I think these activities are wasting a lot of time.
>
> (Interview with Teacher B from the Chinese team;
> literal translation no. 37)

The following different concerns were recorded in the interviews: organizational efficiency, intra- and inter-group social political dimension, and provision of professional and emotional support to the new participants in the innovation project. Each of the above factors has potential damaging effects on the degree of successful implementation of the reforms. Therefore, these factors should be considered in curriculum change and planning.

Meanwhile, the concerns raised by the mathematics team in the interview were fewer than those mentioned by the Chinese team. Time constraint is the most popular topic among the teachers. Spending six hours on three collaborative lesson preparation meetings for one lesson was unacceptable for most of the teachers.

> We spent two hours in each of the three meetings to prepare only one lesson. The meetings were time-consuming.
>
> (Interview with Teacher H from the mathematics team;
> literal translation no. 20)

102 *Case studies: a team approach*

Table 5.5 Concerns raised by the teams

	Chinese team	Mathematics team
Time constraint	No	Yes
Organizational efficiency	Yes	No
Collaboration	No	Yes
Preparation	Yes	No
Internal consensus	Yes	No
Social effects	Yes	No
Coaching new members	Yes	No

> The pressure of completing the entire curriculum was heavy. This type of learning cannot be sustained if we want to complete the entire syllabus.
>
> (Interview with Teacher H from the mathematics team; literal translation no. 24)

Other members mentioned the problem with how to collaborate even more effectively and how to share workload deriving from preparing the lesson and designing teaching materials (interview with Teacher I from the mathematics team; literal translation no. 6). However, some teachers thought the time spent was worthwhile.

> We improved and achieved this progress step by step . . . one topic after the other, not the whole curriculum . . . We did it collaboratively, spending a lot of time, but it is worthwhile . . . because improving pupil learning.
>
> (Interview with Teacher I from the mathematics team; literal translation no. 43)

The concern with time available to teachers has often been mentioned or used as an excuse by teachers for not participating in any forms of reform and innovation activities. Therefore, this issue with time has been a key consideration in planning the innovation project. In fact, some teachers who participated in the first action cycle of the project were released in the second action cycle for fear that they might be overloaded with work and develop a feeling of being burned out. The concerns raised by the two teams are listed in Table 5.5.

Students' perspectives on the innovation

A group of six students who had experienced the three trial lessons was selected for group interview before and after each trial lesson for each team. The interviews focused on the experiences of students with the teacher and the latter's trial lesson. Thus, the findings on each teacher and his or her trial lesson were integrated. The identities of these students remain anonymous throughout the description. Their views and opinions will be supplemented by the observations of the videotaped trial lessons.

What are the conceptions of students of teaching style?

Before the trial lesson, the students in each class already had substantial experience with the trial teachers. They knew the teachers well in terms of their pedagogical preferences and styles of teaching. In the group interview, the data showed vividly that the students had full knowledge about their teachers. Below are summaries of the teaching styles of each trial teacher embedded in the interview data of the students of the Chinese team.

The students from the class of Teacher A mentioned that being in her class was relaxing without the pressure of homework and assignments, as well as fostered a pleasant atmosphere. The teacher used several strategies, such as storytelling, group discussions, drama, and reading activities through the semester. She did not use a variety of methods in one lesson, and preferred spreading her methods throughout a semester. When asked about the trial lesson in particular, the students were unable to determine the contrasting elements between the trial lesson and any other lessons of this teacher. However, they were able to fully describe the flow of the trial lesson.

> We learned the history of dragon boat festival. We read and discovered many stories about the dragon boat festival, especially the alternative stories about its origin. Many say poet Wat jumped into the river to commit suicide; some say it is about General Ng; some rejected the story and said it has no scientific evidence for its existence – people only created the story.
>
> (One student from Class 5R; literal translation no. 1)

> In the beginning, she gave us some materials, asked us to read, and spoke about the history of dragon boat festival. Then, she gave us time to develop our creativity and asked us to design an activity about the festival.
>
> (One student from Class 5R; literal translation no. 2)

Meanwhile, the students of Teacher B enjoyed a variety of learning activities in his class. Methods mentioned in the interview include games, group activities, storytelling, and debate. The pupils provided details about the language-specific learning activities that this teacher had given them such as writing a summary for each paragraph, poem reading, and revising school regulations in groups. Judging from the tone of the interview, this teacher had used these methods quite regularly in his class. Although the students of this class had lower ability levels, they were able to give many details about the trial lesson in the interview. Therefore, the trial lesson left a great impression upon the students.

> The teacher asked as choose to play a certain role, such as the wife of poet Wat and the fisherman, and then persuade poet Wat not commit suicide by jumping to the river.
>
> (One student from Class 5T; literal translation no. 3)

104 *Case studies: a team approach*

> Most impressive is learning the feeling of poet Wat. The reason is because we can remind other classmates of the type of person poet Wat is, why he jumped into the river, and what he did to make other people jealous of him.
>
> (One student from Class 5T; literal translation no. 4)

The students were able to identify a few differences between this trial lesson and the normal lesson. These differences include not using any textbooks, engaging in more activities in the entire lesson, and the addition of prefects to monitor their classroom behavior, and the anxiety of being observed and videotaped.

Class 5U had a rather restrictive experience of Chinese lessons. The students in the interview described the class as noisy, full of misbehaviors, and having much punishment, and a fair amount of disagreements between teacher actions and student experiences.

> The teacher told us not to bring a certain material to class, and then would later on ask to bring them out, but at last he asked to take them out; the whole class has not brought this back. The teacher wrote down names. We only learned a little because the teacher did not teach much.
>
> (One student from Class 5U; literal translation no. 5)

The experience of students of the trial lesson was fairly negative. A summary of the students' descriptions in the interviews is presented below. The teacher asked them to watch a video, which they had already watched in his previous lesson. The students did not know what to learn and they found the trial lesson boring. The teacher sat down in front of the class and only talked about historical figures. The students said they did not understand the lesson. The teacher also did not allow students to ask questions. As a result, the students could hardly remember any details about the trial lesson, except completing worksheets and watching a video. Therefore, the trial lesson led to a rather negative experience for the students.

In all, the experiences of the three classes significantly differed. Some classes were animated by the role play and were impressed by their engagement in the activities. On the contrary, other classes were quite distant about what the teacher had organized for the students. In one class, the trial lesson was excitingly executed. However, in another trial lesson, the students' experiences were negative.

The students from the mathematics trial lessons shared similar feelings about their trial lessons. Notably, they knew their teachers well. The first trial teacher had six years of teaching experience. Her teaching methods as described by her students in the interview before the trial lesson include using daily life materials for illustration, physical games and computer games to arouse interest, motivating students by extrinsic rewards, and inviting students to use their imagination to construct different shapes and work on textbook exercises. One student gave the following remark:

> Her teaching method is interesting. One time, she collected a few drinking bottles and different types of drink to conduct an experiment with us. She

School-based curriculum innovations   105

also asked us to use these materials for measurement. She used a scanner to construct some shapes, played with computers, demonstrated some calculation practices, and used pictures. I think that she is very patient.

(One student from Class 3G; literal translation no. 5)

The students were generally happy with her lessons. In the videotaped trial lesson, all these methods were used and the students participated and were highly engaged in the lesson.

Meanwhile, the second trial teacher had 11 years of teaching experience. Her teaching methods as described by her students include using some activities, competitions, and working exercises on the blackboard. She is also lively and a fair teacher to the students in class. However, the details about her teaching styles and methods given by the students in the interview were less articulated than those for the other trial teacher. Students had negative views about her teaching and said her teaching style was boring and meaningless. Some students said they did not understand some teaching topics and felt sleepy in her class. One student came from Mainland China with a better background in Mathematics. He commented on her lessons negatively.

Some mathematics topics were boring. I do not understand most of them. I felt very sleepy in one of the classes.

(One student from Class 3H; literal translation no. 3)

For the trial lesson, the other interviewed students similarly did not feel much surprised about her teaching arrangements, which included folding papers into different shapes in groups and organizing some competitions. The most strikingly different method for these students was when this teacher asked them to present their works in class. These observations by the students could be found accurately in the videotaped trial lesson. In particular, this teacher left most students behind while focusing only on the two students who were invited to present their work in front of the class in each round. Moreover, other students did not actively participate in this entire class activity that lasted for about 20 minutes.

The teacher handed us some paper. I worked with my group mates collaboratively. The teacher asked me to fold equal shares but I folded the paper many times.

(One student from Class 3H; literal translation no. 4)

According to the interview, only one or two students in the class were successful in completing the task of folding different shapes in line with the requirements of the teacher in the trial lesson.

The interview data showed little evidence about the effects of the trial lessons. The innovation aspect of these trial lessons had slight impact on what their teachers were normally doing with them in their lessons. This lack of contrast between the trial lessons and the normal lessons may emphasize the need for advocates of the school-based curriculum development and teacher leadership to reflect on the goals and essence of school-based reforms.

106 *Case studies: a team approach*

What are the conceptions of learning among this group of younger learners?

Students from both teams had clear conceptions about the learning or learning patterns they prefer. For the mathematics team, the students in the interview knew their preferred pedagogical practice. Teaching these younger learners referred to activities connected with textbooks and exercises only. However, these students accepted games and activities as motivating factors. One student from the first trial teacher class provided the following comment:

> I think the best learning model is a combination of games and lectures. We expect games in every lesson but not too much of them. In this way, we think of the lesson as only game lessons and not mathematics lessons. Honestly, we enjoy games but not mathematics lessons. Teaching with some games is interesting.
> (One student from Class 3G; literal translation no. 6)

This student also made a distinction between a game, which was closer to "play," and learning, which was equivalent to reading textbooks and conducting exercises solitarily.

The interviews conducted after the two trial lessons aimed to elicit information about how students reacted to their experience of an innovation lesson. This expectation was not realized, and the students could hardly distinguish the difference between the trial lesson and the previous practices of their teacher even after continuous prompts by the interviewer. For the first trial lesson, the most significant difference observed by all students was not the pedagogical change, which was the original aim of the innovation, but the teacher's change of personality because s/he was being observed by many of her colleagues. One student gave the following comment:

> Several teachers were watching, and thus, we had to be calm. My hands were shivering, and I noticed that every student was also nervous. We were afraid to make mistake because she might scold us.
> (One student from Class 3G; literal translation no. 8)

The second group of the students interviewed also had clear conceptions about what effective learning would be appropriate to them or what pedagogical approaches they prefer. In addition, the reasons behind their preferences were clear. For example, one student preferred the atmosphere of being involved in competition in class because "winning gives her satisfaction" (one student from Class 3H; literal translation no. 1). Another student enjoyed working out solutions on the blackboard. The reason is because other students could determine her mistakes publicly, and thus, she would be aware of her own problems.

> Like competition, very little competition, very rare, teaching is not very much understood. If you make mistakes and write them on blackboard, you understand what is wrong at least.
> (One student from Class 3H; literal translation no. 2)

School-based curriculum innovations 107

Another student was even more critical about the traditional rote learning and preferred activity approaches. This student had the following opinion:

> I enjoy more activity teaching because I understand more methods in this way. The teacher also teaches us, so we do not have to memorize and memorize the textbook.
>
> (One student from Class 3H; literal translation no. 5)

When asked to compare the teaching style before and after the trial lesson, the students were unable to recognize the major difference or the difference was not strikingly explicit and important to them. They could only acknowledge several differences such as being observed by many teachers and the use of peer presentation in the lesson. One student commented on the adoption of student presentation strategies, which have been used rarely by the teacher in normal lessons. This student believed that such adoption could train the students to be more confident.

The students from the Chinese team shared some common features. Some students were articulate about their pedagogical preferences as well as their related learning outcomes. Meanwhile, other students were less conscious about the relationship between the two. For example, limited data were given from Teacher D's class about their preferential learning activities. The students mentioned briefly that they prefer using the computer to learn, teacher explanation, and reading texts. Surprisingly, this group of students did not mention any learning activities, such as storytelling, group discussions, or any other interactive learning activities that could have been used in other lessons by other teachers if they did not experience these learning activities in the lessons of the Chinese subject teacher. The class of Teacher A was considered by teachers to be more able than other classes at the same level. However, the interview did not show much of their ability to relate learning activities to the intended learning outcomes as in the case of Class 5T, a less able class. For example, when they mentioned they preferred drama, they were unclear about the underlying educational principles of drama, similar to the revelations of students from Class 5T. They only said that drama activities enriched vocabulary, help in understanding texts, give satisfaction, and are humorous. They were unable to indicate the contribution of drama to motivation, learning of social skills, and learning of empathy.

However, students from the class of Teacher B were able to fully describe what they prefer and why they enjoy each pedagogical approach. Students from Class 5T experienced the trial lesson by Teacher B quite differently. They also gave detailed information in the interviews about the kind of learning activities they preferred and the underlying reasons for their interests. Indeed, their conceptions about the relationship between learning activities and intended learning outcomes are congruent with the textbook answers for these educational issues. Table 5.6 summarizes the students' views and expressed reasons for their preferred activities.

The reasons given refer to intrinsic and extrinsic motivational strategies, learning of social and communication skills, and learning of thinking skills. The ability

108 *Case studies: a team approach*

Table 5.6 Students' views on particular pedagogical strategies

Attitude/Preference	Reasons
Dislike	
Direct teacher talk	Boring (motivation)
Like	
Question and Answer	Challenging (achievement motivation)
Games	Interesting and being equated with learning
Activities	Encourage cooperativeness
Debate	Strengthen friendship; Exciting
Group discussion	Motivate the use of thinking; Preparation for secondary education
Play	Equivalent to learning activities

to relate learning activities to the kind of learning outcomes is quite interesting, because this group of students is considered less able than the academically able students in other classes. Below is a transcription of the description in the interview before the trial lesson for illustration.

Student A: "Debate competition is very exciting and fun for me."

Student B: "I enjoy group competitions because we can discuss with our classmates, which strengthens our relationship."

Student C: "I also enjoy debate competitions because such activity is exciting. People often shout out of excitement and are even difficult to control."

Student D: "I prefer debate competitions because people are more involved and enjoy watching. Every participant has a theme to discuss and each of them has to respond and to find something to argue. The atmosphere is very exciting and intense."

Student E: "I also choose debate competitions because such activities are similar to the court case scenario. One participant speaks his or her argument and the other one will reply in rebuttal."

(Students from Class 5T; literal translation no. 2)

Notably, one student emphasized the "play" in the trial lesson. Meanwhile, another student tried to re-orient the focus of our attention from being negative to the trial lesson to regarding the play as having contributions to learning. Traditionally, in Chinese culture, "play" and "game" are considered a waste of time and not related to learning.

The views of the students about their pedagogical preferences and their awareness about what to learn more relevantly, why they must learn in a particular way, and how to learn concepts more effectively are essential ingredients in the deliberation of school-based curriculum development. Eliciting the experiences of students regarding the innovations applied by their respective teachers is also important as the information could form part of the feedback for the evaluation of the school-based innovations. The data outlined above emphasize the diversity of student experiences, and such diversity could be the important mediating effect on how the innovation is perceived and received. This is because the ultimate goal of school-based reforms is to influence the teacher and student learning.

Discussion

The second action cycle of the project adopted the model of the operation developed in the first cycle, as shown in Figure 5.1. This model emphasizes the process and the conditions in which teacher development could be enhanced within a school-based curriculum development model. The organization of the project, the establishment of the curriculum development teams, and the innovation patterns (PER model) employed have created opportunities for teacher engagement in peer collaboration activities, open and reflective professional interactions, and in innovation-oriented pedagogical practices. Whether this project truly succeeded remains unclear. For now, discussions below will focus on leadership style, teacher development, and student learning to illustrate the impact of the project on both teachers and students.

Which type of leadership is more effective?

We conducted a comparison to answer this question not because we wanted to compare other forms of leadership, which are also valuable, but to open up an issue for future exploration. In the findings, the rotation of leadership or a form of distributed leadership to be shared by all members worked well with the teachers and the culture of this team. They enjoyed the participatory form of interactions without the fear of any directives from any person with a hierarchical power or authority over them. They enjoyed a form of interaction that had little implication on what to follow and how to follow. The shifting of the members' roles also allowed each member to emancipate and decenter themselves from their own traditional beliefs, practices, and roles. These cultures have been well framed and accustomed to them, and thus, little room for reflection and contemplation about possibilities has been obtained. This style of leadership encourages and supports teacher learning (MacBeath & Moos, 2004). Notably, the leadership style of the consultant plays the role of a model for other members. He was described and much appreciated as a facilitator, a leader with academic and professional inputs. He was able to stimulate deep thinking about theories, practices, and alternatives.

Is professional development evident?

Considerable evidence from the teacher interviews show that the level of professional awareness is increasing. The teachers' understanding of the aims and targets of the curriculum innovation is also increasingly sharpened. In other words,

110   *Case studies: a team approach*

the impact of the innovation on teacher development in various domains of knowledge and experience has taken a developmental direction from some uncertain state of mind to a higher level of certainty (Sergiovanni, 2001). Teachers in the interviews openly talked to the interviewers in a confessional tone, showing awareness of the inadequacy, and indicating the need for more improvement. This aspect is important because it is the very feature of a learning community, authentically reflective and critical about one's practices and beliefs (Harris & Lambert, 2003; Henderson & Hawthorne, 1995; Miles, Ekholm, & Vandenberghe, 1987).

Did the students gain any benefits?

Whether the students involved in the trial lessons were aware of any changes that their teachers had brought to their learning remained unclear. One possibility that can explain their lack of awareness about the innovation is the prevalence of the activity approach and the use of activities among their teachers in this school. The other reason is that the innovation perceived by the teacher may not match the needs of the students and may be interpreted by the latter in a slightly different manner. Exploring this issue is important for teacher leaders and policy makers when organizing planned changes in pedagogy to enhance student learning and to encourage student participation in school activities (Leithwood & Jantzi, 2000).

Meanwhile, students' awareness of the concepts of learning was also strikingly present in the student interview data. They had a clear notion of the effects of a particular teaching strategy and were conscious of the pedagogical approaches that were more appropriate for them. Thus, teacher leaders and policy makers should incorporate students' opinions in their deliberation of the curriculum and educational change either at the policy level or at the school level. Involvement of students in curriculum decision making is not a new topic, but this certainly needs more empirical and substantial work if its key role in the future curriculum theories is to be acknowledged (Rudduck & Flutter, 2004).

Conclusion

Leadership studies in education have focused mainly on a positional and hierarchical basis to an extent that teachers in schools are only considered peripheral in making pedagogical decisions. Recent studies on curriculum leadership have moved from this model of organizational leadership to one that attempts to recapture the essence of the professional role of teachers in making curriculum decisions within the tradition of school-based curriculum development. Teacher leadership in curriculum decision making in schools is a new phenomenon in both the international and local literature, and its practice is still in its embryonic stage. How this concept and practice could be institutionalized within the infrastructure of the current school ethos still requires substantial theoretical and experimental work.

The report of the first action cycle of a curriculum leadership development project in Hong Kong demonstrated the complexity of the key structures, such as the establishment of curriculum development teams and processes, as well as the three-stage PER model of teacher planning, implementation, and reflection of curriculum practice. This model has been created by the case school in response to the challenges from the community. These structures and processes have yet to find their home within the traditions and the cultures of the school in the study. However, the experience has proven that engaging teachers in curriculum decision making processes enhances the development of professional knowledge and skills among teachers in general.

However, the following two important issues still need to be explored and investigated in both theoretical and empirical studies: how the concept of teacher leadership in curriculum decision making could be effectively practiced schools, and how the structures and processes could be institutionalized in schools on a wider scale. These issues can be tackled by collaboration between researchers on university faculties and teachers in schools. The goal of teacher leadership in curriculum decision making should receive policy priority. Moreover, its successful achievement entails resource and professional support from the government and other stakeholders in the education enterprise.

References

Australian Education Union. (2004). *Educational leadership and teaching for the twenty first century: Project discussion paper.* Retrieved fromhttp://www.aeufederal. org.au/Debates/elat21pap.pdf

Ball, D.L. (1996). Teacher learning and the mathematics reforms: What we think we know and what we need to learn. *Phi Delta Kappa, 77*(7), 500–508.

Ball, D.L., & Cohen, D.K. (1996). Reform by the book: What is – or might be – the role of curriculum materials in teacher learning and instructional reform? *Educational Researcher, 25*(9), 6–8, 14.

Biggs, J.B. (1989). Approaches to the enhancement of tertiary teaching. *Higher Education Research and Development, 8,* 7–25.

Birman, B.F., Desimone, L., Garet, M.S., Porter, A.C., & Yoon, K.S. (2002). Effects of professional development on teachers' instruction: Results form a three-year longitudinal study. *Educational Evaluation and Policy Analysis, 24*(2), 81–112.

Black, P., & Atkin, M. (1996). *Changing the subject: Innovations in science, mathematics and technology education.* London: Routledge in association with OECD.

Borko, H. (2004). Professional development and teacher learning: Mapping the terrain. *Educational Researcher, 33*(8), 3–15.

Brabeck, M.M., Walsh, M.E., & Latta, R. (2003). *Meeting at the hyphen: Schools-universities-communities-professions in collaboration for student achievement and well being.* Chicago: National Society for the Study of Education.

Carr, W., & Kemmis, S. (1986). *Becoming critical: Education, knowledge and action research.* London: Falmer.

Day, C. (1993). Reflection: A necessary but not sufficient condition for professional development. *British Educational Research Journal, 19*(1), 83–93.

Doppelt, Y., Schunn, C.D., Silk, E.M., Mehalik, M.M., Reynolds, B., & Ward, E. (2009). Evaluating the impact of a facilitated learning community approach to professional development on teacher practice and student achievement. *Research in Science & Technological Education, 27*(3), 339–354.

DuFour, R. (2004). What is a "professional learning community"? *Educational Leadership, 61*(8), 6–11.

112 Case studies: a team approach

Elliott, J. (1991). *Action research for educational change*. Buckingham: Open University Press.

Frost, D., & Durrant, J. (2002). *Teacher-led development work: Guidance and support*. London: David Fulton.

Frost, D., & Durrant, J. (2003). Teacher leadership: Rationale, strategy and impact. *School Leadership & Management, 23*(2),173–186.

Fullan, M. (2001). *Leading in a culture of change*. San Francisco, CA: Jossey-Bass.

Fullan, M., & Quinn, J. (2015). *Coherence: The right drivers in action for schools, districts, and systems*. San Francisco, CA: Corwin.

Garet, M.S., Porter, A.C., Desimone, L., Birman, B.F., & Yoon, K.S. (2001). What makes professional development effective? Results from a national sample of teachers. *American Educational Research Journal, 38*(4), 915–945.

Harris, A. (2003a). Teacher leadership and school Improvement. In A. Harris, C. Day, D. Hopkins, M. Hadfield, A. Hargreaves, & C. Chapman (Eds.), *Effective leadership for school improvement* (pp. 72–83). London: Routledge/Falmer.

Harris, A. (2003b). Teacher leadership as distributed leadership: Heresy, fantasy or possibility? *School Leadership & Management, 23*(3), 313–324.

Harris, A. (2004). Distributed leadership and school improvement: Leading or misleading? *Educational Management Administration & Leadership, 32*(4), 11–24.

Harris, A., & Lambert, L. (2003). *Building leadership capacity for school improvement*. Milton Keynes: Open University Press.

Henderson, J.G., & Hawthorne, R.D. (1995). *Transformative curriculum leadership*. New York: Teachers College Press.

Hiebert, J., Gallimore, R., & Stigler, J.W. (2003). The new heroes of teaching. *Education Week, 23*(10), 56.

Holye, E. (1969). *The role of the teacher*. London: Routledge & K. Paul.

Hopkins, D. (2001). *School improvement for real*. London: Falmer.

Hord, S.M. (2008). Evolution of the professional learning community: Revolutionary concept is based on intentional collegial learning. *Journal of Staff Development, 29*(3), 10–13.

King, M.B., & Newmann, F.M. (2000). Will teacher learning advance school goals? *Phi Delta Kappan, 81*(8), 576–580.

Law, E.H.F., & Galton, M. (2004). Impact of a school based curriculum project on teachers and students: A Hong Kong case study. *Curriculum Perspectives, 24*(3), 43–58.

Law, E.H.F., & Wan, S.W.Y. (2005). *Developing curriculum leadership in a primary school: A Hong Kong case study*. Proceedings of the International Conference on Education: Redesigning pedagogy: Research, policy, practice, Singapore: Nanyang University National Institute of Education, 30 May–1 June 2005.

Leithwood, K., & Jantzi, D. (2000). Principal and teacher leadership effects: A replication. *School Leadership & Management, 20*(4), 415–434.

MacBeath, J. (2004). Putting the self back into self-evaluation. *Improving Schools, 7*, 87–91.

MacBeath, J., & Moos, L. (2004). *Democratic learning: The challenge to school effectiveness*. London/New York: Routledge/Falmer.

MacDonald, B., & Rudduck, J. (1971). Curriculum research and development projects: Barriers to success. *British Journal of Educational Psychology, 41*, 148–154.

Macpherson, I., Aspland, T., Brooker, R., & Elliott, B. (Eds.). (1999). *Places and spaces for teachers in curriculum leadership*. Deakin West, ACT: Australian Curriculum Studies Association.

Macpherson, I., & Brooker, R. (1999). Introducing places and spaces for teachers in curriculum leadership. In I. Macpherson, T. Aspland, R. Brooker, & B. Elliott (Eds.), *Places and spaces for teachers in curriculum leadership* (pp. 1–20). Deakin West, ACT: Australian Curriculum Studies Association.

Marsh, C. (1997). *Key concepts for understanding curriculum.* London: Falmer.

McLaughlin, M., & Talbert, J. (2001). *Professional communities and the work of high school teaching.* Chicago: University of Chicago Press.

Miles, M., Ekholm, M., & Vandenberghe, R. (1987). *Lasting school improvement: Exploring the process of institutionalization.* Leuven: ACCO.

Ovens, P. (1999). Can teachers be developed? *Journal of In-Service Education, 25*(2), 275–305.

Putnam, R.T., & Borko, H. (2000). What do new views of knowledge and thinking have to say about research on teacher learning? *Educational Researcher, 29*(1), 4–15.

Rayner, S., & Gunter, H. (2005). Rethinking leadership: Perspectives on remodeling practice. *Educational Review, 57*(2), 151–161.

Rudduck, J., & Flutter, J. (2004). *How to improve your school: Giving pupils a voice.* London: Continuum.

Schon, D. (1983). *The reflective practitioner.* London: Temple Smith.

Sergiovanni, T. (2001). *Leadership: What's in it for schools.* London: Routledge/Falmer.

Shatin Tsung Tsin School. (2003). *Quality education fund (7th Call for Application) proposal of "Accelerating School Based Curriculum Development."* Hong Kong: Shatin Tsung Tsin School.

Sherrill, J.A. (1999). Preparing Teachers for Leadership Roles in the 21st Century. *Theory into Practice, 38*(1), 56–61.

Shulman, L., & Sherin, M.G. (2004). Fostering communities of teachers as learners: Disciplinary perspectives. *Journal of Curriculum Studies, 36*(2), 135–140.

Skilbeck, M. (1984). *School-based curriculum development.* London: Harper & Row.

Snow-Gerono, J.L. (2005). Professional development in a culture of inquiry: PDS teachers identify the benefits of professional learning communities. *Teaching and Teacher Education, 21*(3), 241–256.

Stenhouse, L. (1975). *An introduction to curriculum research and development.* London: Heinemann.

Stoll, L., Bolam, R., McMahon, A., Wallace, M., & Thomas, S. (2006). Professional learning communities: A review of the literature. *Journal of Educational Change, 7*(4), 221–258.

Teddlie, C., & Tashakkori, A. (2003). Major issues and controversies in the use of mixed methods in the social and behavioral sciences. In A. Tashakkori & C. Teddlie (Eds.), *Handbook of mixed methods in social & behavioral research* (pp. 3–50). Thousand Oaks, CA: Sage.

Vescio, V., Ross, D., & Adams, A. (2008). A review of research on the impact of professional learning communities on teaching practice and student learning. *Teaching and Teacher Education, 24*(1), 80–91.

Wallace, J.D., Nesbit, C.R., & Miller, A.C.S. (1999). Six leadership models for professional development in science and mathematics. *Journal of Science Teacher Education, 10*(4), 247–268.

6 Effects of leadership styles on distribution of teacher participation on the mathematics curriculum development team

Discourse and social network analyses

Context of change

The decentralization of educational decision making, especially curriculum decision making, has captured the attention of education policy makers over the past two decades (Fullan, 2001; Hopkins, 2001; Leithwood, 2008). The impetus for decentralization emerged from the growing recognition of the limitations of relying on central agencies in designing, planning, and implementing new curricula in schools (Hall & Hord, 2002; McLaughlin, 1990). Similarly, decentralization resulted from a call for more democratic participation of professional teachers in school and curriculum decision making in the 1960s and 1970s (Australian Education Union, 2004).

Policies aligned with the goal of decentralization have sought to empower teachers to become more involved in decisions concerning three aspects: what to teach, how to teach, and how to assess learning. These trends have required a change from conceptualizing the teacher as a curriculum user to the teacher as a curriculum developer. These policies have generally aimed for teachers to assume higher responsibility in realm of curriculum decision making (Craig & Ross, 2008; Frost & Durrant, 2002, 2003; Harris, 2003; Marsh, 1997; Ovens, 1999; Stenhouse, 1975; Wallace, Nesbit, & Miller, 1999).

Although these trends of decentralization and teacher leadership originated in Western societies, a similar trend is notably becoming evident in East Asia, especially in Hong Kong (Law, Galton, & Wan, 2007; Shouse & Lin, 2010). Thus, the Hong Kong Education Department established a new role of curriculum coordinator in all primary schools in 2002. The purpose behind this policy initiative was to recognize the importance of teacher instructional leadership and to provide resources for building additional leadership capacity in schools. After eight years, this role has become institutionalized in schools; however, the patterns and levels of involvement of teachers in assuming higher responsibility for curriculum leadership have yet to be studied in the East Asian context (Law, Galton, & Wan, 2010).

In the current project, a distributed approach is adopted to understand the mechanism of teacher participation in curriculum decision making (Spillane, 2006).

Therefore, we consider curriculum decision making as a process (or a phenomenon) that is shared among all teachers in the school (Ball & Cohen, 1996; Elliott, 1991; McLaughlin & Talbert, 2001; Shulman & Sherin, 2004). From the perspective of distributed curriculum leadership, every teacher should be responsible for making curriculum decisions for pupils in his/her own classroom. By accepting this responsibility, participation should enhance opportunities for teacher development, school improvement, and pupil learning (Goddard, Goddard, & Tschannen-Moran, 2007; Hiebert, Gallimore, & Stigler, 2003).

The study explores how team-level curriculum leadership influences the interaction patterns of teachers and the consequences of those interactions for teacher learning. We employ data drawn from the discourses of the videotaped meetings of the mathematics curriculum development team in a single school. These data are analyzed to shed light on the interaction between leadership and learning at the teacher level.

The research aims to contribute to the growing literature on distributed school leadership by illustrating how policies that are intended for teacher empowerment are interpreted and enacted in practice. Although the current research is a case study, this approach is a suitable methodology to reveal the enactment of teacher leadership in the East Asian context that has traditionally valued hierarchy and status. Given the importance placed on teacher learning in school improvement (Fullan, 2007; Hallinger & Heck, 2010; Robinson, Lloyd, & Rowe, 2008), the study may offer insights into an important outcome of distributed curriculum leadership.

Curriculum leadership innovation project

The project that forms the focus of this research started in September 2004 in a Hong Kong primary school. The goals of this project, as stated in the project proposal, were as follows:

- To develop the abilities and skills of teachers in strategic planning and development, and to use the evaluation for school improvement;
- To enhance the effectiveness of school self-evaluation in school; and
- To develop a quality culture for school self-evaluation for school improvement.

In this section, we describe this project and its approach to school development.

Leadership organization in curriculum development teams

Two curriculum development teams were formed in the school based on two key subjects: Chinese language and mathematics. These subjects comprise over one-third of the curriculum time in Hong Kong primary schools. In the first action cycle of the innovation project, which was during the first semester, the subject panel heads were chosen as they had assumed hierarchical power. Their selection was expected to alleviate certain political tension against the introduction of a new structure in the working lives of the teachers. In the second

116 *Case studies: a team approach*

action cycle, which was during the second semester, the team leaders were changed. Other participating colleagues were also persuaded to take turns in leading the team.

The two arrangements had two advantages. First, the subject-based approach in forming a curriculum development team is used to control the subject content of the interactions among members in teamwork activities. This method is applied to maximize the positive effects of the shared subject identity and working experiences among team members (MacBeath, 2004; Schon, 1983). The second approach is used to eliminate the potential negative influence of hierarchical power relations among team members. This way would set the stage to create a favorable teamwork environment in which professional dialogue among members could occur. As a result, a culture of shared and distributed curriculum leadership among team members can be cultivated (Black & Atkin, 1996; Britt, Irwin, & Ritchie, 2001; Carr & Kemmis, 1986; Fullan, 1993; Putnam & Borko, 2000). The latter advantage can boost the confidence of the teachers in initiating and leading activities regarding pedagogical changes within their domains in the school.

Participants on the curriculum development team were given guidelines about their roles as well as the objectives and procedures of the planning and reflection meetings. In the guidelines, the team leader was expected to motivate and stimulate thinking about experiences in trial lessons, especially how meetings should be conducted, rather than give instructional information alone. Participating teachers were expected to actively join in the meetings. The guidelines emphasized collaborative spirit, shared responsibility, and collaborative leadership in the innovation project.

To expand the professional inputs into the curriculum deliberation of each team, a subject expert from the faculty of education at a local university was invited to assume the chair of each team in the first cycle of the innovation. Notably, this subject expert was not a member of the research team responsible for this report.

Planning, experimentation, and reflection model of change

The project adopted the planning, experimentation, and reflection (PER) model of change (see Table 6.1 and Figure 6.1) as a guiding structure for the project process. In the PER model, the team would begin by collaboratively reviewing, planning, and designing a lesson or a unit of learning in structured team meetings. Teachers would then practice the innovation lesson. Finally, the team would conduct a reflection meeting to examine the lesson and refine the curriculum based on collaborative analysis and discussion.

This model of change is used in the first action cycle and is repeated in the second action cycle in a spiral and continuous process (Law et al., 2007). This organization of the project implementation has several advantages. First, this design creates opportunities for collaboration and teamwork. Second, changes in pedagogy, which are based on the teaching subject, are determined. Third,

Table 6.1 Three-stage model of teacher planning, experimentation, and reflection curriculum practices

Stage	Aims	Teacher Activities
Planning Stage	To identify the goals and design strategies for a plan of innovation	SWOT, entire school conference, action planning meetings, collaborative lesson preparation meetings, production of materials
Experimentation Stage	To put the plan in action inside the classrooms	Trialing, peer observation, and evaluation
Reflection Stage	To review actions and plans for future actions	Post-observation conference and completion of feedback sheets

Source: Law, E.H.F. (2011). Exploring the role of leadership in facilitating teacher learning in Hong Kong. *School Leadership & Management, 31*(4), 391–407.

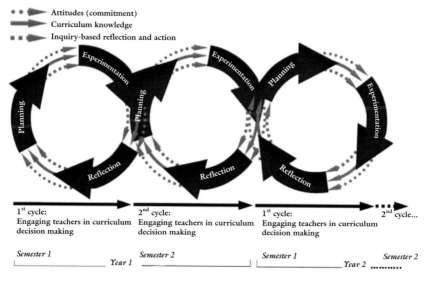

Figure 6.1 Reconceptualizing school-based models of developing teacher curriculum leadership for lifelong education

a critical problem-solving approach is adopted. Fourth, the teacher approaches the change as an open venture rather than as a program designed by external agents for their implementation (Harris, 2004; Macpherson, Aspland, Brooker, & Elliott, 1999).

Methodological approaches

In this study, a design-based approach was adopted to organize curriculum development teams in the case school. This method engaged teachers of mixed backgrounds in cycles of planning, experimenting, and reflecting on curriculum and pedagogical innovations. Data collection involved interviews, videotapes of lessons, lesson and meeting observations, and document analysis. The focus is primarily on the discoursal features of the curriculum team meetings, which can help explore the impact of various leadership styles on teacher learning.

Data analysis

Given that we based each action cycle on the PER model (Law & Wan, 2006), we chose one videotaped planning meeting and two reflection meetings from the second action cycle of the mathematics curriculum development team for the analysis. The approach of using three team meetings allowed for the triangulation of emergent themes and the categorization of data from the curriculum development team, along with the identification of the uniqueness of each of the team meetings (Cohen, Manion, & Morrison, 2000).

Two planning meetings were conducted on April 12 and 25, 2005. One reflection meeting was carried out on May 19, 2005. The two planning meetings were attended by all seven team members, and the durations were 62 and 60 minutes, respectively. The meeting on reflection lasted for about 82 minutes and was attended by seven teachers, including the panel head, the external consultant, the project leader, and four other teachers. One teacher left the reflection meeting at 39 minutes without returning, while another left at 42 minutes but returned to the meeting at 57:50.

We determined in the beginning that we would not be able to exhaust the potential of the visual data embedded in the videotaped meetings in a single viewing. Therefore, we decided to analyze the data in the following manner and procedures. Four researchers simultaneously viewed each of the videotaped meetings in sections of 10 minutes. During each 10-minute segment, each member of the research team focused on identifying the features of the teacher-student interactions and the key points of interests. The team would follow up on these issues in the next 10-minute period. For example, in the first 10 minutes, the roles of the consultant and teachers emerged as points of interest; in particular, the consultant was dominating and directing, and the teachers were passive and attentive. In the subsequent 10 minutes, additional themes emerged. For example, the responses from the consultant provided a clear indication that he was knowledgeable on pedagogical strategies and content knowledge. Although such a behavior was positive, his assertiveness often dominated the discourse and indirectly suppressed opportunities for other team members to raise issues as well as extend or elaborate on the issues at hand.

Although the four researchers watched the videotaped meetings together, a division of labor was employed. One member focused on the accuracy of transcriptions, one on facial expressions and non-verbal behavior, another member focused on dialogue, and the last one on the possible use of the videotaped data and images relevant to the analysis. Beyond these individual foci, all members wrote field notes related to the investigation. They discussed these notes with one another after each viewing. Notably, we viewed the videotaped meetings alongside the written transcriptions of the meetings to check and confirm accuracy. We often revisited sections to deepen our understanding and to allow additional alternative themes to emerge. The four researchers talked aloud and addressed disagreements on alternative interpretations in order to ultimately achieve consensus on the interpretations. When points of departure required certain further investigation, the research team wrote them down for further development.

Data interpretation

The research approach was grounded on the data, with the intention of allowing possibilities and conceptual categories to emerge and undergo refinement. However, the theoretical underpinnings in our design framework should have some impact on the ways we choose to analyze and understand. This practice is normal in qualitative research (Teddlie & Tashakkori, 2003, 2009).

For example, we expect the possible influences of the status, power in the school hierarchy, experience in the teaching profession, and personality of the participants on the ways in which they interact with one another. All these factors have an impact on the negotiation process among the participants. Apart from this predominantly qualitative approach, we include a few quantitative analyses of the visual data on the tapes, such as the distribution of time among participants across the interactions in each meeting, and the counting of the types of discourse features.

Results

The findings are presented in this section. First, we present the detailed discourse analysis of dialogue as it unfolded in the curriculum innovation team meetings. Second, we analyze communication patterns with respect to member participation in the meetings. Finally, we analyze the visual data describing the nature of member participation.

Discourse analysis of the team meetings

In the three meetings chaired by the external consultant, he appeared to use a reflective and exploratory approach in his leadership style when leading the members of the development team in curriculum decision making. His open, collaborative style is illustrated in the following four types of discourses featured in the interactions with the other team members.

120 *Case studies: a team approach*

Guiding exploration

The first type of discourse was evident in the intention of the external consultant to provide guiding questions to lead members toward a new conceptualization of the pedagogical issues in the discussion, rather than being directing or didactic. The three excerpts of discourses below are selected from the three different meetings to illustrate the communicative style of the external consultant. The questions that invited the teachers to explore and speculate in the discourse are presented below.

Excerpt 1

EXTERNAL CONSULTANT: You do not intend to teach the numerical value of fractions in the first lesson; instead, what you want to teach are the properties of fractions. Then why did you choose to ask the children to compare the numerical values of fractions?

(Literal translation from the first co-planning meeting with Teacher Ho, reading from 08:10 to 8:27)

Excerpt 2

EXTERNAL CONSULTANT: Are more examples of fractions of equal numerical value shown to the children? By folding a paper into two halves diagonally, the children cannot always visualize if they are of equal value; if a triangle is divided into two halves by simply drawing a line in the middle, then the children may see that they are of equal value.

(Literal translation from the second co-planning meeting with Teacher Fo, reading from 33:19 to 34:09)

Excerpt 3

TEACHER KWONG: Given that some children were confused in the mid-lesson, the try-out teacher told them to perform division.

EXTERNAL CONSULTANT: Did this phenomenon occur with Teacher Yung?

(Literal translation from the reflection meeting with Teacher Kwong, reading from 05:53 to 06:01)

Reorienting the direction of the discourse

The leadership style of the external consultant was also reflected in the orienting and re-orienting of the discourse when the focus of the discussion became confusing. This consistency is important because his intervention is justified by his professional knowledge and how learning is made possible from the perspectives of the participating teachers. The following excerpts illustrate his interventions in the discourse.

Effects of leadership styles 121

Excerpt 1

TEACHER FO: We chose fractions but can we use new methods?

TEACHER HO: Can we give children something to divide or use any new methods?

EXTERNAL CONSULTANT: This problem has not yet occurred. This question about methods has been asked previously, and there is no answer to this question. We come together to discuss not the method but the content of learning.

> (Literal translation from the first co-planning meeting, reading from 00:13 to 01:40)

Excerpt 2

EXTERNAL CONSULTANT: I am not against using the method of comparing the values (large and small) of fractions. However, this method is difficult because the concept of fractions has not been mastered clearly. Therefore, we should focus on the clarity of fractions first rather than comparing.

> (Literal translation from the first co-planning meeting, reading from 28:15 to 28:59)

Inviting participation from all members

To invite participation from the team members, the external consultant often used open questions without addressing any particular issues raised by the former. This technique was effective to such an extent that in the three meetings, he was recorded using this tactic 30, 34, and 31 times, respectively. This tactic of motivating participation and distributing opportunities for individual contribution was evident in all three meetings. As time progressed, this modeling led other team members to adopt this tactic. For example, we recorded a total of 122 instances of such questions in the second meeting on reflection compared with only 24 times in the first planning meeting. The following examples illustrate this invitational style.

Excerpt 1

EXTERNAL CONSULTANT: When the children were asked to compare the values of the denominators of the two fractions, you also asked them to color the blocks. What did you do to prepare the children for the activity of coloring blocks on the worksheet? You all talked about how you taught them the concepts of fractions in the previous lessons. Did all of you use the same methods? Why did all of you adopt the same method?

> (Literal translation from the first co-planning meeting, reading from 09:00 to 09:37)

122   *Case studies: a team approach*

Excerpt 2

> EXTERNAL CONSULTANT: What can you say about this method? No problems would occur by extending the horizon of the children, but do you think this method would complicate the understanding of the concept? Note that we intuitively felt that this method might not be connected with the concept of fractions of equal value
> > (Literal translation from the second co-planning meeting, reading from 20:43 to 21:10)

Other team members employing this tactic were observed in the following examples.

Teacher Ho: Do we need a pre-test this time?
> (Literal translation from the second co-planning meeting, reading from 09:16 to 09:19)

Panel head: Do you think the students would ask the teachers on how to fold seven times?
> (Literal translation from the second co-planning meeting, reading from 62:26 to 62:28)

Project leader: Do you think changing the order is good? For example, introducing dividing a portion of several pieces first and then dividing a piece?
> (Literal translation from the first co-planning meeting, reading from 57:33 to 58:50)

This type of discourse is more participatory, and the source of practical wisdom can be shared among the members of the team. More importantly, this type of discourse creates expectations of equally valuable contributions from each member. The result is that team and communal spirit is strengthened and enhanced. Another result is that the hierarchical status and its embedded power relationship are suppressed or flattened. Accordingly, the members have more negotiation space in terms of decision making and meeting outcomes.

Reflecting on personal experience

Monologues refer to those utterances that stretch over a longer period of time with one or more communicative purposes, such as instructional and clarification. Monologues are useful in asserting personal and hierarchical power. The numbers of monologues by the external consultant in the three meetings are five, four, and zero times, respectively, which cover a total of 21 minutes and 16 seconds. An excerpt is provided as an example below.

External consultant: Everyone used more than one method. As I mentioned earlier, the problem is not with the method but has to do with the approach you would use to express one concept. We do not have a single general method but employ various methods instead. The problem is still with us. You may ask what is the real problem then? We should think about whether we have misunderstood the issue or whether this learning object is significantly difficult for our students. We could also think about what methods to use to represent the mathematical concepts. In the last few years, I have learned much from my son.

(Literal translation from the first co-planning meeting, reading from 03:50 to 05:53)

This monologue serves several functions as follows:

- Helping members explore the underlying problems in learning the mathematical concept
- Analyzing the issues involved in learning the particular mathematical item logically
- Extending the issue to other possibilities
- Using a real personal case to illustrate the problem
- Clarifying the conceptual problem by using a mathematical concept
- Re-orienting the search for the underlying learning problem
- Identifying the focus of the problem

The instructional monologue in this study is far less didactic; instead, it is reflective and invitational in search of the underlying problems on learning the particular object of learning the mathematical properties of fractions. The leadership style of the consultant illustrates a form of power that is professional and intellectual. In particular, the consultant guides thinking, orients the direction of the discourse, refocuses the pedagogical values of innovation, initiates the use of narratives and personal experiences as forms of resources for curriculum deliberation, and leads the team toward a professional goal hidden in his mind. However, the choice of which communication strategies to employ is invitational, reflective, and open. His choice is also full of team spirit and collaboration, which are realized in his direct language showing frankness and professionalism. This style is contrary to the traditional hierarchical leadership style that is explicit in Asian contexts.

Analysis of communication patterns

In response to the assumed higher professional status of the external consultant, the other members in the team were quite straightforward about their own views and observations. However, the ascribed social power of the consultant is mediated by his slightly flattened leadership style. The panel head in this team played a role similar to that of other members in the team. However, the space for negotiation is flexible, and each response from the members is countered with a challenge in terms of its contents, accuracy, and relevance. This situation may

124   *Case studies: a team approach*

also be evidence of a discourse indicating a flat hierarchy among members of the team. An excerpt is provided below to illustrate this point.

Teacher Ho:	Surprisingly, no student folded the paper in the way we expected. I think we should have told them much earlier. I had reminded myself but forgot to do so. I think some students already got the point.
Teacher Kwong:	I would have also done the same by drawing a line in the middle. Next lesson, the children will use a one-dimensional picture but without a dividing line in the middle. However, I am worried that they may color the other part seeing that the adjacent picture has a color.
Teacher Yung:	She [Teacher Ho] did not emphasize the division in the class. Thus, the students were confused.
External consultant:	Where did the problem occur? You already gave a demonstration yet the students were wrong again.
Project leader:	You can explain [the concept] while you are doing the "ice cream" example in the next lesson. We currently have half a box of ice cream.

(Literal translation from the reflection meeting,
reading from 02:36 to 15:34)

Teacher Ho reflected on the performance of her students and made a concession about her pedagogical decision. In the process, she restated her view about the successful achievement of the learning objective in her lesson. Teacher Kwong was polite to moderate the tone of the pedagogical "mistake" of her colleague by stating that she would have done the same. However, she also extended the analysis by specifying the possible areas of confusion that the students may have encountered. The problem was with the proximity of the two pictures, which could have led to the confusion. Her analysis echoed the insistence of Teacher Ho about the achievement of the learning objective. Compared with the others, Teacher Yung was relatively more straightforward and frank, directly pointing at the problem on pedagogy or lack of pedagogical tactics of Teacher Ho.

Then, the intervention of the external consultant moved the focus of the discussion from the pedagogical strategies to some other possible areas, which may be the real source of the learning problems for students in this case. The project leader further extended the discussion to other possible activities in the future. In this study, a group of teachers engaged in a genuine dialogue that focused on reflecting on a pedagogical act. In addition, each participant expressed his/her own views, expressed reservations about the views of others, subtly supported the views of others, extended the discussion to other possibilities, and re-oriented the focus of the discussion to a new topic or plan of discussion.

The space of discussion and contents served as the focus in the beginning, during which members tried to negotiate this space from different perspectives and angles. Then, the space on which the topic and contents are located is moved to the other possibilities or viewed from another angle. As a result, another space

Effects of leadership styles 125

of topic and contents in relation to the original space is created. Therefore, the members successfully created or added spaces to the original topics and contents as a team of collaborators working toward the same pedagogical goal. No member of the team has any evidence of being superior, or no member appears to play a subordinate role in relation to the others. Hence, a flat hierarchical structure is well exemplified by this example of discourse.

Meanwhile, Figure 6.2 illustrates the pattern of communication style among members in the reflection meeting. The other two planning meetings share major similarities with the reflection meeting. The numbers indicate the number of utterances among members, and the arrows indicate the directions of utterances. One feature that attracts our attention is the active interactions between the consultant and the teachers as well as those between teachers. The intensity of the interactions is shown by the thickness of each line between pairs of interlocutors.

The dialogue of the meeting is multi-structural and elaborated. On the one hand, the external consultant and the panel head, both of whom are assumed to have a higher social status, dominated 53.35% of the total time of the entire meeting. On the other hand, the teachers played an active role in the negotiation process of extracting meanings from the interactions, expressing divergent views on their pedagogical practices and decisions accordingly. The excerpts cited in the above

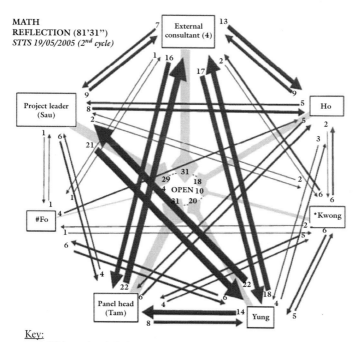

Key:
  *: This teacher left the meeting from 42:21 to 57:50.
  #: This teacher left the meeting at 29:18 and did not return until the end.
  Arrows: directions of utterances showing the person who initiates
  Numbers: show the number of initiations

Figure 6.2 Interaction patterns of the reflection meeting

126 *Case studies: a team approach*

sections illustrate the "expansive" space in the negotiation processes (Engestrom, 2001). This pattern of interactions in terms of the discourse time distribution is re-confirmed when the same graphic is worked out for the three team meetings. Table 6.2 shows the actual time distribution of each member's contribution to the interactions in the meetings and its proportion to the total time of each meeting.

As shown in the time distribution in Table 6.2, the total time occupied by both the panel head and the consultant comprise 53% for all three meetings, which aimed primarily for teacher development and learning. To a certain degree, these quantitative data further support our observation and analysis of the impact of the leadership styles of the consultant and the panel head on teacher participation. The speaking times of the external consultant are consistent across the three meetings, with over 50% in the first planning meeting and around 33% in both the reflection and the second planning meetings. The contributions of the other members of the team are quite evenly distributed, ranging from 7.41% to 11.52%. When the amount of contributions in terms of sheer time is compared with the qualitative features of the contributions indicated in Figure 6.2 and the attached excerpts, the interactions demonstrate the following salient features:

(1) The interactions are divergent in terms of orientation of the contents.
(2) The key feature in the interactions among members is "expansive," stretching and extending to associated areas of concerns and topics.

Table 6.2 Contribution of each participant in terms of time of discourse**

Teacher	First Planning Meeting (minutes)	Reflection Meeting (minutes)	Second Planning Meeting (minutes)	Individual Total (minutes)	Occupation Percentage (%)
Panel head (Tam)	5:14	7:50	2:38	15:42	7.60%
External consultant	35:38	38:29	20:21	94:28	45.75%
Project leader (Sau)	4:22	7:49	5:24	17:35	8.52%
Teacher Yung	4:34	12:23	6:50	23:47	11.52%
Teacher Kwong	0:18	4:04**	10:56	15:18	7.41%
Teacher Ho	5:26	7:25	7:41	20:32	9.95%
Teacher Fo	6:55	3:31#	5:59	16:25	7.95%
Total amount of time (minutes)	62:27	81:31	59:49	203:47	100%

Notes: ˙The curriculum leader briefly attended the beginning of the second planning meeting to clarify certain queries and then left the meeting. Her participation was not associated with the major purpose of the curriculum meeting; thus, this time is not counted as part of the meeting.
˙˙This teacher left the meeting from 42:21 to 57:50. #This teacher left the meeting at 29:18 and did not return until the end.
Source: Law, E.H.F. (2011). Exploring the role of leadership in facilitating teacher learning in Hong Kong. *School Leadership & Management, 31*(4), 391–407.

(3) Contributions or participations in terms of time occupation are comparatively evenly "distributed" among all members.

(4) The discourses are reflective, pedagogy-focused, and problem-solving in nature.

Analysis of visual images and meanings

The visual images with their subtle meanings in the three videotaped meetings have been observed and reported below to triangulate our previous analyses based on discourses in the interactions. In the first meeting, determination can be gleaned from the eyes of the consultant, as he distributed his attention to every member of the team during the discussion. His eyes were wide open and appeared to be smiling to mask the coercive power hidden in his language that incites invitation and reflection (first co-planning meeting, reading from 09:27 to 09:32). He often leaned back in his chair, with one hand supporting his chin. This posture gave an impression of being thoughtful and relaxed. The expression of being relaxed in the meeting might serve to reinforce his imposition of a flattened image contrary to his assumed higher social status in the professional hierarchy of being a teacher educator in the university. Other members seemed relaxed and committed to the conversations; they participated and interrupted the discussions quite freely. Therefore, the atmosphere of the meeting was infused with team spirit and willingness to collaborate. The explanations of the traditional pedagogical strategies and their demonstrations on the whiteboard by two teachers reinforced the focus of the meeting: to reflect upon the personal experiences shared by all members.

The team spirit was further strengthened when the reflection meeting was turned into a conversation laden with commitment and dedication as the members focused on the pedagogical innovation (Foster-Fishman, Nowell, Deacon, Nievar, & McCann, 2005; Somech, 2006; Ticha & Hospesova, 2006). The members laughed "boisterously" without caring much about their mannerisms. One teacher covered her mouth with her hand because she was too excited and spoke loudly. The other three teachers started making body movements giddily, showing their excitement in the discussions about the try-out lessons. Taking turns, which was expected in formal meetings, frequently became interrupted in the reflection meeting. Therefore, the formality in the team was reduced as team spirit increased. The third videotaped meeting shared many similarities with the previous meetings. In the third meeting, loud laughter, random interruptions, and more natural speech were observed. In general, a stronger sense of team spirit and collaboration was noted.

Discussion

The current analysis based on visual data and the interaction patterns from the videotaped meetings of curriculum innovation teams helped identify a specific type of leadership in the three meetings. Notably, a distributed leadership environment was re-created in the mathematics curriculum development team through the insertion of a policy of leadership rotation for the team. The original

128 *Case studies: a team approach*

purpose was to encourage authentic and active participation by team members. The leadership styles of the external consultant and the panel head, who were considered to assert a more Asiatic hierarchical leadership role, appeared to reflect a flat pattern of leadership. This leadership style allowed a significant potential for more "space" for negotiation among members of the curriculum development team. The emergence of space was enhanced by the leadership style of the consultant in several ways listed below:

(1) The discourse is open and elaborated; thus, a "space" for participation is available.
(2) The style of leadership is invitational and reflective, allowing participation to be free.
(3) Contributions from individual members of the team are recognized and valued in the negotiation space.
(4) The leadership style in the traditional sense of "directing" the course of the discourse or the decision making processes and "dictating" the content of the discourse is hidden or is mediated by the liberal style of the consultant.

The effects of the leadership style result in positive and legitimate teacher participation. Therefore, arriving at an ultimate decision is the goal of processes of rational enquiry and discussion among members of the team rather than the judgment of the ascribed leaders in the hierarchy. A few suggestions for policy makers and faculty members with responsibilities in teacher education and training are provided below. These suggestions are also relevant for the management teams of school sectors.

(1) The school management should possess knowledge on how a program of human development among teachers in the school should be developed, designed, and evaluated. In this way, new and experienced teachers could contribute in generating and implementing innovations and policies at the school level.
(2) The school management should possess a macro view and know-how about the strategies that can be employed to enhance a learning and expansive environment in schools, which aim at empowering teacher capacity for leading and planning change and innovations (Fullan, 2008).
(3) Middle managers, such as subject panel heads or curriculum leaders, should receive training and professional development activities in conducting meetings or collaborative activities. The methods should allow opportunities for participants to negotiate meanings in the process of their participation. The emphasis is on the possible consequence of different types of leadership styles and the creation of learning opportunities.
(4) These middle managers should also receive training and educational programs that enhance their ability in conducting school-based research activities with an aim to enhance professional practices and the effectiveness of student learning.

(5) Such middle managers should receive training on leadership through which they can learn how to lead change and innovations among teachers in a professional context.

(6) Awareness of the changing roles of teachers in the teaching profession should be enhanced, and the changing expectations of the society should be clearly conveyed in the teacher education programs. An extended version of teacher professionalism should also serve as the key focus in teacher development programs.

(7) Teacher participation, with focus on teacher capacity in reflective and critical thinking, should be the key to the successful implementation of curriculum and educational innovations. Hence, the culture of a flat hierarchy should become the focus of school reform programs.

(8) The theories and practices of teacher leadership and initiation in school-based curriculum innovations and reforms are still vaguely conceived among participating teachers, especially those who generally look for leadership and wisdom from their hierarchical superiors.

Leadership studies in school-based curriculum development have focused mainly on managerial and hierarchical bases to an extent that teachers in schools have taken a peripheral role in making pedagogical decisions (Andrews & Soder, 1987; Darling-Hammond, Bullmaster, & Cobb, 1995; Hallinger & Murphy, 1986). Recent studies on teacher leadership have focused on a leadership model that attempts to recapture the essence of the professional role and identity of teachers in curriculum decision making. Teacher participation in curriculum decision making appears to have received consensus among policy makers and school management. Meanwhile, teacher leadership in curriculum decision making in schools, the practice of which is still in the infancy stage, is a new phenomenon in both the international and local (Hong Kong) literature.

How this concept and practice could be institutionalized within the infrastructure of the current school ethos, which is dominated by traditions and seniority in Asian countries, still requires substantial theoretical and experimental work (Bush & Qiang, 2000; Walker, 2004; Walker & Dimmock, 2000; Wong, 2006). Our previous reports on the first and second action cycles of a curriculum leadership development project in Hong Kong have demonstrated the complexity and inter-relationship of the key structures.

These new leadership structures and processes have yet to find their home within the culture of the case school in the study. However, experience suggests that engaging teachers in curriculum decision making processes enhances the development of their professional knowledge and skills (Marks & Louis, 1997; Silins & Mulford, 2002). Two important issues must be explored and investigated in both theoretical and empirical studies: how the concept of teacher leadership in curriculum decision making could be practiced more effectively in schools, and how the structures and processes could be institutionalized in schools on a wider scale. Such objectives can be achieved through the collaboration of researchers in university faculties and teacher-leaders in schools. The current study focuses on determining the meditational effects of the consultant's leadership style on the negotiations occurring among teachers in curriculum decision making processes. The analysis of the discourse features of the interactions indicates the power relationship between the positional leaders and the teachers. These features demonstrate that the participation of the teachers was oriented by the consultant's leadership style in terms of the quantitative time distribution and the qualitative control measures realized by the implicit imposition of power and status.

The panel head and the consultant allowed more time for teacher participation. Accordingly, an image of flexibility was imposed onto the teacher participants. This implicit control was strengthened by the language of knowledge and professionalism. The discourse features illustrate this observation and support our argument concerning the effects of the leadership styles of the panel head and the consultant, especially on the amount of opportunities for teacher participation and development. The facilitation can also be understood qualitatively in that teacher participation was shaped toward a role of being the active creators of knowledge and professionalism (Paavola & Hakkarainen, 2005). Teacher participation was extended to a multi-structural question and response type, requiring creative answers in most cases. This communicative style made teacher participation more engaging and gave teachers more room for negotiation and exploration. Therefore, development opportunities were "given" by the leadership style in a much more subtle manner. School-based curriculum development has been a consensus in educational policy studies for many years in international education and in Hong Kong since the 1980s. Policy makers and school management should revisit its conceptualization and its realization in various types of school situations and milieus across countries with different cultural backgrounds and traditions (Law, Wan, Galton, & Lee, 2010).

Focusing solely on teacher leadership development, without a concurrent suitable program of leadership education based on research findings for both middle management and school management, can diminish the effectiveness of any teacher education program. Such strategy can also weaken the initiatives of innovative teachers in creating and expanding spaces for development work in schools. The leadership program should include key concepts of extended professionality, strategies for developing human potentiality in schools, school-based research strategies, as well as comparative and socio-cultural studies in leadership. Extending and stretching the educational and human horizon of middle managers and school management personnel, including school heads, can complement and support an enhancement program of teacher leadership in schools. Doing so can usher in a new era of quality education for children within a holistic view of reforming school education. Distributed leadership as a part of the conceptualization of school-based approaches to curriculum development has been practiced for the past 30 years; however, the process by which this kind of leadership works effectively across nations with diverse socio-cultural backgrounds remains a critical issue in an era of global education (Hofstede, 2005). The current study is our preliminary attempt to contribute to the international discussion of this critical issue from an Asian perspective.

References

Andrews, R., & Soder, R. (1987). Principal leadership and student achievement. *Educational Leadership, 44*(6), 9–11.

Australian Education Union. (2004). *Educational leadership and teaching for the twenty first century: Project discussion paper.* Retrieved from http://www.aeufed eral.org.au/Debates/elat21pap.pdf

Ball, D.L., & Cohen, D.K. (1996). Reform by the book: What is Á or might be Á the role of curriculum materials in teacher learning and instructional reform? *Educational Researcher, 25*(9), 6–8, 14.

Black, P., & Atkin, M. (1996). *Changing the subject: Innovations in science, mathematics and technology education.* London: Routledge.

Britt, M.S., Irwin, K.C., & Ritchie, G. (2001). Professional conversations and professional growth. *Journal of Mathematics Teacher Education, 4*(1), 29–53.

Bush, T., & Qiang, H. (2000). Leadership and culture in Chinese education. *Asia Pacific Journal of Education, 20*(2), 58–67.

Carr, W., & Kemmis, S. (1986). *Becoming critical: Education, knowledge and action research.* London: Falmer.

Cohen, L., Manion, L., & Morrison, K. (2000). *Research methods in education.* London: Routledge/Falmer.

Craig, C., & Ross, V. (2008). Cultivating the image of teachers as curriculum makers. In F.M. Connelly, M.F. He, & J. Phillion (Eds.), *The Sage handbook of curriculum and instruction* (pp. 282–305). London: Sage.

Darling-Hammond, L., Bullmaster, M.L., & Cobb, V.L. (1995). Rethinking teacher leadership through professional development schools. *The Elementary School Journal, 96*(1), 88–106.

Elliott, J. (1991). *Action research for educational change.* Buckingham: Open University Press.

Engestrom, Y. (2001). Expansive learning at work: Toward an activity theoretical reconceptualization. *Journal of Education and Work, 14*(1), 133–156.

Foster-Fishman, P., Nowell, B., Deacon, Z., Nievar, M.A., & McCann, P. (2005). Using methods that matter: The impact of reflection, dialogue, and voice. *American Journal of Community Psychology, 36*(3–4), 275–291.

Frost, D., & Durrant, J. (2002). *Teacher-led development work: Guidance and support.* London: David Fulton.

Frost, D., & Durrant, J. (2003). Teacher leadership: Rationale, strategy and impact. *School Leadership and Management, 23*(2), 173–186.

Fullan, M. (1993). *Change forces: Probing the depths of educational reform.* London: Falmer.

Fullan, M. (2001). *Leading in a culture of change.* San Francisco, CA: Jossey-Bass.

Fullan, M. (2007). *The new meaning of educational change.* New York: Teachers College Press.

Fullan, M. (2008). *The six secrets of change: What the best leaders do to help their organizations survive and thrive.* San Francisco, CA: Jossey-Bass.

Goddard, Y., Goddard, R., & Tschannen-Moran, M. (2007). A theoretical and empirical investigation of teacher collaboration for school improvement and student achievement in public elementary schools. *Teachers College Record, 109*(4), 877–896.

Hall, G., & Hord, S. (2002). *Implementing change: Patterns, principles, and potholes.* Boston, MA: Allyn and Bacon.

132 Case studies: a team approach

Hallinger, P., & Heck, R.H. (2010). Collaborative leadership and school improvement: Understanding the impact on school capacity and student learning. *School Leadership and Management, 30*(2), 95–110.

Hallinger, P., & Murphy, J. (1986). The social context of effective schools. *American Journal of Education, 94*(3), 328–355.

Harris, A. (2003). Teacher leadership and school improvement. In A. Harris, C. Day, D. Hopkins, M. Hadfield, A. Hargreaves, & C. Chapman (Eds.), *Effective leadership for school improvement* (pp. 72–83). London: Routledge/Falmer.

Harris, A. (2004). Distributed leadership and school improvement: Leading or misleading? *Educational Management Administration and Leadership, 32*(4), 11–24.

Hiebert, J., Gallimore, R., & Stigler, J.W. (2003). The new heroes of teaching. *Education Week, 23*(10), 56.

Hofstede, G. (2005). *Cultures and organizations: Software of the mind.* New York: McGraw-Hill.

Hopkins, D. (2001). *School improvement for real.* London: Falmer.

Law, E.H.F., Galton, M., & Wan, S.W.Y. (2007). Developing curriculum leadership in schools: Hong Kong perspectives. *Asia Pacific Journal of Teacher Education, 35*(2), 143–159.

Law, E.H.F., Galton, M., & Wan, S.W.Y. (2010). Distributed curriculum leadership: A Hong Kong case study. *Education Management Administration & Leadership, 38*(3), 286–303.

Law, E.H.F., & Wan, S.W.Y. (2006). Developing curriculum leadership in an elementary school: A Hong Kong case study. *Curriculum and Teaching, 21*(2), 61–90.

Law, E.H.F., Wan, S.W.Y., Galton, M., & Lee, J.C.K. (2010). Managing school based curriculum innovations: A Hong Kong case study. *The Curriculum Journal, 21*(3), 313–332.

Leithwood, K. (2008). *Educational accountability and school leadership.* Retrieved from http://www.ncsl.org.uk/media-415-ca-educational-accountability-and-school leadership.pdf

MacBeath, J. (2004). Putting the self back into self-evaluation. *Improving Schools, 7*(1), 87–91.

Macpherson, I., Aspland, T., Brooker, R., & Elliott, B. (1999). *Places and spaces for teachers in curriculum leadership.* Deakin West, ACT: Australian Curriculum Studies Association.

Marks, H.M., & Louis, K.S. (1997). Does teacher empowerment affect the classroom? The implications of teacher empowerment for instructional practice and student academic performance. *Educational Evaluation and Policy Analysis, 19*(3), 245–275.

Marsh, C. (1997). *Key concepts for understanding curriculum.* London: Falmer.

McLaughlin, M. (1990). The Rand change agent study revisited. *Educational Researcher, 19*(9), 11–16.

McLaughlin, M., & Talbert, J. (2001). *Professional communities and the work of high school teaching.* Chicago, IL: University of Chicago Press.

Ovens, P. (1999). Can teachers be developed? *Journal of In-Service Education, 25*(2), 275–305.

Paavola, S., & Hakkarainen, K. (2005). The knowledge creation metaphor: An emergent epistemological approach to learning. *Science and Education, 14*(6), 535–557.

Putnam, R.T., & Borko, H. (2000). What do new views of knowledge and thinking have to say about research on teacher learning? *Educational Researcher, 29*(1), 4–15.

Robinson, V., Lloyd, C., & Rowe, K. (2008). The impact of leadership on student outcomes: An analysis of the differential effects of leadership types. *Educational Administration Quarterly, 44*(5), 564–588.

Schon, D. (1983). *The reflective practitioner.* London: Temple Smith.

Shouse, R.C., & Lin, K.P. (2010). *Principal leadership in Taiwan schools.* Baltimore, MD: Rowman and Littlefield.

Shulman, L., & Sherin, M.G. (2004). Fostering communities of teachers as learners: Disciplinary perspectives. *Journal of Curriculum Studies, 36*(2), 135–140.

Silins, H., & Mulford, B. (2002). Schools as learning organisations: The case for system, teacher and student learning. *Journal of Educational Administration, 40*(5), 425–446.

Somech, A. (2006). The effects of leadership style and team process on performance and innovation in functionally heterogeneous teams. *Journal of Management, 32*(1), 132–157.

Spillane, J. (2006). *Distributed leadership.* San Francisco, CA: Jossey-Bass.

Stenhouse, L. (1975). *An introduction to curriculum research and development.* London: Heinemann.

Teddlie, C., & Tashakkori, A. (2003). Major issues and controversies in the use of mixed methods in the social and behavioral sciences. In A. Tashakkori & C. Teddlie (Eds.), *Handbook of mixed methods in social and behavioral research* (pp. 3–50). Thousand Oaks, CA: Sage.

Teddlie, C., & Tashakkori, A. (2009). *Foundations of mixed methods research: Integrating quantitative and qualitative approaches in the social and behavioral sciences.* Thousand Oaks, CA: Sage.

Ticha, M., & Hospesova, A. (2006). Qualified pedagogical reflection as a way to improve mathematics education. *Journal of Mathematics Teacher Education, 9*(2), 129–156.

Walker, A. (2004). Constitution and culture: Exploring the deep leadership structures of Hong Kong schools. *Discourse: Studies in the Cultural Politics of Education, 25*(1), 75–94.

Walker, A., & Dimmock, C. (2000). Insights into educational administration: The need for a cross-cultural comparative perspective. *Asia Pacific Journal of Education, 20*(2), 11–22.

Wallace, J.D., Nesbit, C.R., & Miller, A.C.S. (1999). Six leadership models for professional development in science and mathematics. *Journal of Science Teacher Education, 10*(4), 247–268.

Wong, K.C. (2006). Contextual impact on educational management and leadership. *Journal of Educational Change, 7*(1–2), 77–89.

7 Managing school-based curriculum innovations in a Chinese curriculum development team

Discourse and social network analyses[1]

Context of change

For the past several decades, the decentralization of educational decision making in general and curriculum decision making in particular has become a key issue in the broad discussion on change strategies to enhance school improvement, teacher development, and student learning among policy makers (Fullan, 2001; Hopkins, 2001; Leithwood, 2008; Skilbeck, 1984). Some studies have argued that the urge for decentralization is a result of the failure of central agencies to design and plan new curricula for implementation in schools, as well as the call for more democratic participation of professional teachers in school and curriculum decision making processes in the 1960s and 1970s in developed countries, such as the United States and Australia (e.g., Australian Education Union, 2004). However, England and Wales experienced a contrasting shift from a model of education influenced by local educational authorities to a more centralized model of a national curriculum in 1988 (Lawton, 1992). Some reform initiatives have focused on the leadership of principals in bringing about changes in schools, but these have largely neglected equally important roles and shared responsibilities of individual teachers and the transformative role of the teacher community as a whole in schools in the 1980s (Day, Harris, & Hadfield, 2001; Jackson, 2000).

Decentralization has to do with deciding on what to teach more relevantly, how to teach more effectively, and how to assess more accurately where learning takes place. Such decision making is done to meet the diverse needs of pupils in mixed-ability classrooms in response to the introduction of homogenous compulsory education for all in the 1970s. Therefore, decentralization essentially means changing the traditional roles of teachers from being curriculum users to curriculum developers, thus entailing teachers' enhanced responsibilities and initiatives in making curriculum decisions for student learning (Frost & Durrant, 2002, 2003; Harris, 2003; Marsh, 1997; Ovens, 1999; Stenhouse, 1975; Wallace, Nesbit, & Miller, 1999).

In Hong Kong, the traditional practice consists of using a centralized curriculum where decisions about aims, content, pedagogy, and assessment are largely in the hands of the centralized agencies, such as the former Education Department in the British colony. However, the movement towards decentralization has focused on a school-based model of involving and engaging teachers in a wider range of curriculum responsibilities, which have been taken up formally by the Llewellyn report in 1982 and more systematically by various education reports in Hong Kong. However, patterns and levels of involvement and commitment of teachers to participate have yet to be defined and elaborated with empirical data on what works and what does not work in the Hong Kong context (Law, 2003; Law & Galton, 2004; Law & Wan, 2005, 2008). The establishment of a curriculum coordinator at the senior level in primary schools in 2002 demonstrated the government's determination to institutionalize previous policy orientations and invest in additional resources for their implementation. However, efficiency and effects on teacher development and student learning remain largely undocumented empirically. The current project adopts a distributed approach on teacher involvement, which refers to a shared phenomenon and responsibility to be realized collectively in school settings. Curriculum decision making, therefore, is not the sole responsibility of a few key personnel appointed by the school hierarchy, but a process (or a phenomenon) that is shared equally among all teachers in the school (Ball & Cohen, 1996; Elliott, 1991; McLaughlin & Talbert, 2001; Shulman & Sherin, 2004). All teachers should be responsible and accountable for making their own curriculum decisions for their students in their respective classrooms. By taking up this responsibility, participation creates opportunities for school improvement, teacher development, and enhancement of student learning (Conley, 1991; Hiebert, Gallimore, & Stigler, 2003).

Distributive approaches to leadership practices

Distributed leadership is frequently used to label all kinds of shared and collaborative leadership activities (Harris, Leithwood, Day, Sammons, & Hopkins, 2007). Previous leadership practices and research have focused mainly on the managerial approach and have emphasized the hierarchical and positional structure of roles and relationships among personnel in schools. Decision making processes are top-down and likely to be oriented towards a power-coercive model (Burns, 1978). Therefore, leadership practices and their concomitant modes of operation are inadequate in providing an effective model for all schools and their management boards, which are engaged in different stages of the school developments with different foci in their strategic plans (Levin, 2000; Taylor, 2001). Different schools have varied socio-political backgrounds that shape their own development plans and practices. Therefore, schools need models of leadership that cover their needs in their different stages of the school development work (Elmore, 2004). For the last 20 years, the emergence of a complementary model of leadership practice has diluted the uniformity of the power-coercive model of leadership (Foster, 1989; Fullan, 2008b). The new model emphasizes the following three key development features:

(1) Leadership is distributed across different layers of the hierarchical structure (shared responsibility).
(2) The sources of power are non-ranking and non-status-oriented.

136   *Case studies: a team approach*

(3) The professional aspirations of individuals are given space for development.
(4) Teamwork and collaboration are preferred.
(5) Professional discourse prevails.
(6) Decision making is evidence-based.

Therefore, "distributed leadership" refers to leadership practice characterized by "reciprocal interdependency between the actions" of participants in a social activity (Spillane, 2006).

Curriculum leadership innovation project

The project was started in September 2004 in a Hong Kong primary school. As stated in the project proposal, its goals are as follows:

*   To develop abilities and skills of teachers in strategic planning and development and using evaluation for school improvement;
*   To enhance the effectiveness of a school's self-evaluation system; and
*   To develop a quality culture of school self-evaluation for school improvement.

Curriculum development teams

Two curriculum development teams were formed on a key subject basis, namely, Chinese language and mathematics, which comprise over one-third of the curriculum time in Hong Kong primary schools. The selection of team leaders was deliberately manipulated and "chosen" based on their observed commitment and professional attitudes towards curriculum reforms and innovations. In the first action cycle of the innovation project, which was conducted in the first semester, the subject panel heads were chosen as they had assumed hierarchical power. Their selection was expected to alleviate some political tension against the introduction of a new structure in the working lives of the teachers within the infrastructure of the school. However, in the second action cycle, which was conducted in the second semester, these team leaders were replaced and other participating colleagues were "persuaded" to take turns in leading the team. These two arrangements have two advantages. First, the subject-based approach in the formation of a curriculum development team is intended to control the subject content of the interactions among members in teamwork activities to maximize positive effects of the shared subject identity and working experiences among team members (MacBeath, 2004; Schon, 1983). The second one is to eliminate the potentially negative influences of any hierarchical structure and power relationship among team members to create a conducive teamwork environment for the emergence of professional dialogues among members, therefore cultivating a culture of shared and distributed curriculum leadership among team members (Black & Atkin, 1996; Britt, Irwin, & Ritchie, 2001; Carr & Kemmis, 1986; Fullan, 1993; Putnam & Borko, 2000). The latter advantage was thought to develop confidence in teachers in initiating and leading activities on pedagogical changes in schools. These two factors were essential because they allowed the development of a common yet open educational language and the strengthening of a shared yet democratic identity among a group of professional teachers, thus allowing us to focus on a collective action to solve the problem of an identified pedagogical issue (Day, 1993).

The project emphasized the need for collaboration with professionals from university faculties. Thus, each subject-based curriculum team was assigned a subject consultant to provide professional support and advice on pedagogical innovations. The role of the appointed subject consultant was to join the collaborative lesson preparation meetings, observe trial lessons, attend reflection meetings, as well as provide advice and feedback on the focus of pedagogical innovations. In some sense, consultants were expected to play the role of change agents in the development process of the innovation project with the participating teachers. This process was a form of professional leadership that consultants were expected to fulfill.

Planning, experimentation, and reflection model of change

The innovation pattern adopted the planning, experimentation, and reflection (PER) model (Table 7.1), in which the team reviewed, planned, and designed a lesson or a unit of learning in collaborative meetings. This model could be considered as the "lesson plan" approach (Taylor, Anderson, & Meyer, 2005). The team then assigned teachers to try the planned innovation lesson. In the third stage, the team conducted a reflection meeting.

This model of change was used in the first action cycle and repeated in the second action cycle in a spirally continuous structure (Law & Wan, 2005, 2008). This organization has several advantages. First, opportunities were created for collaboration and teamwork. Second, changes in pedagogy were located based on the teaching subject. Third, problem-solving and critical approaches were

Table 7.1 Three-stage model of teacher planning, experimentation, and reflection curriculum practices (PER model)

Stage	Aims	Teacher Activities
Planning stage	To identify the goals and design strategies for a plan of innovation	SWOT, whole school conference, action planning meetings, collaborative lesson preparation meetings, production of materials
Experimentation stage	To put the plan into action in classrooms	Trialing, peer observation, evaluation
Reflection stage	To review actions and plan for future actions	Post-observation conference, completion of feedback sheets

Source: Managing school-based curriculum innovations: A Hong Kong case study. *The Curriculum Journal, 21*(3), 313–332.

138   *Case studies: a team approach*

adopted. Fourth, the change became an open venture. Therefore, school knowledge is taken as a matter of possibility and is open for challenge, rather than as a group of definitive subjects that are merely imposed from external agents for professional deliberation at school sites (Harris, 2004; Macpherson, Aspland, Brooker, & Elliott, 1999).

Focus of innovation

Each curriculum development team was free to choose between two directions of change. Each team then selected a teaching topic and decided between using the same pedagogical approach for all trial lessons and adopting a different pedagogical approach in each trial lesson. For example, the Chinese curriculum development team chose the "Dragon Boat Festival" as a topic in targeting the development of reading comprehension skills and the creativity of five children. The creation of internal variations in pedagogical approaches to teaching and learning was geared towards the generation of opportunities for contrast and comparison in the discussions in planning and reflection meetings. In addition, the realization of these pedagogical approaches in trial lessons provided teachers with concrete experiences for subsequent discussion and analysis (Ball, 1996; King & Newmann, 2000). Therefore, curriculum reforms and change did not remain as some abstract language or concept in policy documents, but became authentic experiences not too distant from the real lives of most teachers (Garet, Porter, Desimone, Birman, & Yoon, 2001).

Procedures of analysis

As we based each action cycle on our PER model, we chose one videotaped planning meeting and two reflection meetings from the second action cycle of the Chinese curriculum development team. This approach of using three team meetings allowed for the triangulation of emergent themes, the categorization of data from the curriculum development team, and the identification of the uniqueness of each of the team meetings (Cohen, Manion, & Morrison, 2000).

We determined from the very beginning that we would not exhaust the potentiality of the visual data embedded in the videotaped meetings from one viewing. Therefore, we decided to adopt a more organized but collaborative approach in analyzing the data using the procedures described in the following sub-sections.

Emerging themes in each phase of the analysis

Four researchers viewed each of the videotaped meetings in sections of 10 minutes together, but with a similar pattern of procedures and actions. In each 10-minute section, each member of the research team worked together to identify the features of the interactions and key points of interest that would be followed up in the next 10 minutes. For example, in the first 10 minutes, we identified the roles of the consultant and the teachers in the interactions. The roles of the consultant tended to be dominating and instructive, while the teachers were passive and attentive. Then, in the next 10 minutes, some emerging themes appeared. For example, responses from the consultant clearly showed that he was the source of pedagogical strategies and wisdom. With his assertiveness, he often dominated the discourse and indirectly suppressed opportunities for other team members to raise issues and extend their thoughts. This developmental approach exhausted as much as possible the enriching layers of meanings and their interpretations in the analysis process, while observations could be confirmed, rejected, identified, refined, and ultimately decided among a team of researchers (Banks, 2007).

Division of labor and confirming the accuracy of the transcriptions

Although all four researchers watched the videotaped meetings together, we made some form of a division. One focused on accuracy, one on facial expressions and non-verbal behavior, another on the dialogues, and the last researcher focused on the potentiality of videotaped data and images. However, we all wrote down field notes of whatever we felt was essential and related to our investigation and discussed these notes after each viewing. We viewed the videotaped meetings alongside written transcriptions of the meetings to ensure accuracy. We often revisited the sections to deepen our understanding and allow more alternative themes to emerge. The four researchers discussed with one another and sought consensus; sometimes, disagreements could arise with regards alternative interpretations. When points of departure required some further investigation, the research team would write them down for further development.

Methods of analysis

Our major approach was a grounded one, with the intention of allowing possibilities to emerge and categories of concepts derived from the videotaped data to be refined. However, we cannot deny that the theoretical underpinnings of our design framework had some impact on the methods we chose to employ to analyze and understand them. We tended to view this method as normal practice in qualitative research approaches. For example, we considered the possibility of the effect of the participants' status and power in the school hierarchy, experience in teaching, and personality in terms of how they interacted with one another. All these factors had an impact, one way or another, on the negotiation process among participants. However, themes or categories of data were compared and triangulated among the four researchers and from the data of the three-videotaped meetings in the second action cycle. Selections of interactions were analyzed and used to illustrate the key features of each participant in the meetings. Aside from qualitative approaches, the team strengthened their arguments by organizing quantitative analyses of the visual data in the tapes, such as the distribution of time between the participants across the interactions in each meeting and the counting of the types of discourse features.

Findings and analyses

The planning meeting was conducted on April 22, 2005, and the two reflection meetings were held on June 10 and June 17, 2005, respectively. The first meeting was attended by all six team members and lasted for 51:04. Meanwhile, the second and the third meetings on reflection lasted 29:59 and 51:21, respectively. These meetings were attended by four teachers, including the panel head, consultant, project leader, and one teacher.

External consultant and the impact of his leadership style

In these three meetings, one striking feature was the assertion of authority by the external consultant, who was a senior academic in the faculty of education at a local university. His execution of his ascribed authority can be classified as a source of information, pedagogical strategies, wisdom, and power (Hofstede, 2005). His expression of authority was communicated through verbal medium. Specifically, his domination of the interactions was expressed mostly through monologues, the contents of which were instructive and directive. Furthermore, he assumed a sense of superiority in pedagogy and knowledge, which allowed little opportunity for the negotiation of meanings among the participants. One of the discourse features was the emphasis on his personal contribution by using the first person pronoun "I" frequently. His use of "da" as a discourse marker to signify his symbolic role in making professional judgments concerning the practice of the participating teachers was also an explicit expression of his overriding power in the meetings. The following selections from his monologues at the two meetings illustrated the nature of his delivery. The duration is about eight minutes.

> I am pleased after watching the trial lesson. In the lesson, three steps were completed clearly. Without the last step, the effects would not be as satisfactory as one would expect. Afterwards, talking about the worksheet can finally give the pupils opportunities for reflection. In group discussions, they are informative and pedagogical. In the next lesson, remember to remind the pupils of the time "BC" for all the events they discussed. . . . About the term "dragon boat," why not call it the "dragon canoe"? Afterwards, the teacher could work with them. I have thought about the possibility of asking the pupils to write down vocabulary. However, I am worried about the fact that their inability to write quickly would eliminate opportunities for thinking activities. You could, however, tell the pupils to jot down the main points or they will forget what they have in mind. The pupils' views are not too bad. In fact, many things can be further developed. You can talk with them more . . . let them talk more. . . . Some are about moral and affective. . . . Finally, can we ask them to access the Internet and search for more information? Working in pairs and groups can benefit the pupils.
>
> (Literal translation from a selection of the reflection meeting, reading 03:14–11:20)

Managing school-based curriculum innovations 141

To illustrate how his perceived role and style of leadership were realized in the discourse, the following is a selected comment from him in the third meeting after the try-out lesson:

> . . . about the learning problem with speech . . . speaking ability, habit and attitude are important. The curriculum guideline is very clear already . . . if you want to train them, you have to teach them more characters and sentence patterns . . . and what you proposed a moment ago ought to have started from junior primary with the children. . . . I can give you materials and information . . . training starts early when they are young . . . ask them to answer in full sentences, this will train them to organize and to think . . . every lesson, four in each group, ask them to speak, they find a topic to speak about . . . can be something about the school, news, they choose freely, they may write down notes and speak from notes . . . ask them not to read from notes directly, each follows the other to repeat the contents of the previous one in turn . . . this is the best model to train students about speech, especially for those who have fear about public speaking. Let them speak about others first, then you teach them some specific communications patterns and sentence patterns.
>
> (Literal translation from a selection of the meeting,
> reading 3:20–10:00)

The consultant concentrated his discourse on speech training, which was the focus in the practice lesson that he had observed. He then subtly rejected the current practice of the teacher in the trial lesson by proposing an alternative approach of emphasizing training "characters and sentence patterns." He then gave an example on how to teach and pointed out the importance of "teaching full sentences." Afterwards, he reiterated the pedagogical objective of this strategy and pointed out that the purpose was to "train them to organize and think." The consultant then gave a detailed example to demonstrate how his proposed alternative was a viable one.

The above analysis of a selection of his monologue illustrates three aspects related to his personality and style. First, he rejected the pedagogical practices and decisions of the teachers. Second, his rejection was not based on pedagogical evidence and was not justified professionally. Third, he continued his commentary for around 10 minutes without inviting the participation of teachers. Thus, his style gave no negotiation space and allowed no interaction with the other parties in the meeting. He imposed his pedagogical theories on the practicing teachers without considering the professional autonomy and development of those teachers. His imposition delimited participation and allowed little room for the active learning of teachers. Thus, his consultancy can be considered as a form of external coercive agency, which reproduced a discourse of power and status within the culture of the school (Gee, Michaels, & O'Connor, 1992). Rather than engaging the participating teachers in a reflective and critical discourse, revisiting deeply rooted beliefs embedded in the current practice, his

142   *Case studies: a team approach*

agency reinforced a "legitimate" form of professionalism that is hierarchical and submissive (Woods, Jeffrey, Troman, & Boyle, 1997).

Internal panel head and the impact of his leadership style

The panel head seemed to indulge in his status and positional role in the subject. His participation was a form of reassertion of his hierarchical status and his superiority in the subject matter. He deliberately joined the "side" of the external consultant by sharing the legitimate power of the overt leader in the meeting. For example, he started a topic but concluded it without facilitating the participation of other teachers. He was often conclusive in his speech, and he assumed his role as the ultimate decision maker in this collaborative lesson preparation. Further, he proposed a topic for the trial lesson without expecting further discussion on its suitability, thereby blocking the negotiation space among participating teachers. His assertive style clearly gave a strong sense of his hierarchical role in his interactional patterns, such as interrupting others and nodding his head to show his recognition of the consultant's view. These actions exhibited his share of the consultant's professional power. As shown below, his emphatic use of "you" in his discourse marks his distant role from the practicing teachers, who assumed a subordinate role in teaching in schools:

> I talk a little here, but not those mentioned by Dr. Ho. . . . The term "new traditions" is problematic linguistically . . . but you need to explain this term clearly. . . . This topic was handled well in the try-out lesson, having included a modern perspective and also the contemporary movements in thoughts, having considered the moral principles in actions. . . . Poet Wat was a leading figure in Chu literary styles in ancient China. This is an important topic even for primary pupils and deserves a lesson on its own.
>
> (Literal translation, a selection of the monologues
> in the reflection meeting, reading 11:20–18:00)

We selected for analysis a series of utterances from his monologue to illustrate how the discourse features showed the underlying principles of his communication beliefs. The panel head:

(1) shows another available perspective
(2) states what that perspective is
(3) continues to explain
(4) gives pedagogical advice
(5) indicates an alternative pedagogical strategy
(6) gives alternative pedagogy
(7) gives the purposes
(8) moves to another topic
(9) offers possibilities

(First meeting, 24:45 to 26:10)

As shown in the above analysis, the panel head did not intend to engage the teachers in an interactive mode of discussion. Instead, his discourse shows his dominating power in dictating professional judgment and wisdom. His form of leadership was far less inquiry-based, and he tended to restrict the space for authentic negotiation and participation among the other teachers. Coincidentally, his leadership style matched the imposing style of the external consultant.

The consultant and the panel head met with the participating teachers, who were expected to play the role of the juniors in the professional decision making processes and in the eyes of those in the hierarchy. Four teachers behaved differently in the three videotaped meetings. The project leader had little leadership role, and she tended to be very reserved. Raising a few questions in the planning meeting and responding to a request from the panel head in the reflection meetings, she had little to contribute in terms of pedagogical wisdom and strategies. She apparently ignored the instructions and advice in the guidelines about her role in conducting meetings. In the planning meeting, one participating teacher remained silent, while another teacher only whispered into the ear of the project leader next to him from time to time. The third one murmured one or two utterances publicly. The overall participation of the teachers was minimal. In the reflection meeting, the discourse was explicitly initiated and led by the panel head or the consultant. The project leader and the participating teacher only responded passively to the requests of the panel head.

The division of the two camps is clearly identifiable. On the one hand, we have a camp of authority with a higher status, assuming the role of being an overall source of information and solutions. On the other hand, we have a group of teachers who were passive and contributed little to the meetings. The meanings negotiated in the interaction were extremely limited, and the opportunities for extending thinking were restricted. One side assumed the role of the source of wisdom, while the other side assumed the role of recipients.

Interactional patterns

One effective way to illustrate the power relationship among members of the meeting is to microscopically analyze the nature of the participation of each member and the pattern of the "flow" of interaction in the discourse structure of the meetings (Locke, 2004). We followed several procedures to achieve a good level of validity. Four researchers watched the three videotaped meetings and stopped every 10 minutes to discuss the content first. The purpose of this step was to deepen our understanding of the contextual meanings of the interactions. While watching, the researchers drew on a piece of paper their own tentative graphic representation of the interaction patterns derived from their own views and interpretation. Afterwards, we compared all the drawings and sought consensus and agreement. From time to time, when we had disagreements, we would return to the videotapes for confirmation and verification.

The following figures show some of the interaction patterns we finalized with agreement and consensus. Figure 7.1 illustrates the pattern of communication

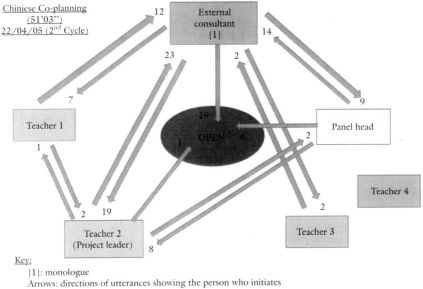

Figure 7.1 The interactional pattern of the planning meeting

style among the members in the planning meeting. The numbers indicate the number of utterances initiated by each interlocutor, and the arrows indicate the directions of utterances. Two features that attracted our attention were the lack of interaction between the teachers and the uni-structural dialogue of the meeting. On the one side, we have the external consultant and the panel who dominated 87.82% of the total time of the whole meeting. On the other side, we have the teachers who played the role of mere recipients of information and advice from the superior person in the hierarchy. This pattern of domination in terms of the discourse time distribution was reconfirmed when the same graphic was worked out for the two reflection meetings.

In addition, the pattern of communication of the reflection meetings was similar to that in the planning meeting, which was uni-structural without cross-interaction between the teachers (Figure 7.2). Again, the consultant and the panel head dominated the discourse in terms of time, which occupied 78.71% of the entire first reflection meeting time. The lack of interaction among teachers was still significant. The aim of the meeting was to reflect on the trial lessons conducted by the teachers. However, the lack of teachers' participation in the reflection and the sheer domination of the discourse by the two leaders turned the meeting into a non-reflective discourse. This indirectly demonstrated the lack of opportunities for teacher reflection and, therefore, for teacher learning because of the imposing leadership style of both the panel head and the consultant.

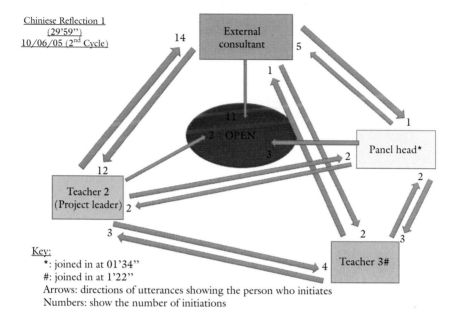

Figure 7.2 The interactional pattern of the first reflection meeting

Meanwhile, the analysis of the communication pattern of the second reflection meeting time confirmed the consistency of the leadership style and the domination of the discourse of the two hierarchical leaders of the meeting (Figure 7.3). Both occupied 90.43% of the total meeting time. Interactions between the teachers were scarce, but extreme cases were found in teachers 3 and 4, who were silent throughout the meeting. The panel head was very late and came during the last 10 minutes of the meeting. The results further support our observation on the effects of leadership styles on the negotiation space of the meetings for teachers who are less experienced and with junior hierarchical status in the curriculum development team.

Table 7.2 shows the time distribution of the participation of each participant in the three meetings. Looking at Table 7.2, particularly at time distribution, we can easily determine that the total time occupied by both the panel head and the consultant was 86.85% for all three meetings, which were primarily for teacher development and learning. To a certain degree, these quantitative data further support our observation and analysis of the impact of the dominating leadership style of the consultant and the panel head on teacher participation. The quality of teacher participation becomes a critical issue for any model of school-based approaches to educational change, and innovations in general, and to the development of professionalism among teachers in schools. The latter will be further discussed in the section below.

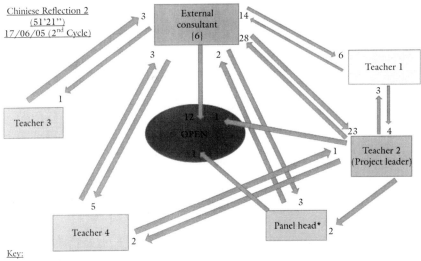

Figure 7.3 The interactional pattern of second reflection meeting

Table 7.2 Time distribution of the participation of each participant in each meeting

	Planning Meeting	First Reflection Meeting	Second Reflection Meeting	Total Amount of Time of the Meetings (minutes)	Occupation Percentage (%)
Panel head	5:32	8:26	0:06	14:04	10.63%
External consultant	39:18	15:10	46:26	100:54	76.22%
Teacher 1	1:07	Absent	1:31	2:38	1.99%
Teacher 2 (Project leader)	4:20(chair)	3:56(chair)	3:18(chair)	11:34	8.74%
Teacher 3	0:46	0:46	0:00	3:13	2.43%
Teacher 4	0:00	Absent	0:00	0:00	0.00%
Total amount of time (minutes)	51:03	29:59	51:21	132:23	100%

Source: Managing school-based curriculum innovations: A Hong Kong case study. *The Curriculum Journal*, 21(3), 313–332.

Discussion

The current analysis, which is based on visual data from videotaped meetings, shows that a specific type of leadership can be identified between the panel head and the external consultant in the three meetings. We bear in mind that a distributed leadership environment was re-created in the Chinese curriculum development team through the insertion of a policy of rotating the leadership for the team. The original purpose was to allow and encourage authentic and active participation of all team members. However, the assertion of professional authority by both the external consultant and the internal panel head proved to be "too suppressive" of any opportunity to engage the participating teachers in the reflective and creative dialogues in the team meetings. Such domination may not be the original intention of the two leading figures in the team. The discourse features, however, show underlying principles of pedagogy and communication among the leaders. The features also indicate the uni-structural nature of interactional patterns, a type of question and response communication pattern, between the sources of pedagogical authority and recipients of the pedagogical wisdom. Therefore, the optimism we generally collect from popular proponents of school-based curriculum development and a team or collaborative approach to curriculum development in schools should at least be considered with some reservation with regards to the constraining elements embedded in the traditional organizational leadership and professional leadership styles of our school systems. Herewith, we provide several suggestions for the policy makers and faculty members responsible for teacher education and training. These suggestions are relevant for the management teams in the school sector.

For the individual teachers

(1) The teachers should be well aware of their changing roles in curriculum development and should thus take a more active role in curriculum deliberation.
(2) The teachers should be proactive and reflective in curriculum development activities; they should see curriculum as an entity that can be shaped by teachers for the good of the students themselves.

For middle managers

(1) Middle managers, such as subject panel heads or curriculum leaders, should receive training and professional development courses for conducting meetings or collaborative activities that allow opportunities for participants to negotiate meanings in the process of their participation. The emphasis is on the likely consequence of having different types of leadership styles and creation of learning opportunities.
(2) They should receive training and educational programs that could enhance their ability in conducting school-based research activities, with the aim of enhancing professional practices and effectiveness of student learning.

148   *Case studies: a team approach*

For partnership with external faculties of education

(1) Consultants should adopt a professional and liberal approach to the current practice of the schools while playing the role of being a change agent in the process of development and innovation.
(2) Generally, consultants should possess knowledge and skills to enhance and create a positive learning environment for teacher participants, guided by the ultimate goal of empowering their capacity for leading and planning change and innovations (Fullan, 2008b).

Conclusion

Leadership studies in school-based curriculum development have focused mainly on a managerial and hierarchical basis to the extent that schoolteachers have been considered peripheral in making pedagogical decisions (Andrews & Soder, 1987; Hallinger & Murphy, 1986). Recent studies on curriculum or teacher leadership have moved our bias away from this model of organizational leadership to a leadership model that attempts to recapture the essence of the professional role and identity of teachers in making curriculum decisions within the tradition of school-based curriculum development (Lasky, 2005; Law, Lee, Wan, Ko, & Hiruma, 2014; Zhao, Li, & Law, 2016). Teacher participation in making curriculum decisions seems to have obtained consensus among policy makers and school management (Camburn, Rowan, & Taylor, 2003). Meanwhile, teacher leadership in curriculum decision making in schools is a new phenomenon in both the international and local (Hong Kong) literature, and its practice is still in embryonic stage. How this concept and practice could be institutionalized within the infrastructure of the current school ethos, with its domination by traditions and seniority, still requires substantial theoretical and experimental work.

Our previous reports on the first and second action cycles of a curriculum leadership development project here in Hong Kong have demonstrated the complexity and interrelationship of key structures. Specifically, the establishment of curriculum development teams and processes, such as the three-stage PER model of curriculum practice, is a response of the case school to the challenges of the community. These structures and processes have yet to find their home within traditions and cultures of the case school in the study. However, experience has proven that engaging teachers in curriculum decision making processes enhances the development of professional knowledge and skills among teachers in general. Nevertheless, implementing the concept of teacher leadership in curriculum decision making more effectively in schools and institutionalizing structures and processes in schools on a wider scale remain important issues. Such issues should therefore be explored and investigated in both theoretical and empirical studies through collaboration between researchers on university faculties and teacher leaders in schools.

The current study discusses the meditational effects of the leadership style of both the panel head and the consultant on the negotiation process among teachers in curriculum decision making processes. The analysis of the discourse features of the interactions indicates the power relationship between positional leaders and teachers. These features indicate that the participation of teachers is "dominated" by the panel head and the consultant in terms of quantitative time distribution, as well as the interactions in the meetings being shaped by their imposing power and status. The panel head and the consultant allowed little time for teacher participation. Therefore, an image of a passive participant was imposed on teacher participants; however, the effect was mediated by the language of knowledge and professionalism. Discourse features illustrate this observation, thus supporting our argument about the constraining effects of the leadership styles of the panel head and the consultant on the number of opportunities and space given to the teacher to facilitate the latter's participation and development. The constraints can be understood qualitatively: teachers are shaped into the role of being the recipients of the knowledge and professionalism of only the positional leaders. Teacher participation is restricted to uni-structural question-and-answer-type interactions, and, in most cases, this type is closed and requires factual answers. This communicative style made the teacher participation one-sided and left teachers with little room for negotiation and exploration. Therefore, development opportunities were taken away by the leadership style imposed upon the teachers. School-based curriculum development has been the consensus in educational policy studies for many years in international education and in Hong Kong since the 1980s. Based on the results stated above, it is high time for policy makers and school management to revisit its conceptualization and its realization in various types of school situations and milieus across countries with different cultural backgrounds and traditions.

Focusing solely on teacher leadership development, without a concurrent suitable program of leadership education based on research findings for both middle management and school management, can diminish the effectiveness of teacher education programs and initiatives of innovative teachers in creating and expanding spaces for development work in schools. The leadership program should include key concepts of extended professionalism, strategies for developing human potential in schools, school-based research strategies, as well as comparative and socio-cultural studies in leadership. Extending and stretching the educational and human horizon of middle managers and school management personnel, including school heads, can also complement and support an enhancement program for teacher leadership in schools towards a new era of quality education for our children within the holistic view of reforming school education.

Distributed leadership, as part of the conceptualization of school-based approaches to curriculum development, has been with us for the past 30 years, but how it works effectively across nations with diverse socio-cultural backgrounds remains a critical issue in this era of global education. This article is our first attempt to contribute to the international discussion of this critical issue.

Note

1 Another version of Chapter 7 has appeared in: Managing school-based curriculum innovations: A Hong Kong case study. *The Curriculum Journal, 21*(3), 313–332.

References

Andrews, R., & Soder, R. (1987). Principal leadership and student achievement. *Educational Leadership, 44,* 9–11.

Australian Education Union. (2004). *Educational leadership and teaching for the twenty-first century: Project discussion paper.* Retrieved from http://www.aeufed eral.org.au/Debates/ elat21pap.pdf

Ball, D.L. (1996). Teacher learning and the mathematics reforms: What we think we know and what we need to learn. *Phi Delta Kappan, 77*(7), 500–508.

Ball, D.L., & Cohen, D.K. (1996). Reform by the book: What is – or might be – the role of curriculum materials in teacher learning and instructional reform? *Educational Researcher, 25*(9), 6–8, 14.

Banks, M. (2007). *Using visual data in qualitative research.* London: Sage.

Black, P., & Atkin, M. (1996). *Changing the subject: Innovations in science, mathematics and technology education.* London: Routledge, in association with OECD.

Britt, M.S., Irwin, K.C., & Ritchie, G. (2001). Professional conversations and professional growth. *Journal of Mathematics Teacher Education, 4*(1), 29–53.

Burns, J. (1978). *Leadership.* New York: Harper and Row.

Camburn, E., Rowan, B., & Taylor, J.E. (2003). Distributed leadership in schools: The case of elementary schools adopting comprehensive school reform models. *Educational Evaluation and Policy Analysis, 25*(4), 347–373.

Carr, W., & Kemmis, S. (1986). *Becoming critical: Education, knowledge and action research.* London: Falmer.

Cohen, L., Manion, L., & Morrison, K. (2000). *Research methods in education* (5th ed.). London/New York: Routledge/Falmer.

Conley, S. (1991). Review of research on teacher participation in school decision making. *Review of Research in Education, 17,* 225–266.

Day, C. (1993). Reflection: A necessary but not sufficient condition for professional development. *British Educational Research Journal, 19*(1), 83–93.

Day, C., Harris, A., & Hadfield, M. (2001). Challenging the orthodoxy of effective school leadership. *International Journal of Leadership in Education, 4*(1), 39–56.

Elliott, J. (1991). *Action research for educational change.* Buckingham: Open University Press.

Elmore, R.F. (2004). *School reform from the inside out: Policy, practice and performance.* Cambridge, MA: Harvard University Press.

Foster, W. (1989). Toward a critical practice of leadership. In J. Smyth (Eds.), *Critical perspectives on educational leadership* (pp. 39–62). London: Falmer.

Frost, D., & Durrant, J. (2002). *Teacher-led development work: Guidance and support.* London: David Fulton.

Frost, D., & Durrant, J. (2003). Teacher leadership: Rationale, strategy and impact. *School Leadership & Management, 23*(2), 173–186.

Fullan, M. (1993). *Change forces: Probing the depths of educational reform.* London: Falmer.

Fullan, M. (2001). *Leading in a culture of change.* San Francisco, CA: Jossey-Bass.

Fullan, M. (2008a). Curriculum implementation and sustainability. In F.M. Connelly, M.F. He, & J. Phillion (Eds.), *The Sage handbook of curriculum and instruction* (pp. 113–122). Thousand Oaks, CA: Sage.

Fullan, M. (2008b). *The six secrets of change: What the best leaders do to help their organisations survive and thrive.* San Francisco, CA: Jossey-Bass.

Garet, M., Porter, A., Desimone, L., Birman, B., & Yoon, K.S. (2001). What makes professional development effective? Results for a national sample of teachers. *American Educational Research Journal, 38*(4), 915–945.

Gee, J., Michaels, S., & O'Connor, M. (1992). Discourse analysis. In M. LeCompte, W. Millney, & J. Preissle (Eds.), *The handbook of qualitative research in education* (pp. 227–291). San Diego, CA: Academic Press.

Hallinger, P., & Murphy, J. (1986). The social context of effective schools. *American Journal of Education, 94*(3), 328–355.

Harris, A. (2003). Teacher leadership and school improvement. In A. Harris, C. Day, D. Hopkins, M. Hadfield, A. Hargreaves, & C. Chapman (Eds.), *Effective leadership for school improvement* (pp. 72–83). London: Routledge/Falmer.

Harris, A. (2004). Distributed leadership and school improvement: Leading or misleading? *Educational Management Administration and Leadership, 32*(4), 11–24.

Harris, A., Leithwood, K., Day, C., Sammons, P., & Hopkins, D. (2007). Distributed leadership and organisational change: Reviewing the evidence. *Journal of Educational Change, 8*(4), 337–347.

Hiebert, J., Gallimore, R., & Stigler, J.W. (2003). The new heroes of teaching. *Education Week, 23*(10), 56.

Hofstede, G. (2005). *Cultures and organisations: Software of the mind* (2nd ed.). New York: McGraw-Hill.

Hopkins, D. (2001). *School improvement for real.* London: Falmer.

Jackson, D. (2000). The school improvement journey: Perspectives on leadership. *School Leadership & Management, 20*(1), 61–78.

King, M.B., & Newmann, F.M. (2000). Will teacher learning advance school goals? *Phi Delta Kappan, 81*(8), 576–580.

Lasky, S. (2005). A sociocultural approach to understanding teacher identity, agency and professional vulnerability in a context of secondary school reform. *Teaching and Teacher Education, 21*(8), 899–916.

Law, E.H.F. (2003). In search of a quality curriculum for the 21st century in Hong Kong. In W. Pinar (Eds.), *International handbook of curriculum research* (pp. 271–283). Mahwah, NJ: Lawrence Erlbaum.

Law, E.H.F., & Galton, M. (2004). Impact of a school-based curriculum project on teachers and students: A Hong Kong case study. *Curriculum Perspectives, 24*(3), 43–58.

Law, E.H.F., Lee, J.C., Wan, S.W.Y., Ko, J., & Hiruma, F. (2014). Influence of leadership styles on teacher communication networks: A Hong Kong case study. *International Journal of Leadership in Education, 17*(1), 40–61.

Law, E.H.F., & Wan, S.W.Y. (2005). *Developing curriculum leadership in a primary school: A Hong Kong case study.* Paper presented at the International Conference on Education: Redesigning pedagogy: Research, policy, practice, Nanyang University National Institute of Education, Singapore, May–June.

Law, E.H.F., & Wan, S.W.Y. (2008). Impact of a school-based curriculum leadership innovation upon teachers and pupils: A case study in Hong Kong. In J. Lee,

152 *Case studies: a team approach*

L. Lo, & L.P. Shiu (Eds.), *Developing teachers and developing schools in changing contexts* (pp. 177–206). Hong Kong: Chinese University Press.

Lawton, D. (1992). *Education and politics in the 1990s: Conflict or consensus?* London: Falmer.

Leithwood, K. (2008). *Educational accountability and school leadership.* Retrieved from http:// www.ncsl.org.uk/media-415-ca-educational-accountability-and-school-leadership.pdf

Levin, B. (2000). *Educational reform.* New York: Routledge/Falmer.

Locke, T. (2004). *Critical discourse analysis.* London/New York: Continuum.

MacBeath, J. (2004). Putting the self back into self-evaluation. *Improving Schools, 7*(1), 87–91.

Macpherson, I., Aspland, T., Brooker, R., & Elliott, B. (1999). *Places and spaces for teachers in curriculum leadership.* Deakin West, ACT: Australian Curriculum Studies Association.

Marsh, C. (1997). *Key concepts for understanding curriculum.* London: Falmer.

McLaughlin, M., & Talbert, J. (2001). *Professional communities and the work of high school teaching.* Chicago, IL: University of Chicago Press.

Ovens, P. (1999). Can teachers be developed? *Journal of In-Service Education, 25*(2), 275–305.

Putnam, R.T., & Borko, H. (2000). What do new views of knowledge and thinking have to say about research on teacher learning? *Educational Researcher, 29*(1), 4–15.

Schon, D. (1983). *The reflective practitioner.* London: Temple Smith.

Shulman, L., & Sherin, M.G. (2004). Fostering communities of teachers as learners: Disciplinary perspectives. *Journal of Curriculum Studies, 36*(2), 135–140.

Skilbeck, M. (1984). *School-based curriculum development.* London: Harper & Row.

Spillane, J. (2006). *Distributed leadership.* San Francisco, CA: Jossey-Bass.

Stenhouse, L. (1975). *An introduction to curriculum research and development.* London: Heinemann.

Taylor, A. (2001). *The politics of education reform in Alberta.* Toronto, ON: University of Toronto Press.

Taylor, A.R., Anderson, S., & Meyer, A. (2005). Lesson study: A professional development model for mathematics reform. *Rural Educator, 26*(2), 17–22.

Wallace, J.D., Nesbit, C.R., & Miller, A.C.S. (1999). Six leadership models for professional development in science and mathematics. *Journal of Science Teacher Education, 10*(4), 247–268.

Woods, P., Jeffrey, B., Troman, G., & Boyle, M. (1997). *Restructuring schools, reconstructing teachers.* Buckingham: Open University Press.

Zhao, M., Li, C., & Law, E.H.F. (2016). Intentions and influences of teachers' school based curriculum development in primary and secondary schools in Northwest China. In J.C.K. Lee, Z. Yu, X. Huang, & E.H.F. Law (Eds.), *Educational development in Western China* (pp. 233–245). Rotterdam: Sense Publishers.

8 Curriculum leadership functions and patterns of distribution[1]

Context of change

Educational change and innovation have been characterized by their orientation towards the needs of a contemporary society. Society demands equality among those who have and those who have not, comradery between those who hold one set of beliefs and those who hold another, as well as liberty from being dominated economically or ideologically. These ideas are highlighted as the key values underlying the assumptions of many proposed innovations. Changes in education necessarily require variations in professional qualities of the teaching force and its organizations. Hence, schools become the focal point of many planned departures from the traditional role of being teaching communities towards communities searching for improvement and enhancement (Benham & Murakami-Ramalho, 2010; Day, 2000; Garet, Porter, Desimone, Birman, & Yoon, 2001; Giles & Hargreaves, 2006; Knight & Wiseman, 2005; McCormick, Fox, Carmichael, & Procter, 2011; Stoll, 2009; Stoll & Louis, 2007; Walker, Edstam, & Stone, 2007; Zeichner, 2005). This radical re-orientation of the role of schools as a community of learning and social reconstruction has been recently received in the last 20 years in the West (Campbell & Groundwater-Smith, 2010; Hord & Sommers, 2007). Consequently, this re-orientation has become more familiar with Eastern countries in recent years (Chan & Pang, 2006). However, little is known about how schools and teachers should respond to these changes and their concomitant challenges. In particular, additional responsibilities given to schools and teachers seem to subvert their traditional roles of being conservative and promoting the building of society and its economy. The current study aims at experimenting with instigating changes among teams of teachers in reforming their pedagogical work in schools and trying to determine how teachers respond to changes and how such changes have been mediated by socio-cultural variables embedded in human discourse.

Pedagogical innovation projects

The original project, which was completed in 2006, was a teacher-initiated project that began in 2004 in a Hong Kong elementary school. The goal of the project was to enhance the capabilities of the schools and their teachers by developing the

154   *Case studies: a team approach*

curriculum leadership skills among elementary schoolteachers. The project was exploratory, design-based, and an attempt to incorporate key features from contemporary literature on teacher development and learning. The following summary presents the key features of effective models for teacher learning:

a   Actively engaging teachers in curriculum decision making processes (Hoban, 2002; Mayer, Donaldson, LeChasseur, Welton, & Cobb, 2013; Rogers, 1996; Rogers & Horrocks, 2010; Papa & Papa, 2011);

b   Teachers working in teams of colleagues preferably within their own subject teaching in the initial stage before moving to a more collaborative and integrative approach across subjects in the school curriculum (Borko & Putnam, 1998; Shulman & Shulman, 2004);

c   Teacher activities should be action-oriented with a reflection of practical experiences in innovative pedagogical strategies (Elliott, 1991; Schon, 1987; Stringer, 2007); and

d   A team approach based upon "flattened" or "distributive" leadership, allowing sufficient space for actualization of individual experimentation (Chrispeels, Castillo, & Brown, 2000; Gronn, 2000, 2002; MacBeath, 2005; Spillane, 2006; Spillane, Halverson, & Diamond, 2001; Spillane et al., 2004).

Following this line of thinking, the project organized development activities in the schools in several ways, as listed below:

a   Various curriculum development teams were formed on the subject base of participating teachers, three subject-based teams in the first project, and two subject-based teams in the replication study. The purpose is to orient the focus of the activities and the contents of the discourses in the communicative networking systems of each team (McCormick et al., 2011).

b   Each team comprised teachers of various groups based on experience, age, and gender. The purpose is to re-create situations wherein potential "information gaps" would encourage exchanges and possibly create tensions for problem solving (Groundwater-Smith & Campbell, 2010).

c   Leadership was rotational, and therefore, the effects of power types would affect the human relationship among members realized in the discourses of meetings (Engestrom, 1999, 2001). This time, no external consultant from the education faculties was invited, so more internal interactions were expected without external intervention.

This model of instigating or bringing interventions among teachers in school-based settings was replicated in another elementary school in Hong Kong in 2007–08. This study aims to report on the analysis of interactions among members in each of the curriculum development teams. The analysis thus reveals the nature of each individual teacher's participation in the team meetings. Such participation shows the dynamism of human relations mediated by socio-political factors, including power, status, and leadership styles, but realized in the meeting discourses. We assume that a greater degree of negotiation among members leads to greater space for learning and therefore, strong evidence of the emergence of a "distributive form of teacher leadership."

Effective model of teacher learning in schools

Different models of teacher development and change have been proposed and discussed in the last 30 years apart from the critical features of necessary conditions for effective teacher learning outlined in the above section. However, our PER (Planning, Experimenting, and Reflecting) model is simple, convenient, and encompasses all essential features of effective teacher learning. This model engages teachers in a series of spirally cyclical actions on planning, experimenting, and reflecting upon pedagogical innovations in school settings (Law, Galton, & Wan, 2010). Embedded in this PER model is our progressive view about the role of the school as a learning community for students and teachers. Table 8.1 summarizes the key activities at each stage of the cycle.

As mentioned earlier, this model of engaging teachers in a series of processes to enable them to initiate pedagogical and curriculum innovations assumes a holistic and continuous approach, which is adopted in schools to foster learning culture among teachers. The graph below depicts the holistic strategy underlying this model of engineering changes among teachers (Law et al., 2010).

Research design and data collection

This study used a multi-methods approach, in which quantitative and qualitative data were gathered from video recordings of the planning and reflection meetings of the English and General Studies teams in the first and second innovation cycles. This multi-method approach was chosen in order to understand the process of innovation from different perspectives (Meijer, Verloop, & Beijaard,

Table 8.1 A three-stage model of teacher planning, experimentation and reflection curriculum practices (PER model)

Stage	Aims	Teacher Activities
Planning stage	To identify the goals and design strategies for a plan of innovation	SWOT, whole school conference, action planning meetings, collaborative lesson preparation meetings, production of materials
Experimentation stage	To put the plan into action in classrooms	Trialing, peer observation, evaluation
Reflection stage	To review the actions and plan for future actions	Post-observation conference, completion of feedback sheets

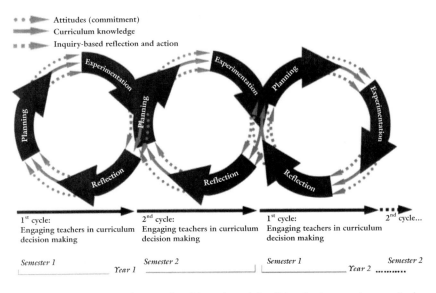

Figure 8.1 Reconceptualizing school-based models of developing teacher curriculum leadership for lifelong education

2002; Tashakkori & Teddlie, 2003). Re-creating situations would require allowing teachers comparatively free space without the potential images of hierarchical figures, such as panel heads and school heads, in the school bureaucracy. Hence, the research team decided to deliberately withdraw the participation of the panel and school heads in the second innovation cycle, while the first innovation cycle was still under traditional leadership in the school hierarchy. The process of quantifying data was carried out by calculating the number of initiations of responses of each member of the English and General Studies teams. The quantified data were compared with the qualitative data of video recordings in terms of time distribution among the participants across the interactions in each meeting as the well as frequency and percentage of the counting of discourse features of each meeting. Four sets of data collected in the first and second innovation cycles were compared in a multi-dimensional way. Then, themes or categories were generated through comparisons of data and then cross-examined by three researchers. Triangulation was enhanced by time (two innovation cycles), space (two elementary schools), and investigators.

Findings and discussions

The framework of presentation and analysis follows broadly our previous studies that report the findings and analyses of the first study done in 2003–05, identify key features, and determine the nature of "participation" in team meetings (Law, 2010; Law, Galton, et al., 2010; Law & Wan, 2006; Law, Wan, Galton, & Lee, 2010). We see each meeting and its discourse as a realization of human relationships embedded in the socio-cultural historical milieu with a common object in its activity. Meanwhile, the team and its concomitant meetings are considered systems of communication networking (Fox & McCornmick, 2009; James & McCormick, 2009; McCormick et al., 2011).

Distribution of teacher participation in meetings

For the English team, four formal meetings, one planning meeting, and one reflection meeting were held during the two cycles of pedagogical innovations in October and November 2006, respectively. All members of the team were young graduates with an average age of around 35 years. One member was the subject head of the English department, while another member served as the project leader. All participating teachers were female. Given that all five members participated in the first planning meeting, only three participated in the rest of the meetings. Hence, we separately reported our analysis of the planning and reflection meetings in the first and second innovation cycles.

In the first innovation cycle, the panel head played a dominant role in terms of the participation time in the planning meeting, accounting for about 41.42%. When she was absent for the reflection meeting, the "effect" on the distribution was obvious. The rest of the team shared their "time" evenly, and each remaining participant in the reflection meeting accounted for about 28.14% to 38.31% of the total time. This effect further gained some concrete evidence in the second innovation when the absence of the panel head was planned. The time was shared quite evenly among the three members of the team. Table 8.2 shows the time distribution of teacher participation.

Table 8.2 Time distribution for the English team

Innovation Cycle	Meeting	Time Contribution of Each Member (minutes) (%)					Total Amount of Time of Each Meeting (minutes)
		Teacher Teacher 023	Project Leader Teacher 119	Teacher Teacher Star	Panel Head Me	Teacher Teacher 007	
1	Planning	6:11 18.56%	6:39 19.96%	3:45 11.26%	13:48 41.42%	2:56 8.80%	33:19
	Reflection	2:10 28.14%	2:35 33.55%	Absent	Absent	2:57 38.31%	**7:42**
2	Planning	7:43 44.86%	4:24 25.58%	Did not involve	Did not involve	5:05 29.55%	**17:12**
	Reflection	2:14 46.85%	0:52 18.18%	Did not involve	Did not involve	1:40 34.97%	**4:46**

158   *Case studies: a team approach*

Table 8.3 Time distribution for General Studies team

Innovation Cycle	Meeting	Time Contribution of Each Member (minutes) (%)					Total amount of time of each meeting (minutes)
		Principal	Teacher 1 Panel head	Teacher 2	Teacher 3	Teacher 4	
1	Planning	5'23 (62.96)	0'3 (0.58)	3'2 (35.48)	0'3 (0.58)	0'2 (0.39)	8'33
	Reflection	13'52 (70.51)	0'21 (1.78)	4'37 (23.47)	0'20 (1.69)	0'30 (2.54)	19'39
2	Planning	Did not involve	1'18 (19.85)	4'59 (76.08)	0'4 (1.02)	0'12 (3.05)	6'33
	Reflection	Did not involve	0'8 (6.25)	1'28 (68.75)	0' (0.00)	0'32 (25.00)	2'08

For the General Studies team, all members were young except for the school head, who was close to retirement age. The distribution patterns were similar in all four meetings in both the first and second innovation cycles. The school head dominated the planning meeting, with occupation times of about 62.96% and 70.51% in the planning and reflection meetings, respectively. Similar to the English team, the school head was withdrawn from the second innovation cycle, thus allowing more space for individual teachers. However, the time was not shared evenly by other members of the team. Instead, the project leader dominated the discourse during the planning and reflection meetings.

One must bear in mind that the total time for each meeting was comparatively short and, therefore, the "domination" of the hierarchical figures of the two teams during the meetings should be interpreted with caution. More data should be made available to triangulate. Table 8.3 shows the time distribution of each member in all meetings.

Establishing communicative networking patterns

English team

For the English team, the communicative networking pattern from the first to the second innovation cycle showed some significant changes. In the planning meeting in the first cycle, the participation of the panel head was significantly dominant in terms of time. However, upon a closer look at the communicative patterns among members in the interaction in the planning meeting, the networking pattern was much more complicated. The following diagram shows communicative networking patterns of the team in the planning meeting with the presence of the panel head. The values indicate the number of utterances initiated by each interlocutor, and the arrows indicate the directions of the utterances.

Curriculum leadership functions and patterns 159

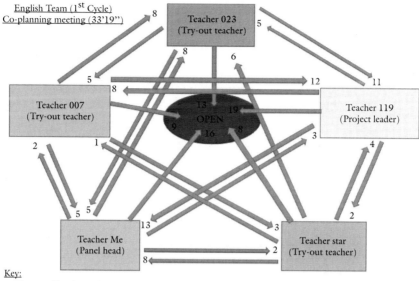

Figure 8.2 Communication-networking patterns in the first planning meeting in the first innovation cycle

Several points should be considered:

a   Initiation from each of the members was evenly distributed and this phenomenon was significant in demonstrating the comparatively free atmosphere in the meeting that was chaired by the panel head. Thus, we may assume a rather "open" style in the conduct of the meetings.
b   Initiations that were open to all members in the meeting were numerous. In fact, each member posed open questions in rhetorical form to invite member contributions and responses. This result temporarily supports our previous assumption that the meeting was conducted democratically and, comparatively speaking, allowed freer participation by all members regardless of status and power. The number of these open questions is stated in brackets in Table 8.4.
c   The networking pattern is not restricted to a few members but rather diffused among all members, although some took more initiatives than others. The pattern is multi-structural and multi-dimensional in terms of the nature of initiations among members. However, we need further evidence from the analysis of the discourse nature of the meetings in the next section to deepen our understanding and allow us to establish the nature of the two teams' communicative networking systems. Table 8.4 shows the distribution of the initiations of each member.

160 Case studies: a team approach

Table 8.4 Distribution of initiations among members of the English team in the planning and reflection meetings of the first and second innovation cycles

Members	Number of Initiations			
	First Innovation Cycle		*Second Innovation Cycle*	
	Planning meeting	Reflection meeting	Planning meeting	Reflection meeting
Teacher Teacher 023	23 (13)*	22	58 (14)*	13 (2)*
Teacher Teacher 119 (Project leader)	47 (19)	20	32 (3)*	10 (2)*
Teacher Teacher Star	27 (8)	Absent	Not involved	Not involved
Teacher Teacher Me (Panel head)	31 (16)	Absent	Not involved	Not involved
Teacher Teacher 007	37 (9)	22	52 (4)*	18 (2)*

( )* Number of open questions or statements inviting free participation

English Team (2nd Cycle)
Co-planning meeting (16'17")

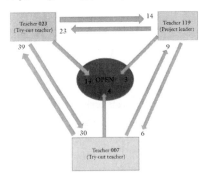

English Team (2nd Cycle)
Reflection meeting (4'56")

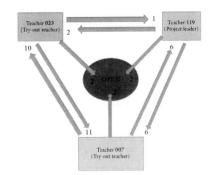

Key:
Arrows: directions of utterances showing the person who initiates;
Numbers: show the number of initiations

Figure 8.3 Communication-networking patterns of the planning and reflection meetings of the second innovation cycle

The reflection meeting shows a similar distribution pattern of initiations among members in Table 8.4. The communicative networking pattern in the second innovation cycle changed after the planned withdrawal of the panel head from participation. Diagram 2 shows the patterns in the planning and reflection

Curriculum leadership functions and patterns 161

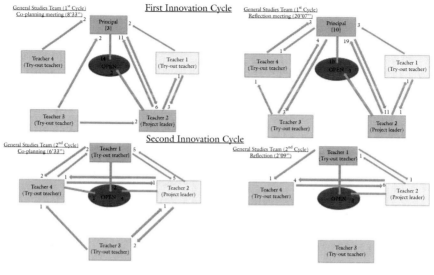

Figure 8.4 Communication-networking patterns in the first and second innovation cycles

meetings in the second innovation cycle, along with the distribution of the number of initiations of the members in the meetings.

The above diagrams clearly show that "leadership" has become even more "distributed," indicating the full and active participation of all members of the team. The distribution of the initiations shows open communicative networking patterns in the two meetings held by the team.

General Studies team

The communicative networking pattern of this team shows the strong leadership effect of the school head. The diagrammatic representations of communicative networking patterns of the four meetings of the General Studies team are presented in Figure 8.4 and Table 8.5.

Table 8.5 shows that the number of initiations was comparatively fewer than that in the English curriculum development team. Specifically, intercommunications among members of the team were rarely found in the four meetings. However, the effect and the nature of the leadership style are still inconclusive because the durations (6:33 and 2:08) of the two meetings without the school head were short. Hence, we need further proof directly from

162　*Case studies: a team approach*

Table 8.5 Distribution of initiations among members of the General Studies team in the planning and reflection meetings of the first and second innovation cycles

Members	*Number of Initiations*			
	Planning meeting	*Reflection meeting*	*Planning meeting*	*Reflection meeting*
Principal	20 (14)*	25 (10)*	9 (2)*	2
Teacher 1	5	4	12 (4)*	8 (3)*
Teacher 2 (Project leader)	14 (2)*	21(1)*	2	0
Teacher 3	4	5	4 (1)*	6
Teacher 4	2	3		

Note: ()*: Number of open questions or statements inviting free participation

discourse analysis among members to identify significant changes in the patterns of the communicative networking systems of the team.

Establishing functional patterns of the meeting discourses

English team

The previous discussion presented the communicative networking system of the meetings of the English team based on time distribution among members and the multiple distributive patterns of initiations in the meetings. The discussion indicates that a more open and elaborated style of communicative networking system is realized in the meetings. However, we need more specific evidence to establish whether an elaborated code is actualized in the meetings of the English team (Bernstein, 1999). This step requires microscopic analysis on the functions of each utterance in the discourse. The results indicate the underlying and embedded assumptions on the roles and responsibilities of each participating teacher. For convenience, in our discussion, we selected only the co-planning meeting for our analysis given that the duration (33:19) of the meeting was the longest and all members of the team participated.

Discourse features of leadership

Two hierarchical leaders – the panel head and the project leader – worked in the first innovation cycle. In the second innovation cycle, the panel head was deliberately withdrawn from participation to compare the effects of diminishing leadership.

First, we study the leadership style of the project leader (Teacher 119), who was less than 25 years old at that time and only had several years of teaching experience. In the meeting, she led the discussion and changed the topics regularly and smoothly. In most cases, the changes she proposed concerned the efficiency

Curriculum leadership functions and patterns 163

and the direction of the meeting and the discussions. She made 14 changes of this nature. The following are some examples of the proposed changes she wanted to move in the meeting:

1 Propose a change in object of learning (using gerund);
2 Seeking proposals for consolidating learning (learning activities);
3 Proposing pedagogical alternatives (proposing chess game);
4 Relating to the content of learning activities (seeking ideas);
5 Checking accuracy of the proposal and seeking clarification (homework for students); and
6 Checking whether the proposed activity can consolidate student learning (consolidating student learning).

The following excerpt shows how she proposed changes in pedagogical content knowledge and pedagogical alternative strategies.

Teacher 119:	This is the sentence with the use of "for."
Teacher 023 and Teacher 119:	"Thank you for . . ." – this is for students to complete.
Teacher 119:	To be followed by using "gerund" – is it true?
Teacher Star:	Yes, or they may use "noun."

(Literal translations from a selection of the meeting, reading: 01:35–01:42, 10/19/2006)

The switch to the application of "gerund" in organizing learning activities for students in the practice lesson is significant in demonstrating how the project leader led the discussion on planning the innovation. The following is another excerpt from the same meeting.

Teacher 119:	After teaching this topic, we should use more examples. This means we should highlight the topic in the textbook, talk about the daily life examples; for example, we greet each the teachers after finishing the lesson, using "thank you for teaching us," that is leading the students to the teaching object about using language in greetings. Let them understand we regularly use the language of greetings. Now we use some activities for consolidation purpose.
Teacher 119:	We used "board game" before.
Teacher 023:	Because it concerns many conversations, in other words, that means, we give responses to others, we thought about using board game, we may design some game cards, a student may draw one card, you give him a response, he may win and he may gain some moves on the board, something like this one.

(Literal translation from a selection of the meeting, reading: 02:05–02:58, 10/19/2006)

164   *Case studies: a team approach*

The example above shows how the project leader changed the plan of the discussion topic deliberately. However, her leadership in managing and leading the discourse direction met some objections from the members during the meeting. The following is an excerpt in which her proposal was rejected in the meeting.

Teacher 119:	Asking students to pick a card, this is possible, we may add a few more on the card, and enlarge the board for the game as well. . . .
Teacher 119:	Four in a group to use A4 size paper, this is enough, ok?
Teacher 007:	A3.
Teacher 023 *and Teacher 119:*	A3.
Teacher 119:	Four students?
Teacher Star:	A3 size is better.
Teacher 023:	A3 size is better.
Teacher 119:	Then we use A3.

(Literal translation from a selection of the meeting, reading: 03.43–04.03, 19/10/2006)

The panel head gave full details in her discourse and tried to re-orientate the directions of the discussions in deciding the key object of learning as well as the details of the lesson plan. She had the longest monologue (over 3 minutes) and occupied 41.42% of the meeting discourse. This occurrence was reported above. Our concern here is with the nature of her monologues first. The following is a simplified but literally translated version of her longest monologue, in which she gave details about her views on pedagogical strategies in designing the lesson.

We can arrange games at each focus of learning, like beginning with e-book, then ask students to return to their game, then practice using "thank you" for five minutes, then ask students to return to the game. . . . we use role play like attending a party, before the class, we give each one an invitation card tomorrow, then they arrive at the party, they have to thank the host, this gives them situations to practice the target language, next, they may play games like spelling game, or board game. Teach them pronunciation as well. . . they are given chances to practice all forms of greetings and expressing gratitude. Then they may show appreciations of the costumes of the other people like using "what a huge party," "what a wonderful dress." Let them feel they need to show appreciation. Then after finishing the game, open the textbook or we may watch a video about attending a party.

(Literal translation from a selection of the meeting, reading: 17.39–20.51, 19/10/2006, Teacher me)

This incident is significant because the discourse shows her underlying assumption about her role, her participation in the meeting, and her duty as a leader, that is, to lead those who may not be well informed and knowledgeable as she may have assumed. Indeed, she dictated the methods and design of the innovation lesson in detail.

Another critical observation was made about her role in the direction of the discussion concerning the design of the lesson plan: she made decisions or spoke with authority in key decision points about the selection of learning contents as well as the organization of the lesson. She made suggestions on the inclusion of language items (e.g., the phrases "what a surprise," "what a beautiful dress") and expressions of gratitude and appreciation (e.g., "congratulations," "well done"). She decided on the overall structure of the lesson, such as suggesting a party to recreate a situation in which students are required to use language items of appreciation and gratitude.

Teacher Me: You may upset your plan, but if using board game allows the students to use group work or pair work, you may try it in other situations . . . they may collect presents and then say "what is surprise!", **or attending a party** and saying "what a nice dress", . . . or you may ask them to think about attending a party . . . what do they see? And what do they say? For example, seeing a baby, say "what a cute baby"

(Literal translation from a selection of the meeting, reading: 15.47–16.46, 19/10/2006, Teacher me)

After she suggested using a party as the learning context for the acquisition of language items in the domain of expressing gratitude and appreciation, the discussion turned sharply to this direction and incorporated the use of a board game in the newly redefined lesson. The details of her proposed lesson plan are quoted above.

Here participation was strange in one sense. She did not intervene in the very beginning of the meeting. She kept silent until the meeting reached 6"27'. Was it a deliberate strategy on her part? One could never know. Her participation was sporadic and spontaneous for the rest of the meeting, except the time when she actively engaged in the discussion. In this sense, her sporadic withdrawal from participation allowed time and space for the participation of others.

Participation styles of other members

In terms of occupation time, the leadership took over 60% of the meeting, and the rest shared the remaining time. Their participation could not be considered inferior or subordinate despite the fact that the decision points and direction were largely dictated by the leadership of the meeting. On the contrary, the members' participation and responses could be considered creative and critical in the meeting discourse.

Teacher 023:   Because it concerns many conversations, that means you have to respond to what others say, I have thought about using board

166 *Case studies: a team approach*

> game, then we design some game cards, you draw a card and then you have to respond, you may win or answer and then you move forward a step, something like this.
>
> > (Literal translation from a selection of the meeting, reading: 02.37–02.58, 19/10/2006, Teacher 023)

This utterance follows the suggestion from the project leader about using a board game. Her participation complemented the initiation of the topic and added more information to the discussion.

> *Teacher Star:* Is it that each card represents a context, each student draws a card which means a context, like giving you something in return . . .
>
> > (Literal translation from a selection of the meeting, reading: 02.58–3.04, 19/10/2006, Teacher Star)

This teacher continued the dialogue but added personal interpretation to the understanding of the suggestion of using the board game as a form of pedagogy.

As we mentioned in the previous section on the leadership style of the project leader, the other members openly rejected the suggestion of this leader and reconfirmed their proposal of using A3 size paper, instead of the original suggestion by the project leader to use A4 size (reading: 03.43–04.03).

The other members, Teacher 023 and Teacher Star, showed some form of creativity when asked what materials students could use in board games. They proposed using rubbers, pencils, or dices in the game. They thought about other alternatives as well (reading: 04.10–04.22).

These members tried to manipulate the direction of the meeting as well. For example, Teacher Star moved the discussion plan to another one, suggesting that the meeting should allow the members to "brainstorm" the content of learning (reading: 04.29–04.31). Teacher 023 also tried to move the course of the meeting by suggesting that they should work on important details for the planned lesson (reading: 06.03–06.05).

These three members often formed their own discourse patterns separately from project leaders and the panel head. For example,

> *Teacher 023:* Have two pages, the last page is about leaving, then they should thank the friends who invited them, using "thank you for . . ."
> *Teacher 007:* This matches what we do, but will they be confused?
> *Teacher 023:* . . . in fact, parents would say thank you, when people leave, they thank the people as well.
> *Teacher Star:* I think we should add something to the board game, besides, birthday party is good as well.
>
> > (Literal translation from a selection of the meeting, reading: 05.20–05.51, 19/10/2006)

This discourse shows that inter-member relationship could be more exclusively built up beyond the reach of the project leader and the panel head.

| Teacher Star: | . . . or we should choose some more phrases, or some that the students are not familiar with, like "welcome to . . ." |

Teacher Star: . . . or we should choose some more phrases, or some that the students are not familiar with, like "welcome to . . ."

Teacher 119: Yes, this phrase is important.

Teacher Star: . . . or I suggest "we hope you will . . ." and then we could use blank.

Teacher 007: I suggest "this looks exciting."

Teacher Star: More examples.

Teacher 007: These are highlighted already.

Teacher Star: But some of these are well known to the students and therefore, we take them away.

(Literal translation from a selection of the meeting, reading: 12.34–12.58, 19/10/2006)

The three members created these "sub-group" discourses among themselves and focused on pedagogical arrangements of the planned innovation. We have no access to the reasons as to why these sub-group discourses regularly occurred throughout the meeting, but we can speculate that these occurrences may be considered a form of excluding members who are perceived as outsiders of the sub-cultural group within the team. Politically speaking, this situation poses danger, but professionally, the exchange symbolizes a form of re-asserting one's own identity and some degree of "autonomy" from the group.

Open questions open invitations

One discourse feature of the meeting had to with the number of open questions or open statements that were realized by members of the meeting. The open questions comprised 39.30% of the total number of initiations made by all members in this single meeting. This figure is substantial. Let us look at some of these "open questions" or "open statements" and find out the underlying intentions of these utterances in the discourse.

Project leader: "Yes, about the contents of the cards, do you have any suggestions?"

(reading: 04.22–04.28)

The question above invites open participation.

Panel head: "Is it possible . . . each section we do not include complicated PowerPoint, because this is a real party, we enter the party, other people invite you to join, you would say . . . express gratitude . . ."

(reading: 24.27–24.46)

In the statement above, first, she raises the possibility, after which she gives a concrete suggestion, provides reasons, extends her reasons, and then gives examples.

Teacher 023: ". . . or we may brainstorm now what we have . . ."

(reading: 06.04–06.05)

168   *Case studies: a team approach*

The teacher above suggests and proposes what the team should do.

Teacher Star: "I feel the board game can have additional activities . . . besides
having the birthday party . . ."

(reading: 14.48–14.54)

In the statement above, the project leader recommends additional changes to the
original proposal by other members.

Teacher 007:   "How long do we do it?"

(reading: 23.31–23.32)

Here, the project leader is seeking clarification from the meeting attendees.

All these examples illustrated the kind of questions and statements that were used
regularly in the meeting. This feature is crucial in dictating the flow of the meeting
and in eliciting "participation" in discourse. All these utterances show the active participation of members, which implies that each member assumes an active role, seeks
clarification, suggests alternatives, recommends proposals, and facilitates efficiency in
managing the direction of the meeting. All these roles seem to show that the team
shares collaborative spirit and each member plays its role actively and constructively.
At least, we see little evidence of withdrawal and silence except the panel head.

Summary

The leadership style of the English team focuses on the efficiency of the meeting. This focus helps in identifying the focus of work for the planned innovation,
determining the object of learning for the students, and finalizing the organizational strategies of the planned lesson. The project leader offered alternative
pedagogical strategies and affirmed the content knowledge of the planned innovation. Her leadership is a soft one, which mediated the direction and focus of the
discussion, given her subtle skills in managing the meeting. In comparison, the
panel head was more direct and made obvious departures in terms of the selection of the object of learning and its organization at critical points of decision
making. She adopted a "harder" approach than the project leader.

Having described the leadership in this authoritarian way, we must still exercise
caution in making conclusions regarding our observations about the communicative networking system of the English team. The system still showed evidence
of genuine teacher participation, and the decisions were mediated from time to
time by the hidden assertiveness of the other members of the team. However,
we did not see a deliberate attempt of the leadership in offering members space
for experimentation from time to time, although some of the suggestions of the
members were taken up in the meeting.

General studies team

The school head led the General Studies team. Known to be assertive and powerful in her style of management, she was well respected by the educational

community for her innovations in the school. Therefore, her occupation time in the two meetings in the first innovation cycle at well over 60% was not surprising. Her planned withdrawal in the second innovation cycle was replaced by the project leader whose occupation time was over 68% of the meeting discourse. Let us look at the discourse features of the meetings closely. We particularly chose the longest meeting (19'39") in the first innovation cycle for our analysis.

Discourse features of the leadership

The school head spoke with instructional authority and hierarchical authority. Her tone was evaluative and, in some cases, could be intimidating.

Example One

Principal "I watched Miss Ding's lesson, I feel you are not clear enough, and the learning place is not appropriate. I have already told you my views, you said it looks like a ball, what is a ball? In fact this is very abstract, I think it should need a picture to illustrate clearly."

(Literal translation from a selection of the meeting, reading: 01.10–01.47, 13/11/2006)

Example Two

Principal: "You should have a systematic thinking . . . not talking about the lung separately from respiratory track . . . or it is not taught holistically . . . when a ball is broken, what does it mean? What does it mean when the ball is blocked . . ."

(reading: 03.24–04.09)

Example Three

Principal: "Indeed you should use the special room for teaching this topic with the facilities of maps, diagrams and models which help students to learn . . . the room has microphone, projector, do you understand? The students can see the intestine . . ."

(reading: 10.09–10.25)

In the first example, the school head directly used the name of the teacher and then she moved to "blame" all teachers by using "you." She also gave suggestions on improving the lesson. The first one above is instructional with suggestions for improvement. The second example points out the knowledge problem of teachers, specifically indicating inadequacy in understanding the content knowledge of the topic. The third example is organizational. Here, the school head was unsure why the teachers did not use the special room that housed all necessary equipment and facilities for teaching and learning the topic effectively. She reiterated in detail the facilities that researchers deemed should be known to the teachers. Teachers must find the room inconvenient for some reason.

170 *Case studies: a team approach*

Meanwhile, the project leader was the major interlocutor with the school head in the meeting. She formed a sub-group discourse with the school head. In other words, the two members here, to a certain extent, excluded the participation of others so that they would not be bothered to participate in the dialogue.

Teacher K: We shall talk about "digestion." (refocusing).

Principal: Would you teach some of these again, like respiring? (ascertaining the direction of thinking)

Teacher 2: Yes, we shall cover those items. . . (reconfirming)

Principal: No, this one . . . inhale. . . (re orientating)

Teacher 1: Respiratory capacity, talked [about] already. . . (reconfirming)

Teacher 2: Taught already (confirming).

Principal: Any addition about this lesson? (seeking additional information and thoughts)

Teacher 2: Thank you, miss Principal! (expressing gratitude)

Principal: [Did] you learn? (assuring learning)

Teacher 2: Next lesson we do. . . (moving forward to next lesson)

Principal: In this lesson, what did we learn? (asking information about learning)

Teacher 2: We apply this in our next lesson, first, we should have pictures of real objects, next lesson we use respiratory system (confirm learning and the object of improvement).

(Literal translation from a selection of the meeting, reading: 07.42–08.30, 13/11/2006)

As can be seen from the excerpt above, the meeting was not multi-directional but rather concentrated on the dialogue between the school head and the project leader. This phenomenon was in contrast with the English team, wherein sub-group exchanges were not made between the leadership. Comparatively, the other members were speaking and engaged in dialogues or genuine exchanges of views and information.

Let us return to the planning meeting. Here, the exchanges were between the school head and the project leader only. The long monologues of the school head were instructive with many ideas and suggestions on pedagogical strategies.

Principal: Not to give students the experiences of failure . . . after some experiences of failure, let them experience success . . . being happy . . . we should show the film first, then some practical work in the laboratory . . . first time may fail but do a successful experiment . . . let the students understand how we can protect the lung . . .

(Literal translation from a selection of the meeting, reading: 02.47–04.07, 17/10/2006)

The school head employed a didactic approach during the meeting. Instead of open discussion, she dominated the discussion and, in many cases, offered explanations and suggestions related to such innovations. Early in this section, we mentioned that the school head and the project leader have established a sub-group interaction, which excluded the participation of the others. The following excerpt illustrates the exclusivity of the dialogue between the two.

Principal: I think we do not tell them . . .
Teacher 2: Leave the students to finish it . . .
Principal: In other words, let them discover . . . we can use enquiry based methods . . . leave them to discover why it failed.. do we need a whole page worksheet?
Teacher 2: Good.
Principal: We can use a whole worksheet.
Teacher 2: Hypothetically

(Literal translation from a selection of the meeting, reading: 06.09–06.37, 17/10/2006)

Towards the end of the planning meeting, the three other members finally indicated their preference regarding the division of labor during planning the lesson.

Summary

Compared with the English team, the General Studies team is rather restrictive in terms of space for negotiation among the members. In the latter, most of the decision points were controlled by the leadership, and little opportunities were given by the leadership. We also see few deliberate attempts by the leadership to allow teachers to experiment and explore alternatives. The leadership was rather didactic in the General Studies team.

Discussion and conclusion

In our previous studies on the impact of leadership styles upon meeting discourses for our first leadership project in 2003–04, two models of communicative networking patterns were observed. On the one hand, we observed an elaborated or extended mode shaped by the leadership in the Mathematics curriculum development team. This study was characterized by its accommodation for teacher participation, which allowed space for negotiation and teacher experimentation. On the other hand, we observed another contrastive mode: the restrictive mode, which was shaped by the other form of leadership in the Chinese curriculum development team and did not allow teacher suggestions and proposals to be developed and become fruition in practice lessons for experimentation. As mentioned earlier, the experimentation of teacher suggestions and proposals is considered essential for enhancing the space of teacher learning.

In the replication study in 2007–08, external consultants from the university faculties were not invited deliberately, with an intention to allow more genuine and authentic interaction among internal members of the school without external intervention. The above presentation of the findings and observations of the communicative

172 *Case studies: a team approach*

Table 8.6 Characteristics of leadership styles

	English curriculum development team	General Studies curriculum development team
Leadership style	Distributed (administratively)	Centralized
Mediating factors	Directed by the project leader and the panel head	Didactic principal
Effects	Stronger team spirit	Less team spirit
	Developing a collaborative pattern	Receptive
Discourse style	Open and exploratory	Closed and informative
	More expressive	Less expressive
	More interactive	Full of stories by the principal
Participation style	More interactive	Less interactive
	Active	Less active
Teacher learning	More effective professionally	Less effective professionally

networking systems of the two curriculum development teams, the English and the General Studies teams, shows a similar restrictive mode is established in the GS team and a variation of the extended mode in the English team (see Table 8.6).

The reason why we use the term "administratively" to qualify the form of distributive leadership in the English team is that both the panel head and the project leader did not have an instructional role similar to the external consultant from the university faculty in the first project in 2003–05. Therefore, they did not have the expectations of a "leading role" in helping the participating teachers to "learn" as was the case with the consultant from the university faculty. However, we still observed a variation of the extended mode in the second project, which we also found in the first project.

In all, the findings suggest that an effective leadership program ought to include components that train future curriculum leaders to become effective managers in leading the development of innovations administratively and instructionally.

Note

1 Another version of Chapter 8 appeared in Law, E.H.F., Lee, J.C.K., Wan, S.W.Y., Ko, J., & Futoshi, H. (2014). Impact of leadership styles on communication networking in subject teams: A Hong Kong perspective. *International Journal of Leadership in Education*, *17*(1), 391–407.

References

Benham, M., & Murakami-Ramalho, E. (2010). Engaging in educational leadership: The generosity of spirit. *International Journal of Leadership in Education*, *13*(1), 77–91.

Bernstein, B. (1999). Vertical and horizontal discourse: An essay. *British Journal of Sociology of Education*, *20*(2), 157–173.

Borko, H., & Putnam, R. (1998). Professional development and reform-based teaching: Introduction to theme issue. *Teaching and Teacher Education, 14,* 1–3.

Campbell, A., & Groundwater-Smith, S. (Eds.). (2010). *Connecting inquiry and professional learning in education: International perspectives and practical solutions.* London: Routledge.

Chan, C.K.K., & Pang, M.F. (2006). Editorial: Teacher collaboration in learning communities. *Teaching Education, 17,* 1–5.

Chrispeels, J.H., Castillo, S., & Brown, J. (2000). School leadership teams: A process model of team development. *School Effectiveness and School Improvement, 11*(1), 20–56.

Day, C. (2000). Beyond transformational leadership. *Educational Leadership, 57*(7), 56–59.

Elliott, J. (1991). *Action research for educational change.* Buckingham: Open University Press.

Engestrom, Y. (1999). Expansive visibilization of work: An activity-theoretical perspective. *Computer Supported Cooperative Work, 8,* 63–93.

Engestrom, Y. (2001). Expansive learning at work: Toward an activity theoretical reconceptualization. *Journal of Education and Work, 14*(1), 133–156.

Fox, A., & McCornmick, R. (2009). Events and professional learning: Studying educational practitioners. *Journal of Workplace Learning, 21*(3), 198–218.

Garet, M., Porter, A., Desimone, L., Birman, B., & Yoon, K.S. (2001). What makes professional development effective? Results for a national sample of teachers. *American Educational Research Journal, 38*(4), 915–945.

Giles, C., & Hargreaves, A. (2006). The sustainability of innovative schools as learning organizations and professional learning communities during standardized reform. *Educational Administration Quarterly, 42*(1), 124–156.

Gronn, P. (2000). Distributed properties: A new architecture for leadership. *Educational Management and Administration, 28*(3), 317–338.

Gronn, P. (2002). Distributed leadership as a unit of analysis. *Leadership Quarterly, 13,* 423–451.

Groundwater-Smith, S., & Campbell, A. (2010). Joining the dots: Connecting inquiry and professional learning. In A. Campbell & S. Groundwater-Smith (Eds.), *Connecting inquiry and professional learning in education: International perspectives and practical solutions* (pp. 200–206). London: Routledge.

Hoban, G.F. (2002). *Teacher learning for educational change: A systems thinking approach.* Buckingham, Philadelphia: Open University Press.

Hord, S.M., & Sommers, W.A. (2007). *Leading professional learning communities: Voices from research and practice.* Thousand Oaks, CA: Corwin Press.

James, M., & McCormick, R. (2009). Teachers learning how to learn. *Teachers and Teacher Education, 25,* 973–982.

Knight, S., & Wiseman, D. (2005). Lessons learned from a research synthesis on the effects of teachers' professional development on culturally diverse students. In H. Waxman & K. Tellez (Eds.), *Improving teacher quality for English language learner* (pp. 71–98). Hillsdale, NJ: Lawrence Erlbaum.

Law, E.H.F. (2010). Space for teacher learning: A case study on developing teacher curriculum leadership in Hong Kong. In K. Yamazumi (Ed.), *Activity theory and fostering learning* (pp. 87–110). Osaka, Japan: Center for Human Activity Theory.

Law, E.H.F., Galton, M., & Wan, S.W.Y. (2010). Distributed curriculum leadership in action: A Hong Kong case study. *Educational Management Administration and Leadership, 38*(3), 286–303.

Law, E.H.F., & Wan, S.W.Y. (2006). Developing curriculum leadership in a primary school: A Hong Kong case study. *Curriculum and Teaching*, 21(2), 61–90.

Law, E.H.F., Wan, S.W.Y., Galton, M., & Lee, J.C.K. (2010). Managing school based curriculum innovations: A Hong Kong case study. *The Curriculum Journal*, 21(3), 313–332.

MacBeath, J. (2005). Leadership as distributed: a matter of practice. *School Leadership and Management*, 25(4), 349–66.

Mayer, A.P., Donaldson, M.L., LeChasseur, K., Welton, A.D., & Cobb, C.D. (2013). Negotiating site-based management and expanded teacher decision making: A case study of six urban schools. *Educational Administration Quarterly*, 49(5), 695–731.

McCormick, R., Fox, A., Carmichael, P., & Procter, R. (2011). *Researching and understanding educational networks*. London: Routledge.

Meijer, P.C., Verloop, N., & Beijaard, D. (2002). Multi-method triangulation in a qualitative study on teachers' practical knowledge: An attempt to increase internal validity. *Quality and Quantity*, 36(2), 145–167.

Papa, R., & Papa, J. (2011). Leading adult learners: Preparing future leaders and professional development of those they lead. In J. Papa (Eds.), *Technology leadership for school improvement* (pp. 91–107). London: Sage.

Rogers, A. (1996). *Teaching adults* (2nd ed.). Milton Keynes: Open University Press.

Rogers, A., & Horrocks, N. (2010). *Teaching adults*. Milton Keynes: Open University Press.

Schon, D. (1987). *Educating the reflective practitioner: Toward a new design for teaching and learning in the professions*. San Francisco, CA: Jossey-Bass.

Shulman, L.S., & Shulman, J.H. (2004). How and what teachers learn: A shifting perspective. *Journal of Curriculum Studies*, 36(2), 257–271.

Spillane, J.P. (2006). *Distributed leadership*. San Francisco, CA: Jossey-Bass.

Spillane, J.P., Halverson, R., & Diamond, J.B. (2001). Investigating school leadership practice: A distributed perspective. *Educational Researcher*, 30(3), 23–28.

Spillane, J.P., Halverson, R., & Diamond, J.B. (2004). Towards a theory of leadership practice: a distributed perspective. *Journal of Curriculum Studies*, 36(1), 3–34.

Stoll, L. (2009). Connecting learning communities: capacity building for systemic change. In A. Hargreaves, A. Lieberman, M. Fullan, & D. Hopkins (Eds.), *Second international handbook of educational change* (pp. 469–484). The Netherlands: Springer.

Stoll, L., & Louis, K.S. (Eds.). (2007). *Professional learning communities: Divergence, depth and dilemmas*. London: Open University Press.

Stringer, E.T. (2007). *Action research: A handbook for practitioners*. Newbury Park, CA: Sage.

Tashakkori, A., & Teddlie, C. (Eds.). (2003). *Handbook of mixed methods in social and behavioral research*. Thousand Oaks, CA: Sage.

Walker, C.L., Edstam, T., & Stone, K. (2007). *Two years, three kinds of educators, and four schools: Improving education for English language learners*. Paper presented at the annual meeting of the American Educational Research Association, Chicago, IL.

Zeichner, K. (2005). Becoming a teacher educator. *Teaching and Teacher Education*, 21, 117–124.

Section 3

Activity theory and curriculum leadership

An alternative perspective

9 Mediational functions of power and status on emergence of leadership properties

Context of innovation

The decentralization of educational decision making in developed countries for the past decades, particularly in the domain of school curriculum, has been perceived as a core strategy that enhances school improvement, teacher development, and pupil learning (Fullan, 2001; Gamage & Zajda, 2005; Hopkins, 2001; Skilbeck, 1984). In general terms, decentralization refers to the transfer of the power to make pedagogical and curriculum decisions from the central agencies to peripheral schools. Decentralization also implies that school teachers take up new curriculum responsibilities, and that their roles have moved from curriculum users to curriculum developers whose assigned functions could be understood as a form of curriculum leadership (Harris, 2003, 2004; Marsh, 1997; Ovens, 1999; Stenhouse, 1975; Wallace, Nesbit, & Miller, 1999). In Hong Kong, the decentralization movement took its embryonic form in the Llewellyn report in 1982, which highlighted the need for school teachers to involve themselves in curriculum decision making processes to enhance teacher professionalism and pupil learning (Law & Galton, 2004; Llewellyn, 1982). In 2002, teacher participation in curriculum decision making reached an institutional approach. Leadership in organizing the school curriculum was assigned to a senior teacher, who was appointed as curriculum coordinator in each primary school in Hong Kong (Education Department, 2002). However, limited empirical studies have indicated the real meaning of teacher participation in school-based curriculum decision making to teacher learning or the manner in which participation is being mediated by various forms of artifacts within the socio-cultural contexts of schools (Harris, 2005).

> The analysis of teacher learning in our efforts has moved from a concern with individual teachers and their learning to a conception of teachers learning and developing within a broader context of community, institution, polity, and profession.
>
> (Shulman & Shulman, 2004, 269)

At the same time, we can conceive of teacher communities in which shared visions (often called myths or religious images in other contexts), community

178 *Activity theory and curriculum leadership*

commitments, a shared knowledge base (which may be common or a form of distributed expertise), a community of practice and established rituals or ceremonies for joint reflection and review either serve to enhance the development of particular accomplishments, actively inhibit their development, or are neutral with respect to them.

(Shulman & Shulman, 2004, 267)

This study is based on data from interviews and videotaped meetings with members of two curriculum development teams in the second action cycle of a teacher leadership development project in a case school in April 2005. The organization and design of the project (Design-Based Research Collective, 2003) were based on the principles and framework of activity theory.

> There has been very little concrete research on creation of artifacts, production of novel social patterns, and expansive transformations of activity contexts.
>
> (Engestrom & Miettinen, 1999, 27)

Therefore, outlining the key principles and theoretical assumptions would be appropriate in this case.

Activity theory: its principles and analytical framework

Activity theory originates from the social learning theory of Vygotsky, who advocates learning in social actions mediated by various material and psychological forms of cultural and social artifacts. These artifacts refer to tools, signs, language, beliefs, traditions, schema, and discourse that shape the object of learning and are being created and shaped in the interactions among different parties in the activity system. These artifacts also represent a primary unit of analysis in activity theory. Activity theory is also a developmental theory that seeks to explain and influence qualitative changes in human practices over time (Daniels, 2001, 91). The first generation of activity system includes only the subject, the object of the activity, and the mediation artifacts, whereas the third generation develops into an interaction model that depicts the emergence of new artifacts because of interactions between two activity systems. In the third generation, the rules, division of labor, and the community are included (Engestrom, 2001).

The motivation to learn and develop or the driving force to change emerges when contradictions that lead to tensions and dynamics, in the form of instability arising from institutional contexts, trigger actions for change on the part of participants in culturally valuable collaborative practices where something useful is produced.

> If we want to successfully confront the various actors involved in the care, we must be able to touch and trigger some internal tensions and dynamics

Mediational functions of power and status 179

in their respective institutional contexts, dynamics that can energize a serious learning effort on their part.

(Engestrom, 2001, 140)

Expansive learning encompasses a cycle of learning actions in response to a series of contradictions that the subjects encounter, and includes the following stages:

1 Primary contradiction encourages questioning the current practice.
2 Secondary contradiction allows further analysis.
3 Modeling the new solution begins (a new pattern of activity).
4 A new model is examined.
5 A new model is implemented.
6 Reflections on the process are conducted.
7 The practice is consolidated.

Learning to activity theory differs in kind with a Piagetian model of learning, which highlights the vertical progression toward a higher level of cognition and competence in the course of a study. On the contrary, activity theory advocates a complementary model of situated learning (Lave & Wenger, 1991) that focuses on expanding learning experiences horizontally. Therefore, transformative learning emerges when participation and involvement are expanded and when participation assumes rotations and changes in responsibility and role in the community of practice (Daniels, 2001, 39).

The change in responsibility and role of each member in the object-oriented unit of activity, such as teamwork or leadership activities, assumes changes in the power structure and division of labor in the team. Therefore, the change in power and division of labor, that is, the mode of control, entails changes in discourse features of interactions within the team (Bernstein, 1995; Daniels, 1995). These features shed light on the mechanisms or strategies used by members of the team to restrict the scope of the dialogue or release the constraints to engage in genuine and authentic negotiation processes. The interaction features, namely, discourse shifts, also indicate the processes in which the division of labor, power and control, and social relations are to be negotiated or mediated (Daniels, 2004). In other words, the study of the interaction processes in the activity system will disclose the social processes, which are mediated in discourses by the hierarchical structure of social relations among the members of the activity system. Therefore, the study will show the manner in which a piece of innovative initiation by a subject in the activity system is resisted or developed into a form of acceptable primary, secondary, or tertiary artifact. The study will also highlight the manner in which a piece of experience or belief is reproduced or transformed. This model of thinking sounds deterministic and does not allow individual autonomy, but our concern here is the extent to which the power, as a form of psychological artifact, leads to changes in the communicative patterns and the extent to which the changed pattern facilitates or constrains (mediation functions) the space for negotiations of meanings among members of a team. We assume that a greater

180 *Activity theory and curriculum leadership*

negotiation space indicates greater potential for individual transformation and teacher learning.

Application of activity theory

The following diagram is recreated based on the three generations of activity theory to show the relationship of an activity system to communal traditions and expectations at large. The mutual interaction relationship within and without the activity system is depicted by the different types of arrows in the diagram.

The recreated diagram of an activity system is adopted from three generations of activity theory and used for analysis in the current study (see Figure 9.1).

Instead of using triangles to indicate the inter-relationships among subjects, objects, artifacts, and outcomes, I prefer using a circle in the center of the diagram to include the composition of a Curriculum Development team in my research project, showing the potentially multi-directional interactions among members in each team. The position of the object or focus of the activity remains central, and the artifacts are placed in the middle of interaction paths between members of the team, symbolically and practically showing their mediation role(s) and

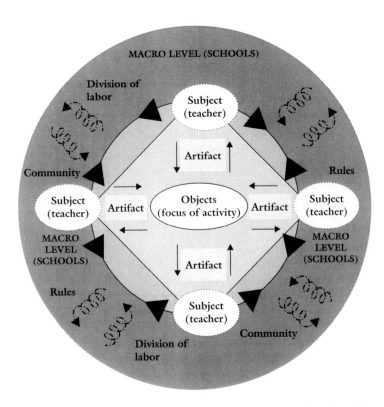

Figure 9.1 Activity system curriculum development teams in schools at the macro and micro level

function(s) in the production of the artifacts. The circle of the activity system is covered with another circle that indicates the inter-relationship between micro-activity systems, where each curriculum development team is located, and macro-societal systems, which represent the rules, division of labor, and community of a school. The relationship between micro-activity systems (inner circle) and macro-sociological and cultural – historical systems in the school (outer circle) is shown with spiral lines in shade to illustrate the hidden and implicit mutual influences of individuals or groups of people as activity systems and the socio-cultural contexts of the community where individuals or groups operate.

At the micro-level of analysis, an activity system is composed of the following key components:

Subjects: teachers
Object of the activity: the focus of the innovation (outcome)
Artifacts: discourse, lesson plans, languages, values, roles, and others
Process of interaction: mediation

At the macro-level of analysis, an activity system is composed of the socio-cultural contexts of the school community, including the following key components:

Rules: regulations
Community: social ethos, beliefs, values, traditions, and others
Division of labor: organizational structure
Process of interaction: socialization

Research design and organization

School curriculum leadership development project

The school was established in 1975, which has 700 students, has a religious background and is located in Shatin District in Hong Kong. Similar to many other primary schools, the school has been under tremendous pressure because of the decrease in birthrate over the period and faces the fear of closure. Under the circumstances of change and challenge, the school leadership has initiated a number of development projects in recent years, including participation in partnership schemes with the Education and Manpower Bureau, peer observation of teaching, teacher appraisal scheme, and collaborative lesson preparations to gain parents' confidence and to improve performance in the school evaluation exercise.

The development project was supported financially by the Hong Kong Quality Education Fund in September 2004. The support lasted for two years to develop teachers' leadership skills and capacities in reviewing, planning, designing, implementing, and evaluating the school's curriculum.

This project aimed to create innovation opportunities for the professional development of teachers in a primary school in Hong Kong, China within a reform context of change and innovation initiated by the government in 2000.

182 *Activity theory and curriculum leadership*

Professional development activities included workshops, seminars, reports, presentations, and the most importantly, the formation of three curriculum development teams to review, plan, design, implement, and evaluate pedagogical aspects of the school's subject-based curriculum (Hiebert, Gallimore, & Stigler, 2003). All activities were organized into "a cycle of actions," and each semester in two years' time had one cycle. The purposes were to sustain innovations among participating teachers and to manipulate core variables, such as the rotation of leadership in the project for observations.

The conceptualization of the team approach and its organization originated from the major principles and research practice of activity theory outlined in the paragraphs above. However, the core elements in effective professional development program were derived from the principles on teacher development, the activities of which should be the following:

1 School-based and problem-solving in nature, with a pedagogical focus;
2 Collaboratively designed and implemented by teachers involved with their ownership in the innovations in a flattened leadership context;
3 Reflective and action-oriented; and
4 Organized in a series of cycles of actions and activities to sustain change and innovation

(Carr & Kemmis, 1986; Darling-Hammond & McLaughlin, 1995;
Day, 1993; Elliott, 1991; Fullan, 1993; Harris, 2003, 75;
Henderson & Hawthorne, 1995; MacBeath & Moos, 2004;
Schon, 1983).

Curriculum development teams: formation and process

Three Curriculum Development teams based on major school subjects were organized as a form of intervention that sought to alter the socio-cultural context of schooling through the development of a culture of collaborative peer problem solving (Daniels, 2004). This time, the agent of change is not located in the leadership of head teachers or experienced teachers but rather in the recreation of socio-cultural situations in which regulative discourse as a form of artifact becomes problematic. Therefore, members (subjects) of the team would encounter internal tensions, dilemmas, conflicts, and contradictions that stimulate the probable emergence of critical moments for solutions, which are considered as a new form of artifact or product or the outcome of the activity system (Engestrom, 2001, 142).

Membership and the roles of each member in object-oriented team meetings became critical to the focus of the research, and therefore were manipulated to create contrasts among experience, seniority, and occupational hierarchy in the team. For example, the Chinese and Mathematics subject-based Curriculum Development teams consisted of their department heads and other participating teachers with less practical experience but were recommended because of their commitment and enthusiasm. The rotation of leadership was also a core variable in the design, with subject heads leading the team in the first cycle, while another team member took the "leadership" role in the second cycle. This arrangement was intended to create a flattened leadership context (Harris & Lambert, 2003). Therefore, observations could be made on the manner in which the change of power structure stimulated change in discourse among members in each development team. Negotiation processes among team members could also be observed and recorded. Thus, the concept of leadership in the project is re-conceptualized as

> A shared phenomenon at a teaching/learning site, and acknowledges the teacher as a curriculum maker, located within a context charged with possibilities for engagement.
> (Macpherson & Brooker, 1999, p. 1; Spillane, Haverson, & Diamond, 2004; Timperley, 2005)

The process of activities for members in each Curriculum Development team had to follow a simplified three-stage model of conducting action research that aimed to identify an innovation for their lesson in the planning stage, attempt the planned innovation in their classroom teaching in the implementation stage, and review actions and propose new directions in the final stage of reflection. In this way, the object of the professional activities for all members in each team became focused and oriented toward input-driven or product-driven pedagogical innovations. All members were also bound to some form of expectations of working in teams and collaboration (Law, Galton, & Wan, in press).

Methodology and data collection

A mixed-method approach was adopted to ensure that a wide range of direct experiences with the innovation was collected and the effects of the innovation could be understood from the various perspectives of the participants in the project (Johnson & Onwuegbuzie, 2004). Interviewing the key participating teachers and videotaping the planning and reflection meetings as well as all tryout lessons were conducted. All videotaped meetings were transcribed verbatim. However, this paper only reports the findings based on the analysis of the interviews with individual members as well as the videotaped meetings of the Mathematics and Chinese Curriculum Development teams, which were considered as two distinct activity systems in the second action cycle. We use activity theory approaches with a focus on the concept of the mediation effects of the two artifacts, namely, the roles of the consultants and the leadership styles in a distributed model in the activity systems.

Findings and analyses

No attempt was made to present all findings and analysis of the project in this paper. However, the main purpose of this study is to use the empirical data relevant

184 *Activity theory and curriculum leadership*

to our discussion of the fundamental theoretical premises of activity theory as a framework for the analysis of situated learning in the context of school-based curriculum development in general and the development of teacher curriculum leadership in particular. Attempts were made to illustrate the extent to which some of the artifacts such as power, role, and leadership style, serve as psychological and communicative instruments in the mediation of the interaction pattern or discourse among members of the two Curriculum Development teams. The findings and analyses below seek to shed light on the call for empirical studies on mediation processes in activity systems specific to teacher participation in forming curriculum decisions.

Mediation functions of the professional styles of the consultants

Partnership with the university faculty in education has been considered as a key factor in the successful implementation of educational reforms. This view is particularly true when the style of collaboration fits well with the professional needs of the school-based innovation being taken in a developmental perspective instead of an ad hoc and unsustainable manner. The current project also emphasized the need for collaboration with professionals from university faculty members, and each subject team was assigned an expert in the field to provide professional support and advice on pedagogical innovations. The appointed experts worked with the Curriculum Development teams, joined in the collaborative lesson preparation meetings, observed tryout lessons, attended reflection meetings, and provided advice and feedback on the focus of the pedagogical innovations. The functions and practice of having an appropriate consultant from outside the school environment to work with the school-based Curriculum Development team or projects have not been well-documented in many school improvement or curriculum development project reports. Unlike in the present study, most of these types of reports do not provide detailed evidence on the manner in which their functions have been realized in practice and in some cases the manner in which their prescribed effectiveness could have been mediated by other micro-political considerations within each of the development team and the professional style of the consultants themselves. The purpose of this project was to provide a source of potential contradictions and tensions to the conventional practice of the teachers.

The consultants appointed for the two Curriculum Development teams had been working with each of the teams in the first action cycle and had developed some form of mutual understanding with the participating teachers. Members of both teams found the consultants to be useful, appreciated their professional inputs in the discussions before and after the tryout lessons, enjoyed the opportunities to ponder on the pedagogical issues and explore possible alternatives for future. However, the effect of the mediation roles of the two consultants on the curriculum deliberation in the two teams appeared to differ in a significant number of dimensions. Below, we present each case separately with some emergent themes, such as the emerging collaboration models and models of personality or professional style.

Mediational functions of power and status 185

Chinese curriculum development team

The consultant for the Chinese team appeared to have taken a confrontational model and presented his views in direct contrast with the team members. Whether or not he was conscious of this act requires further investigation. Conflicting views were recorded in the following interview.

> He does not understand us yet . . . like we want a lesson to teach pupils about festivals in China . . . but he thought a lesson is not enough . . . he possibly wanted us to use a whole module . . . we had only one meeting . . . last meeting we had some initial idea about the topic for the tryout lesson . . . and how to develop . . . design instructional plan successful . . . we are busy very busy.
> (Chinese Team: Teacher A interview, literal translation no. 5)

The conflicting views might have been handled smoothly in the planning meeting by the team leader or in discussion to arrive at a consensus or in the formulation of achievable solutions. Unfortunately, this approach should not have been used to solve the problem. The conflicts appeared to have been left untouched, and each teacher took his or her own views to action in the tryout lesson.

> We had many mistakes because we were not well prepared . . . we had not any consensus . . . the consultant suddenly arrived . . . we did not have the guidelines but suddenly Phoebe (teaching assistant) gave us many guidelines; we need time to digest; we did not follow the guideline; . . . we could have only one lesson . . . we also had some internal arguments . . . the consultant then gave some suggestions . . . asked us to give him the plan by email; he was suggesting we need not think by ourselves but can use website materials developed by other schools; many schools are doing the same thing with different topics; we could download them and teach them in our classes; we did not have any conclusion and we followed that up later.
> (Chinese Team: Teacher C interview, literal translation no. 58)

The style of the consultant's professional input and relationship with the team has been salient and explicit in the videotaped planning and reflection meetings. The videotaped planning meeting shows some agreement with the teacher observations on the relationship between the consultant and the Curriculum Development team. The consultant had given significant professional input on pedagogical principles and practices in relation to the Chinese curriculum in the planning meeting as well as in the reflection meetings after the tryout lessons. He tended to dominate and direct the discourse, which was closed, instead of being open to more alternatives and seeking possibilities from the perspectives of the participating teachers.

> Problems with speaking . . . speaking ability, attitude and habit are important, indeed the curriculum guide is very clear about this, listening, speaking, reading and writing . . . if you want them to master these skills, you need to

186 *Activity theory and curriculum leadership*

train them on character and word construction, sentence patterns, etc., . . .
speaking ability starts with early age, . . . in a lesson, four pupils in one group,
they have to speak, they have to find a topic themselves, like school issues,
news, let them speak free, can speak for two minutes, . . . other groups follow.

> (Consultant, literal transcription, Video Taped Consultation
> Meeting on 22 April 2005)

Responding to the teachers' pedagogical questions, the consultant elaborated on
the issue, offered general advice on alternatives, compared experiences of other
schools, and proposed strategies. This communicative pattern is observed consistently throughout the three videotaped meetings that he had with the team.
His discourse style matched the features of an elaborated code, whereas the other
members in the meetings adopted a restricted code (Bernstein, 1995).

The observations given by the teachers were also congruent with the discussion contents in the planning meeting, indicating that the focus of the meeting
was not on the instructional design or innovative aspect of the tryout lessons but
on general issues with curriculum and teaching in the primary schools in Hong
Kong. The lack of clarity in focus appeared to be a consequence of his professional style and the perception of his own role in the team.

In the reflection meeting, a few reflections on the tryout lessons made by the
teachers were recorded, and the comments were taken solely from the observations of the consultant. Therefore, the reflection meeting failed to create opportunities for the teachers to share experiences and seek improvements from their
practical experiences of attempting to use the innovation. In other words, the
space for participatory or expansive learning is limited, and in extreme cases suppressed or at least constrained by the dominating role of the consultant. Evidence
in the videotaped meetings shows that when a teacher initiated three discourse
shifts to essential pedagogical issues, such as integrating learning with the life
experience of the pupils and sources for support learning materials for pupils,
the consultant responded didactically, basically following the previous discourse
pattern. The teacher initiations were not used to improvise further reflections
among members in the team on the object of learning in the lesson, although the
consultant did most of the talking in the videotaped meetings.

Teacher S: We had talked about different abilities, actually should we train all
skills, or concentrate on one first?

Consultant: First, we better do one first, because we do not have a clue how
to move, now we work on one, and when mature, we can extend,
from festivals to food culture, religion, music etc.

> (Literal transcription, Video Taped Reflection Meeting
> on 17 June 2005)

The mediated interaction pattern becomes largely uni-structural and closed, and
the object of the activity system is blurred (Biggs & Moore, 1993). We have a
distorted or twisted activity system, which may be termed a uni-structural activity

system in the case of the Chinese Curriculum Development team. This interaction pattern is similar to coordination (Edwards, 2005), showing that each member contributes individually without strong evidence of the mutual negotiation of the object of learning. Therefore, participation in the case of team members appears to remain at the surface level, although one might argue that the experiences with the consultant may expand the horizon of the team members. However, the responses are largely restricted and uni-structural without evidence on the pedagogical issues being extended, challenged, and explored and on the solutions being proposed and sought.

Mathematics curriculum development team

The contribution of the consultant in the Mathematics team moved toward the other end of the dichotomy. The consultant served not only as a mentor for some members but also as a mediator between colleagues in a school in case of embarrassments such as peer observation. The following quotations from the teacher interviews demonstrate the socio-political functions of the consultant in the implementation of a curriculum innovation.

> We colleagues did peer observation, but because we were colleagues, we tend to be lenient and more accommodating . . . but Mr. Wong is an outsider, he does not have our tradition, he is able to observe many problems that we are so used to . . .
> (Mathematics Team: Teacher G interview, literal translation no. 32)

> Mr. Wong gave us many good ideas . . . his role is a mentor, not a higher authority, he is thinking with you, his attitude is good.
> (Mathematics Team: Teacher G interview, literal translation no. 35)

For the panel head, the contributions of the consultant led her to reflect deeply on her own traditional practice in classroom teaching and indicated deep learning from her participation in the curriculum decision making process.

> To look at the same topic and how to teach from a different angle, learned very much . . . particularly learned from Mr. Wong, the consultant, discovered that what we thought and practiced may not be correct . . . using different angles would see different things . . . discovered what pupils think is different from what we think they know in mind . . .
> (Mathematics Team: Teacher I interview, literal translation no. 42)

The videotapes of the planning and reflection meetings were used to triangulate the various roles played by the consultant in the various stages of the innovation project. He was a facilitator, leading the discussions and initiating topics for discussions of great pedagogical significance in both the planning and reflection meetings. Below is a selection of the questions that the consultant used to stimulate professional reflection among team members in the videotaped meetings.

188 *Activity theory and curriculum leadership*

He performed the following in the planning meetings:

- He emphasized the conceptual issues by teaching the concept of "fractions," and that the meeting should focus on the manner in which the concept of fractions can be taught with clarity and accuracy. He reiterated that teachers are not short on methods, but rather had issues on whether the methods used are related closely with learning the target concepts in Mathematics remains unknown.
- He used communication skills such as clarification, probing, asking for explanations and concrete examples, and seeking alternatives. He challenged the traditional practices of the team members.

He singled out the following points during the reflection meeting:

- He pointed out the conceptual problems for the younger learners in the tryout learning sessions when a generic issue with fractions is contextualized with the use of paper, shapes, and folding as main elements in learning the concept.
- He moved the focus of the discussion from blaming the inability of the pupils to the inability of the teachers to clarify the various key properties of the concept of fractions for their pupils.
- He also pointed out that the transition from one activity to another should be linked strongly in conceptual terms or the pupils would not be able to appreciate the values and links between activities.

The following statement is a literal transcription of a series of leading and probing statements that the consultant posed to the teachers to stimulate reflections among members, and he readdressed the learning issue with pupils:

> The teacher did give two examples to pupils . . . one using square and one circle . . . pupils are still unable to conceptualize the issue or generalize the principles . . . from one example, (restricting to the use of square and circle only) and then move to something general . . . the pupils may not understand how this task is related to the second task or the task of colouring . . . the problem is with transition . . . how to give more background information to support learning . . . it is the flow or the transition from one task to the second task which matters . . .

He facilitated the discussion and invited members to participate in the exploration of the fundamental issues in teaching the topic and attempt to identify the focus of the innovation lesson or the object of the activity system. His discourse feature is open, stimulating, and inviting. The following are some questions that he posed:

> What about other teachers?
> This means it is not the problem with methods.

Mediational functions of power and status   189

Fraction big or small is not the first lesson on fraction, before, must teach others about fraction. Why did we choose to teach to compare fraction big and small? According to your method, do we have problems in the process?

(Literal translation, Consultation Meeting, 12 April 2005)

This feature is also illustrated below through a functional analysis of the exchanges among members in the consultation meeting and a graphical representation of the multi-structural nature of a portion of the interaction pattern of the discourse.

Consultant:	explain issues, challenge traditional views, explore, analyze, present alternative views
Teacher 1:	attempt to find a focus of innovation, explain procedure
Consultant:	put the proposed focus in a tentative mood
Teacher 1:	agree on the possible explanation
Consultant:	explain, elaborate in exploratory and tentative ways
Teacher 2:	explain the focus of teaching the topic
Consultant:	reiterate, pose questions
Teacher 3:	explain what the normal teaching practice is, and express the difficulty in teaching
Consultant:	rephrase the issues, pose three questions
Teacher 1:	state in the meeting that some teachers have no experience of teaching the topic
Teacher 4:	participate, explain, state in the meeting how she teaches
Consultant:	pose another question
Teacher 4:	give example how to teach the topic
Consultant:	direct to other teachers who are silent; inviting participation
Teacher 3:	explain how he teaches the topic and difficulty
Teacher 4:	give examples how he teaches
Teacher 3:	Illustrate how
Teacher 4:	illustrate how pupils perform the task
Consultant:	pose another question
Teacher 4:	respond and give examples
Teacher 3:	give examples
Consultant:	pose questions
Teacher 3:	use the blackboard to illustrate
Teacher 4:	give examples
Consultant:	confirming
Teacher 3:	express difficulty
Consultant:	invite teachers to focus on the difficulty and pose questions
Teacher 1:	agree on the difficulty
Teacher 4:	confirm the teaching approach, give examples

This series of exchanges illustrates the multi-structural nature of the communication, and nearly all members participated. The sources of information do not come largely from the consultant but from various members of the team,

190 *Activity theory and curriculum leadership*

and information was given from time to time. The focus of discussion concentrated intensely on the object of the activity system, that is, the exploration of the pedagogical problems and their solutions. This pattern of communication among the members of the team is observed consistently in the co-planning and reflection meetings conducted on 25 April 2005 and 19 May 2005, respectively. We may label this pattern as a multi-structural activity system in consideration of the nature and characteristics of the mediated interaction pattern. This interaction pattern is similar to a cooperation where each member contributes to the communal discourse, with strong evidence of the mutual negotiation of the object of learning (Edwards, 2005).

An important note shows that various members of the meeting responded to the teacher initiation, as opposed to the consultant who assumed professional superiority with a restricted type in the Chinese team.

The contributions of the consultant in the Mathematics Curriculum Development team are twofold: offering professional and academic inputs concerning pedagogical issues on the topic that the teachers wanted to explore and leading the team to reflect on personal pedagogical experiences and practices. He facilitated discussions in an open yet professional manner, allowing expressions of views, highlighting key pedagogical concerns such as links between learning activities and learning sessions, extending members' understanding of the underlying issues with deep learning, and moving the focus of the discussion from accusations of pupil inability to the reconsideration of the appropriateness of the selection of pedagogical strategies in relation to the achievement of the content knowledge gained by pupils. He demonstrated in practice a form of professional leadership without dictating the directions to the team.

In summary, two contrasting modes of professional inputs are observed from two consultants with similar backgrounds. The former mode exemplified by the consultant for the Chinese team is called a restricted mode of professionality; whereas the latter mode is called an extended mode of professionality. Table 9.1 summarizes the characteristics and potential effects of their mediation functions on curriculum deliberation.

Table 9.1 Models of mediation of the two modes of professionality

Domains of contributions/effects	*Modes of Professionality*	
	Restricted	*Extended*
Input	personal instructional experience	generic instructional alternatives
Role	informative	exploratory
Discourse style	closed	open
Collaboration	didactic	negotiable
Social cohesion	diffused	converged
Leadership	ascribed; power-coercive	re-educative; social interactive
Interaction pattern	uni-structural	multi-structural

Mediation functions of leadership styles

The project attempted to manipulate the leadership style by rotating the leadership with the panel heads as team leaders in the first action cycle and the committed teachers as team leaders in the second cycle. Therefore, a new concept of shared and participatory leadership is instituted to allow for more genuine, professional, and open-ended dialogues in team interactions on pedagogical issues and to develop teacher leadership in school-based curriculum development. In such a reconstructed situation, the power relationship between followers and leaders becomes blurred. This change of leadership is also expected to cause tensions and contradictions during the curriculum deliberation processes.

The teacher interviews showed some evidence of the changes in leadership style and pointed to the mediation effects of this intervention. The team leaders of the Mathematics and Chinese teams regarded themselves as facilitators liaising work with the external consultant, coordinating meetings, searching for discussion materials, motivating colleagues to participate, preparing PowerPoint presentations as learning materials to support teaching, and collecting documents as part of their administrative duties.

> I am a so and so leader, how to contact the consultant, organize meeting, concerned about whether I can motivate colleagues to attend meetings . . . whether we can compromise . . . but colleagues collaborated well . . . more easily than I expected . . .
> (Mathematics Team: Teacher F interview, literal translation no. 13)

They were also very conscious of the changing style of leadership and expressed their agreement with the new style of appointing chairs for the Curriculum Development teams.

> Once we sat down together, we did not have the idea about who was leader, or panel head, or tryout teachers, our roles were loose, we felt relaxed because we were not tryout teachers, panel head and I talked quite freely, not aware of our formal roles, we enjoyed our conversations.
> (Mathematics Team: Teacher F interview, literal translation no. 8)

The Mathematics team leader, Teacher F, saw her role in this way:

> This time I was an observer, last time I was the tryout teacher . . . because now you are an observer you watched and saw more how the tryout teachers handled teaching, are they correct or is there room for improvement, this is learning.
> (Mathematics Team: Teacher F interview, literal translation no. 5)

The perceptions of team leaders matched those of the other members who had worked with them in the second action cycle of the project. The following observations were taken from the Chinese team members.

192 *Activity theory and curriculum leadership*

> Teacher A is responsible for coordination . . . she had lesson plan and package . . . tell us what the problems are. . . . tell us what to attend to . . .
>
> She could not tell us what is the idea about the project but support us in planning lesson . . . learning materials etc.
>
> (Chinese Team: Teacher B interview, literal translation no. 44)

> . . . guide us in the meeting . . . in fact the PowerPoint and the module idea were her ideas . . . she used them before and this time they adapted them for use in each class . . .
>
> (Chinese Team: Teacher C interview, literal translation no. 45)

> She is quick and efficient . . . talk to members.
>
> (Chinese Team: Teacher C interview, literal translation no. 45)

The team leaders were observed by the Curriculum Development team members as supporters and facilitators of the curriculum-making process instead of traditional leaders who assume a more directive role. However, evidence appears to show that the leadership styles of both teams had different effects on the object of the activity system thus created. A tryout teacher from the Mathematics team expressed her observation in the following manner.

> She leads us to think . . . she thinks of many issues . . . lead us to ask the consultant . . . and give us a summary . . . what to attend to . . . a good supporter . . . support us to design a curriculum . . . but her leadership role is not strong . . . I feel we are equal, share work, every one can be a team leader . . . the leader helps collecting information . . . chair meetings.
>
> (Mathematics Team: Teacher H interview, literal translation no. 21)

This observation was triangulated with the videotaped meetings of both teams. The team leader of the Mathematics group tended to be more articulate and willing to pose questions to the meetings, whereas the leader of the Chinese team tended to be less willing to lead the discussions. This observation leads us to view the new roles played by the original leaders (panel heads) of both teams and determine the manner in which they contrast with the new team leaders.

In the second cycle of the innovation, the panel heads of the Chinese and Mathematics departments were deliberately not given a specific role to play. However, both continued to assert varying degrees of influence on the curriculum-making processes. The panel head of the Mathematics team was more subtle in being assertive, whereas the Chinese panel head tended to orient the content of the professional discourse in most of the planning and reflection meetings. He was unwilling to surrender his traditional status in the school hierarchy, and asserted a sense of hierarchical influence in the deliberation of the innovation.

When the consultant directed the focus of the discourse during the consultation meeting on 22 April 2005 toward problem identification, he included information on the curriculum orientation in the school, shifting the discourse away

Mediational functions of power and status 193

from the pedagogical level to another intermental plane on planning within his terms of reference.

> Our situation is like this, level one students are too small, level two students have done this (training in speaking), level three and six students have country standard tests, then we choose level five for this project, or we could ask Miss Wan, the project leader, for clarification, or we should have some consensus.
> (Literal translation, Consultation Meeting on 22 April 2005)

His "disruption" was not adopted by other members, and the chair continued focusing on the original discourse. He also used "you" in referring to other teachers in the project, thereby distancing himself from the team. His use of the language of control and demand enabled him to assume a dominant role in the curriculum decision making processes and deliberately downgrade the role of the team leader as solely a liaison, with the consultant from the outside and a facilitator to discuss design issues with the other members. In the reflection meeting, the team leader openly admitted her team's confusion with the focus of the innovation after the panel head gave detailed explanations on pedagogical issues with cultural studies and invited the team to "brush aside" the instructions from the project leader.

Panel Head: . . . another issue, the studies of culture should be a form of immersion . . ., they can study by themselves. . . . You do not need to be restricted by what Ms. Wan (the project leader) has instructed . . .
Team Leader: possibly we understood wrongly previously . . .
(Literal Translation, Consultation Meeting on 22 April 2005)

Interviews with the new chair indicated her perception of her role in the team, which matched the expectations of the panel head. His assertion of power was also observed in the videotaped planning and reflection meetings, where he made severe criticisms on the links between the studies of a historically tragic figure, Poet Wat, who had committed suicide, and the modern way of viewing the value of life, which the tryout teachers wanted to experiment on in the tryout lesson. He assumed a leadership role in making decisions on the subject content.

> [My role is] To provide knowledge background for the topic.
> (Chinese Team: Teacher E interview, literal translation no. 22)

> There is a division between panel and consultant: panel responsible for content; consultant for pedagogy . . .
> (Chinese Team: Teacher E interview, literal translation no. 22)

His assertion was formally "rewarded and recognized" by the external consultant with an open announcement of the division of labor or professional superiority (expertise) between the two during the reflection meeting.

194   *Activity theory and curriculum leadership*

Me, only focuses on pedagogical issues, while Mr. Chan is an expert in cultural studies, he is able to analyze deeply the problem with culture.

(Literal translation, Reflection Meeting on 17 June 2005)

Members reacted differently to the leadership styles of the two traditional panel heads. For instance, the members of the Chinese team developed negative feelings toward his overt assertiveness in leadership.

He was busy . . . or he gave us pressure because we based our teaching on our pupils . . . but he insisted on subject content . . . quite serious about content . . . but we based on pupil ability to design . . . and this is great difference . . .

(Chinese Team: Teacher C interview, literal translation no. 45)

The team members would have preferred to have their discussions without him, although they acknowledged his positional power in line with accountability. The members of the two development teams also acknowledged the facilitating role deliberately played by their former panel heads and had a stronger sense of team spirit being developed among them.

I feel the panel head was not a panel head anymore. I feel she is a member of the team . . . we share work . . . we are equal . . . we all can solve problems . . . she gives us views and ideas when we are short of . . .

(Mathematics Team: Teacher H interview, literal translation no. 21)

A member of the Mathematics team felt that in putting the plan into action, she was acting on behalf of the Curriculum Development team.

I feel I am acting out the collective decisions . . . I am an actor . . . I am implementing our ideas and decisions . . .

(Mathematics Team: Teacher H interview, literal translation no. 26)

This feeling of a shared community is also observed in the Chinese team. In general, the members felt that the working spirit was collaborative. Despite the clear authority of the panel head, they did not have any feelings of being directed in a way that distanced them from their own expectations and wishes. A team member even felt that he was implementing their collective decisions.

I think we work together and methods and roles are similar; just coordinating, we look at what we have, talked about features of each class to help each teacher, give some ideas, to construct something.

(Chinese Team: Teacher B interview, literal translation no. 42)

. . . like an implementer . . . other wants me to teach this thing . . . then I could adjust accordingly to my class features . . . to revise the lesson plan . . .

(Chinese Team: Teacher B interview, literal translation no. 43)

Teacher thinking here appears to be undergoing some form of changes, from an assertive and dominant leadership caused by the ascribed status of the leaders (subject panel heads) to a collaborative form of leadership that has allowed some room for personal professional expression. Although the members still appreciated the special knowledge of the panel head, nevertheless, they would venture and explore alternative areas beyond the traditions.

In the videotaped meetings and reflections of both teams, the interactions were illustrative of the effects of the social dimension of the interaction among members of the teams. Maintaining social cohesion among members in the team is essential because this cohesion is a means to enhance teamwork and team spirit. Achievement of the team's goals has long-term effects for each member of the teams. Therefore, teachers tended to be less critical and reflective, and comments were milder in tone. Whether this prevailing reservation in terms of assertiveness among team members is a function of the local Chinese culture requires further investigation of a different kind. Even the panel heads and team leaders played a rather secondary role in terms of leadership in professional domains. However, when the discussion on professional matters was initiated by the consultant from outside the school context, the dialogues and interactions became significantly focused on the pedagogical efficiency and conceptual clarity of the learning target. In particular, this instance is explicitly observed in the Mathematics team.

In general terms, the adoption of a form of distributed leadership in the Mathematics curriculum development team encouraged the emergence of a community of professional learners with a focus on formulating a task to achieve pedagogical innovation in action in classroom settings, whereas professional leadership was less salient in the Chinese team because of the assertive and didactic leadership styles of the consultant and the dominating influence of traditional leadership in the curriculum decision making processes. Changing roles have fostered changing perceptions on traditional practices, which gave room for change in beliefs and practice. This style of deliberation of a leadership style based on the collective responsibility of each individual member in curriculum decision enhances personal and professional learning in a public manner, and prepares teachers to assume leadership roles of various domains in the school-based curriculum development in a collective manner. This statement is also true for a team whose collaboration and professional leadership had been mediated by the traditional form of power and influence of the panel head and the didactic style of the consultant, as in the case with the Chinese development team.

Table 9.2 summarizes the different leadership patterns and their mediating effects on the two development teams.

Interviews with the Chinese team members indicate their active participation in the development process despite continuous attempts by the panel head to dominate the agenda and subsequent discussions in the meetings.

196 *Activity theory and curriculum leadership*

Table 9.2 Models of mediation of leadership style

	Chinese Team	Mathematics Team
Leadership style	Distributed	Distributed
Mediating factors	Dominated by assertive panel head; Didactic consultant	Less assertive panel head; Facilitating consultant
Effects	Less team spirit Developing resentment within the team	Stronger team spirit Developing collaborative pattern
Discourse style	Closed and informative; less interactive; Less expressive	Open and exploratory; more interactive; full of stories; expressive
Participation style	Less interactive; less active coordination	More interactive; active cooperation
Teacher learning	Less negotiation space professionally	More negotiation space professionally

Conclusions

Teacher participation in curriculum decision making appears to have received universal consensus in the context of policy change toward decentralization in many developed and developing countries. Calls for empirical studies on the patterns of participation and their effectiveness have also been made. The teacher curriculum leadership project outlined above has attempted to base its design and analysis on the key premises of activity theory, which emphasizes the sociocultural contexts of learning and mediation roles of artifacts in the production of outcomes in activity systems. The innovation project manipulated the formation of the Curriculum Development Teams and rotation of leadership to create potential tensions and contradictions among members. The intention of this project is to enable observations of the mediation functions of two essential artifacts, namely, the roles of consultants and the leadership styles on the interaction patterns or forms of teacher participation in the two teams. A comparison of evidence from the two teams is conducted. Evidence shows that the mediation functions of the two artifacts were explicit, and their effects on the interaction patterns or forms of teacher participation significant. The observations also show that the characteristics of the subcategories of the two artifacts have distinct influences on the communicative processes of the meetings. Restricted professionality exemplified by the consultant from the Chinese team allows less negotiation space for its members, thereby creating a uni-structural pattern of communication (Hoyle, 1974; Hoyle & Wallace, 2009). Its mediation function constrains exchanges of alternatives and possibilities. However, extended professionality identified in the Mathematics team invited cooperative participation and created a multi-structural pattern of communication. These features have become necessary conditions for deep learning among members of the team.

Distributed leadership in the two teams has been mediated by another artifact, that is, the assertiveness of the dominating role of the panel head. However, the mediation functions of the two panel heads appear to differ. On the one hand, the panel head in the Chinese team tended to assert his hierarchical and professional power, thereby containing the possibilities for an open and dialogical interaction pattern and participation among team members. On the other hand, the Mathematics panel head appeared to be more participatory, and her discourse shift in the intra-mental plane in the discussion appeared to be adopted by her members. The discussion moved to the core issues on pedagogical difficulties. The object of the activity system was clearly focused on solutions that emerged toward the end of the meeting.

In the two illustrations on the mediation functions of the two artifacts on the object of the activity systems, the artifacts highlight the mediation effects on the processes of achieving the outcomes. The findings also show that subcategories within a specific artifact differ in mediation effects. This exploration points to the need for further empirical investigation on the classification of subcategories of a specific and essential artifact in the mediation processes as well as on the manner in which these subcategories assert contrastive mediation effects on the interaction pattern in general and on teacher participation in particular. In theory, empirical studies of this nature will disclose further the complexity of the mediation processes in which innovative initiations in response to tensions and contradictions are contained, twisted, regulated, and shifted or explored, extended, enriched, and developed.

References

Bernstein, B. (1995). Code theory and its positioning: A case study in misrecognition. *British Journal of Sociology of Education, 16*(1), 3–19.

Biggs, J.B., & Moore, P.J. (1993). *Process of learning.* Singapore: Prentice Hall.

Carr, W., & Kemmis, S. (1986). *Becoming critical: Education, knowledge and action research.* London: Falmer.

Daniels, H. (1995). Pedagogic practices, tacit knowledge and discursive discrimination: Bernstein and post-Vygotskian research. *British Journal of Sociology of Education, 16*(4), 517–533.

Daniels, H. (2001). *Vygotsky and pedagogy.* London: Routledge/Falmer.

Daniels, H. (2004). Activity theory, discourse and Bernstein. *Educational Review, 56*(2), 121–132.

Darling-Hammond, L., & McLaughlin, M.W. (1995). Policies that support professional development in an era of reform. *Phi Delta Kappan, 76*(8), 597–604.

Day, C. (1993). Reflection: A necessary but not sufficient condition for professional development. *British Educational Research Journal, 19*(1), 83–93.

Design-Based Research Collective. (2003). Design-based research: An emerging paradigm for educational inquiry. *Educational Researcher, 31*(1), 5–8.

Education Department. (2002). *Provision of an additional teacher post for leading curriculum development in primary schools for five years* (Administration Circular No. 13/2002). Hong Kong: Education Department.

Edwards, A. (2005). Let's get beyond community and practice: The many meanings of learning by participating. *The Curriculum Journal, 16*(1), 49–65.

198 *Activity theory and curriculum leadership*

Elliott, J. (1991). *Action research for educational change.* Buckingham: Open University Press.

Engestrom, Y. (2001). Expansive learning at work: Toward an activity theoretical reconceptualization. *Journal of Education and Work, 14*(1), 133–156.

Engestrom, Y., & Miettinen, R. (1999). Introduction. In Y. Engestrom, R. Miettien, & R.L. Punamaki (Eds.), *Perspectives on activity theory* (pp. 1–16). Cambridge: Cambridge University Press.

Fullan, M. (1993). *Change forces: Probing the depths of educational reform.* London: Falmer.

Fullan, M. (2001). *Leading in a culture of change.* San Francisco, CA: Jossey-Bass.

Gamage, D.T., & Zajda, J. (2005). Decentralisation and school-based management: A comparative study of SGS models. *International Journal of Educational Practice and Theory, 27*(2), 35–58.

Harris, A. (2003). Teacher leadership and school improvement. In A. Harris, C. Day, D. Hopkins, M. Hadfield, A. Hargreaves, & C. Chapman (Eds.), *Effective leadership for school Improvement* (pp. 72–83). London: Routledge/Falmer.

Harris, A. (2004). Distributed leadership and school improvement: Leading or misleading? *Educational Management Administration & Leadership, 32*(4), 11–24.

Harris, A. (2005). Leading or misleading? Distributed leadership and school improvement. *Journal of Curriculum Studies, 37*(3), 255–265.

Harris, A., & Lambert, L. (2003). *Building leadership capacity for school improvement.* Buckingham: Open University Press.

Henderson, J.G., & Hawthorne, R.D. (1995). *Transformative curriculum leadership.* New York: Teachers College Press.

Hiebert, J., Gallimore, R., & Stigler, J.W. (2003). The new heroes of teaching. *Education Week, 23*(10), 56.

Hopkins, D. (2001). *School improvement for real.* London: Falmer.

Hoyle, E. (1974). Professionality, professionalism and control in teaching. *London Education Review, 3*(2), 13–19.

Hoyle, E., & Wallace, M. (2009). Leadership for professional practice. In S. Gewirtz, P. Mahony, I. Hextall, & A. Cribb (Eds.), *Changing teacher professionalism: International trends, challenges and ways* (pp. 204–215). New York: Routledge.

Johnson, R.B., & Onwuegbuzie, A.J. (2004). Mixed methods research: A research paradigm whose time has come. *Educational Researcher, 33*(7), 14–26.

Lave, J., & Wenger, E. (1991). *Situated learning: Legitimate peripheral participation.* New York: Cambridge University Press.

Law, E.H.F., & Galton, M. (2004). Impact of a school-based curriculum project on teachers and students: A Hong Kong case study. *Curriculum Perspectives, 24*(3), 43–58.

Law, E.H.F., Galton, M., & Wan, S.W.Y. (2007). Developing curriculum leadership in schools: Hong Kong perspectives. *Asia Pacific Journal of Teacher Education, 5*(2), 143–159.

Llewellyn, J. (1982). *A perspective on education in Hong Kong: Report by a visiting panel.* Hong Kong: Government Printer.

MacBeath, J., & Moos, L. (2004). *Democratic learning: The challenge to school effectiveness.* London: Routledge.

Macpherson, I., & Brooker, R. (1999). Introducing places and spaces for teachers in curriculum leadership. In I. Macpherson, T. Aspland, R. Brooker & B. Elliott

(Eds.), *Places and spaces for teachers in curriculum leadership* (pp. 1–20). Deakin West, ACT: Australian Curriculum Studies Association.

Marsh, C. (1997). *Key concepts for understanding curriculum*. London: Falmer.

Ovens, P. (1999). Can teachers be developed? *Journal of In-Service Education, 25*(2), 275–305.

Schon, D.A. (1983). *The reflective practitioner*. London: Temple Smith.

Shulman, L.S., & Shulman, J.H. (2004). How and what teachers learn: A shifting perspective. *Journal of Curriculum Studies, 36*(2), 257–271.

Skilbeck, M. (1984). *School based curriculum development*. London: Harper & Row.

Spillane, J.P., Haverson, R., & Diamond, J.B. (2004). Towards a theory of leadership practice: A distributed perspective. *Journal of Curriculum Studies, 36*(1), 3–34.

Stenhouse, L. (1975). *An introduction to curriculum research and development*. London: Heinemann.

Timperley, H.S. (2005). Distributed leadership: Developing theory from practice. *Journal of Curriculum Studies, 37*(4), 395–420.

Wallace, J.D., Nesbit, C.R., & Miller, A.C.S. (1999). Six leadership models for professional development in science and mathematics. *Journal of Science Teacher Education, 10*(4), 247–268.

10 Engaging teachers in reflective practice

Tensions between ideological orientations and pragmatic considerations

Reflecting on teaching and learning

Changes in education necessarily require changes in the professional qualities of the teaching force and its organizations – schools, which become the focal point of many planned departures from traditional teaching communities to communities engaged actively in the search for improvement and enhancement (Benham & Murakami-Ramalho, 2010; Borko, 2004; Garet, Porter, Desimone, Birman, & Yoon, 2001; Knight & Wiseman, 2005; McCormick, Fox, Carmichael, & Procter, 2011; Stoll, 2009; Stoll & Louis, 2007; Walker, Edstam, & Stone, 2007; Zeichner, 2005). This radical reorientation of the role of schools as a learning community as well as a community for social reconstruction, together with the expectation of teachers being reflective practitioners, has been ongoing for the past 30 years in the West (Campbell & Groundwater-Smith, 2010; Hargreaves & Shirley, 2008, 2009; Hord, 2009; Hord & Sommers, 2007). In recent years, these concepts have become increasingly familiar in countries in the East (Chan & Pang, 2006; Lee & Feng, 2007). However, little is known of the manner in which schools and teachers should respond to these changes and their concomitant challenges. In particular, the additional responsibilities of schools and teachers are subversive to their traditional roles, being conservative and instrumental to the building of the society and its economy in the Asian context (Hopkins, 2007).

In considering the crisis that arose in the relationship between teaching and learning, the reflection developed in research on education has also affected the teaching discipline. In fact, traditional instructional models now appear to be increasingly inadequate and unable to meet the demands of today's society. This inadequacy has led to the abandonment by the teaching faculty of the traditional mold and has resulted in the establishment of new methodologies, with schools facing fear and uncertainty on which direction to take. In particular, the teaching of mathematics now requires mediation between the theory proposed by the most innovative research and the discussion of practical situations in class, with the need to promote a vision of mathematics education that is better connected to reality (as shown in the studies of Nunes, Schliemann, & Carreher, 1993). In the current landscape, an interesting position is that of Anna Sfard's, who uses two metaphors to describe learning: the acquisition metaphor and the metaphor of participation. As noted by Paavola, Lipponen, and Hakkarainen (2004), the first metaphor emphasizes individual mental processes, while the second metaphor examines the transmission of cultural knowledge and skills from one generation to another. Two complementary processes (Stahl, 2008) emphasize the need for a transition to new forms of learning, where participation, communication, and situated learning perspectives become dominant in the interactions of students and teachers.

Sfard's focus on communication and cognition is synthesized in the new term "commognition," which is intended to indicate the manner in which the dialogue becomes the basis for shared meanings, whereas the thought becomes an individualized form of communication activity. In offering mathematics as a form of communication, the mathematical object becomes the object of discourse, and the result of meaning building is identified as localized in the time and space of specific practices. In other words, as clarified by Stahl (2008), the mathematical object becomes an objectification or reification of a discursive process. Hence, a need for concrete and contextual learning (Lave & Wenger, 1991) is necessary in rethinking the approach to the curriculum that separates the things learned from the way we learn.

Model of teacher learning in schools

Different models of teacher development and change have been proposed and debated in the past 30 years, in addition to the critical features of the necessary conditions for effective teacher learning outlined in the section above. We propose a model called Planning, Experimenting, and Reflecting (PER), which encompass all essential features of effective teacher learning that engages teachers in a series of spirally cyclical actions of planning, experimenting, and reflecting on the pedagogical innovations in the school setting. Embedded in this PER model is our futuristic view of the role of schools as a learning community for students and teachers. Table 10.1 summarizes the key activities at each stage of the cycle.

Figure 10.1 depicts the holistic strategy underlying this model of engineering changes among teachers.

Table 10.1 A 3-stage model of teacher Planning, Implementation, and Reflection curriculum practices (PIR model)

Stage	Aims	Teacher Activities
Planning Stage	To identify a goal for innovation	SWOT, Whole School Conference, Action Planning Meetings, Collaborative Lesson Preparation Meetings, Production of Materials
Implementation Stage	To put the plan in action	Trialing, Peer Observation and Evaluation
Reflection Stage	To review actions and plan for future actions	Post Observation Conference, Completion of Feedback Sheets

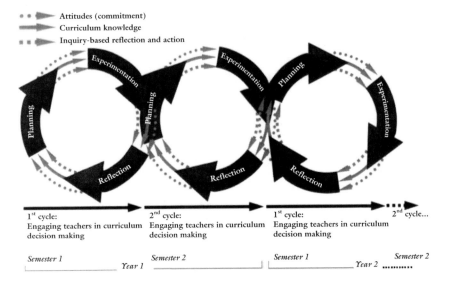

Figure 10.1 Re-conceptualizing school-based models of developing teacher curriculum leadership for life long education

Source: Law, E.H.F., Galton, M., & Wan, S.W.Y. (2010). Distributed curriculum leadership in action: A Hong Kong case study. *Educational Management Administration & Leadership, 38*, 286. Figure 10.1.

Methodology for analysis

Different models or frameworks have been proposed to understand the process of knowledge creation and its realization in human practice. These models are derived fundamentally from different conceptions on human learning. The two most influential models are the Piagetian and Vygotskian models of human learning. The former focuses on the cognitive transformation of an object of learning being assimilated from external sources (internalization) to the realization of that object of learning in actual human activities in response to various types of stimulations and challenges to maintain a state equilibrium psychologically (Piaget, 1953; Vygotsky, 1978). The latter model emphasizes on the socio-cultural aspects of human learning and the functions of the various types of "artifacts" in mediating the effectiveness and nature of the object of human learning (Engestrom, 1987, 1990, 1992, 1994, 1999a, 1999b; Gee, Michaels, & O'Connor, 1992; Yamagata-Lynch, 2010). Both models have generated many sub-models of human learning found in various types of human practices (Lave & Wenger, 1991). We focus on Engestrom's activity theory, particularly on the model of expansive learning cycles based on the social nature of human practices, to specify the functions of conflicts and tensions embedded in human practices in generating the needs (objects) for the search for new solutions (Engestrom, 1987). The functions of various types of human artifacts, such as symbols and

Engaging teachers in reflective practice   203

tools, in the achievement of the object mediate the process and the realization of the object within the activity system, which could be a team of teachers with a specific organizational goal or any other human organization. This study used the key concepts of "expansive learning cycles," "mediation," and "artifacts," in the analysis of the data to uncover key and critical features in the process of creating and generating human knowledge and shed light on a practical theory.

Structure of the project and data collection

The original project, called "Accelerating school based curriculum development," was initiated in 2004 and completed in 2006 in a Hong Kong elementary school. The goal of the project was to develop the curriculum leadership skills among elementary schoolteachers to enhance the capabilities of the schools and their teachers. The project was exploratory and design-based, and attempted to incorporate the key features from contemporary literature on teacher development and learning. The following is a summary of the key features of the effective models for teacher learning.

a   Actively engaging teachers in curriculum decision making processes (Hoban, 2002; Hopkins, 2007; Rogers, 1996; Rogers & Horrocks, 2010; Papa & Papa, 2011).
b   In the initial stage, teachers working in teams of colleagues preferably within their own subject teaching, before moving to a more collaborative and integrative approach across subjects in the school curriculum (Borko & Putnam, 1998; Gallimore, Ermeling, Saunders, & Goldenberg, 2009; Meirink, Imants, Meijer, & Verloop, 2010; Shulman & Shulman, 2004).
c   Teacher activities should be action-oriented with reflection on practical experiences on innovative pedagogical strategies (Calderhead, 1989; Elliott, 1991; Schön, 1983, 1987; Stringer, 2007).
d   A team approach based on "flattened" or "distributive" leadership that sufficiently allows the actualization of individual experimentation should be espoused (Chrispeels, Castillo, & Brown, 2000; Gronn, 2000, 2002; MacBeath, 2005; Spillane, 2006; Spillane, Halverson, & Diamond, 2001, 2004).

Following this line of thinking, the project organized the intervention activities in the schools in the following ways:

a   Various curriculum development teams were formed on the subject base of the participating teachers: three subject-based teams in the first project and two subject-based teams in the replication study. The purpose is to orient the focus of the activities and the contents of the discourses in communicative networking systems of each team (Bernstein, 1999; McCormick et al., 2011).
b   Each team was composed of teachers with various backgrounds such as experience, age, and gender. The purpose is to recreate situations in which potential "information gap" would encourage exchanges and possibly create

204 *Activity theory and curriculum leadership*

tensions for problem solving (Groundwater-Smith & Campbell, 2010; Stein, Smith, & Silver, 1999).

c   Leadership was rotational, and therefore the effects of power types would affect the human relationship among members realized in the discourses of the meetings (Engestrom, 1999a, 1999b, 2001). This time, no external consultant from the education faculty was invited and hence, more internal interaction was expected without external intervention.

Data were collected in (number) meetings and through other methods. We obtained discourse data from the videotaped meetings, teacher and student interviews, videotaped practice lessons, and teacher-reflective journals. We analyze these data following the conceptual framework described above and use discourse analysis method in our analysis.

Objectives of the research

The purpose of the analysis is to highlight the critical features of knowledge creation in teacher-situated learning. In particular, this research aims to engage teachers in reflective practice on commonly used mathematics concepts.

Description of the process: analysis

The data are analyzed according to the phases in the expansion cycle of learning proposed by Engestrom.

First step: stages of knowledge creation (questioning, challenging, criticizing, and rejecting)

Initially, the consultant questioned the traditional wisdom and practice of educators and teachers, arguing with simple logic that the key issue is on the learning content and not on the pedagogy because mathematics educators have been discussing many kinds of methods of learning for many years. In the extract below, the consultant (Extract 1) clarified the issues, identified the fundamental problem, established the direction of the discussion, and therefore clarified the object of the activity system.

Consultant: We have no answer, we sit together now to discuss, the pedagogy is not important but the content issue, generally people would respond the emphasis is on the content, not talking about the method, if we have problems with the methods, people have talked about all these long time ago, mathematics has been well established for many years, we all talked about all methods, if we are involved in methods, we have difficulties.

(Literal translation: reading 0.30–1:15, co-planning meeting of the second innovation cycle, 12 April 2005)

The key features of this stage are the ongoing processes of challenging the traditional practice and rejecting aspects of the accepted practice.

> Most importantly, based on your years of experiences, identify what is the real problem of learning with the students. For example, you talked about the comparison of fraction, we then had to think what is our priority to establish among students, afterwards, we decide what activities to play, without the clear concept of the object of learning, we ask students to fold the papers, divide something, these are superficial, after play, nothing gains. No concept is established among students, if the project leader Miss Wan does not specify what we do, we shall plan and decide freely . . .
> (Literal translation: reading 1:20–1:35, co-planning meeting of the second innovation cycle, 12April 2005)

Second step: analyzing the problem through historical-genetic and actual empirical approaches

This time, the consultant resorts to the historical power of experience among the participating teachers, establishing the groundwork for moving the focus of the exploration of the learning issue to a mathematical problem in the curriculum, that of identifying the real object of learning in the mathematics curriculum. This "search" for the object of learning becomes the real object in the activity system established by the consultant and constitutes the participating teachers. In activity theory, Engestrom (1999b, p.381) suggests four types of artifacts that serve as meditational functions in the process of achieving the object of the activity system. These four types of artifacts can be identified in Table 10.2, which shows the meeting discourse.

In the first extract, the "What" object indicates that the realization of the object of the activity system among teachers is the search for the focus of the learning content for students. In the second and third extracts, the consultant diagnoses and explains the potential properties of the learning content that shapes the direction of the "object" of the activity system but also guides and directs processes and procedures of the activity system in "search" of the learning content. In his analysis, he switches between historical and actual empirical dimensions. In the fourth extract, the focus of the discussion changes from the instructions given by the consultant on the search for the direction of the discussion to the practical issue of realizing the "search" (object of the activity system) in the meeting discourse. The object of the activity system is moved from "searching the focus of the discussion" to "finding out the object of learning for the students on the topic of fraction." This step moves the development of the object to a new dimension.

In the first stage, a change in the thematic development of the discourse of the meeting is observed:

1) The consultant decides on the protocol or direction of the following discussion.
2) The team follows the decision and engages in the exploration and identification of the focus of learning content (substantive).
3) Thereafter, the consultant re-orients the reflection on the relationship between pedagogical strategies and the focus of learning content.

206 *Activity theory and curriculum leadership*

Table 10.2 Four types of artifacts

Use of four types of artifacts in mediating the achievement of the object of the activity system	Extract	Position
First: "What" Object	"Methods are not important but the learning content, the content first in our search"	(Literal translation: reading 4.12–4:55, co-planning meeting of the second innovation cycle, 12April 2005)
Second and third: "Why" and "how" Objects	"You teach the value of fractions from the first lesson, before that, you have already taught about fractions? Then why do you want to choose to teach comparing the value of fractions?"	(Literal translation: reading 2:25–2:45, co-planning meeting of the second innovation cycle, 12April 2005)
Fourth: "Where" Object	"We are not talking about what methods to use, but a "concept" of learning, can each one of you talk about your view first?"	(Literal translation: reading 3:15–3:55, co-planning meeting of the second innovation cycle, 12April 2005)

The "How" artifact (Theme 1) mediates the discussion on clarifying and identifying the object of the activity system, which serves as a guide for the discussion. The "What" artifact (Theme 2) mediates the discussion on clarifying and
identifying the properties of the learning object for students. In the process of
analyzing the situational issues with the learning object, the "historical-genetic"
and "actual-empirical" approaches are used. In fact, the consultant clarified the
misconception and pointed out that the real problem should not be on the pedagogical strategies employed but rather on the identification of the learning content, representing a misplacement of the real learning focus (Excerpt n. X).

> Before we calculate the fraction, but with comparison, it seems difficult.
> When students compare fractions with different (not common) denomina-
> tors, you normally give them worksheets with blocks. I would like to ask you
> what you did before you asked them to do the worksheets with blocks. Why
> did you want them to fill the blocks in the worksheet? Each of us talks about
> how you taught the concept of fractions. Are your methods the same? 006
> (Literal translation: reading 4:25–5:35, co-planning meeting of the second
> innovation cycle, 12 April 2005)

In this excerpt, the historical events (historical-genetic) on teaching the topic
on fractions and empirical experiences of using worksheets (actual-empirical) are

Engaging teachers in reflective practice 207

used as the bases for achieving the object of the activity system, which is the identification of the real learning object in learning the values of fractions decided in Theme 1.

Third step: modeling the new solution

The discussion on deciding the focus of the learning content continues. However, the discussion switches between the application of appropriate methods and the strategies in teaching fractions (using empty blocks, dividing a cake, counting apples, folding paper, cutting pizza, and categorization), the conceptual issues on-learning fractions, and its concomitant concepts ("one," "whole," values of fractions, equal division, and equal fractions). The tension between the consultant and other n. members of the team (how many?) who disagree on the pedagogical strategies and content knowledge continues (how many?).

The following excerpt (number X) illustrates the tension between the consultant and the teachers on deciding the focus of the learning content.

Consultant: . . . dividing requires many methods . . . you may ask pupils to use their own methods to equally divide something . . . you could have some variations on the same learning concept . . . you should highlight the same concept with various methods, this helps, for example, giving students ten pieces and ask them to divide among five children, this is about concept learning.

Teacher S: We do not have time . . . can let them try to fold . . .

Consultant: . . . must think about how to help students to establish concepts . . .

Teacher M: dividing a cake . . . how to divide . . .

Teacher S: Let them divide, and ask them to put them on whiteboard about how to divide . . . then they learn the concept . . .

(Literal translation: reading 42:25–43:35, co-planning meeting of the second innovation cycle, 12 April 2005)

In this excerpt, the teachers in the team switch from the focus of identifying the real learning content for the lesson to the methodological issues on learning fractions.

The solution becomes the following:

1 The team decides not to teach the values of fractions with different denominators. They are too complicated for students without firm foundation on various basic concepts needed prior to learning the values of fractions.

2 The team decides to retreat to the teaching of the basic concepts of fractions in the traditional practice. This decision is a compromised solution to the real issue of identifying the learning content, which was established at the beginning of the meeting in Theme 1.

The perspectives of the participating members of the team shape and mediate the course of the discussion, reconstructing the initial proposal by the consultant.

208 *Activity theory and curriculum leadership*

The conflicting views on the object of the activity system in both sides continue to persist. The emergence of an initiative (focus of the learning content) has undergone a series of changes in its process of development and ended in a compromised form without a change in its original nature.

Fourth step: examining the new model

The second planning meeting confirmed that the focus of the learning content is on learning fractions and its basic concepts. The development of the initiative proposed by the consultant, that is, that the problem of learning is on the misconceptions on the learning content, ascends from an abstract idea (knowledge content) to concrete ideas in learning fractions (knowledge content in concrete forms in mathematics). However, this solution is a retreat by the team to the more fundamental learning issues on fractions. The following excerpt (N. X) illustrates the nature of the discussion.

Consultant: Do you give them examples how to do division in equal proportion? For example, slicing a cake diagonally? Sometimes, pupils do not feel they are of equal share?
Teacher I: Let them observe more, ask them which one is of equal share.
Teacher G: Or we can focus on two equal shares?
Teacher K: more is better.
Consultant: Regardless of the number of divisions, the sum is one.
                  (Literal translation: reading 30:15–32:24, co-planning meeting of the second innovation cycle, 25 April 2005)

This excerpt illustrates that the team examined the compromised solution to teaching the basic concepts of fractions to students.

Fifth step: implementing the new solution

This stage has two sets of data: two lessons and two videotaped practice lessons; they illustrate the realization of the compromised solution in the form of lesson plans and practice lessons.

LESSONS

Two lesson plans were designed by two teachers in the team based on the agreed learning content (basic concepts of fractions):

1)   The first lesson plan demonstrates the key concepts of fractions (for example, what is a fraction? How is it expressed as a number?). In consolidating learning, the students are asked to use a piece of paper and divide it into equal parts. Coloring a part shows the meaning of a fraction in concrete terms. A rectangular shape is given, and students are grouped to design a method to divide the shape into equal parts.

2) In the second lesson, students (how many students) are asked to divide a sheet of paper into two parts. Thereafter, two other students are invited to choose one piece, and each will be awarded a present according to the "size" of the paper. The class is asked whether this action is fair. The class responds negatively. This lesson shows the importance of equal sharing. Thereafter, the teacher asks the students to color one piece and to show the meaning of fractions. In practice activities, students are also given different shapes of paper to design equal divisions. More activities of this nature followed to complete the lesson.

In the two practice lessons, both teachers used different pedagogical strategies, such as folding a piece of paper into equal and unequal parts to teach children the basic concepts of fractions. However, the first teacher did not relate coherently the teaching of "less than one" and subsequent activities on "dividing a piece of paper into equal shares." The second teacher had similar problems with conceptual issues of "fractions." She asked a student to cut a piece of paper into two unequal halves, which were then exchanged for presents of unequal sizes to show the functional value of "equal parts"; to her, the conclusion was that unequal parts for different students mean inequality.

Sixth step: reflecting on the process

After the two practice lessons were conducted, a reflection meeting was conducted on 19 May 2005. In the meeting, the tension arose between the consultant, who insisted that the key mediating artifact in determining the quality of teaching and learning is the lack of clarity on the learning content on "fractions," and the teachers, who were overwhelmed with the issue of pedagogical variations. This conflict in "perspectives" of the two parties persisted, and the practice lessons did not appear to have assisted them in moving from their well-established beliefs on effective learning. The following is an excerpt of the consultant illustrating his beliefs on effective learning in mathematical concepts.

Consultant: You give details in the lesson plan, but you did not teach clearly the concept, you use "about half," or "less than half," and therefore, the students follow your pattern of expressing these concepts. However, you insist on accuracy later and this distract the focus of the learning content . . . we must ask what you want the students to learning from these "activities" of folding paper etc.
(Literal translation: reading 11:23–12:45, reflection meeting of the second innovation cycle, 19 May 2005)

The consultant's line of thinking on the distinction between pedagogy and content knowledge has not changed during the entire process of the PER. Interestingly, the responses of the teachers detracted from the perspectives of the consultant. The defense mechanism is realized in the interactional mode of

210 *Activity theory and curriculum leadership*

discourse, which moves away from the real substance of the transactional mode. For example, *"Breakdown of computers in class, limitations of the paper, my class was astonished to see the video camera. They would not be so quiet in class,"* or eliminating the persuasiveness of his arguments.

Consultant: . . . Sometimes, you say the same "size" but then you say "the same shape," therefore what do you refer to when you say "equal fraction." Is it about size or shape? Normally, when two shapes overlap exactly, they are of equal share. After being divided into eight parts, the shape of each part changes. The students could not understand.

Teacher G: *They are ONLY primary three.*

(Literal translation: reading 20:13–22:05, reflection meeting of the second innovation cycle, 19 May 2005)

The conflicting perspectives between the two parties are clear.

Seventh step: consolidating the new practice

During this process, from the planning and experimenting stages, the "solution" is not concrete but rather a "strategy" of emphasizing a perspective of teacher action and student learning in classroom pedagogy. This "solution" becomes the object of the activity system in the early stage of its development. This "solution" is transformed into a function as the mediating "artifact" in shaping the new second activity system during its development process. However, the vagueness of this solution allows flexibility and individual manipulation on the part of the teachers. What new knowledge is gained by the teachers or generated collectively by this team in the process?

We establish learning by considering the following supplementary data analyzed through discourse analysis: the reflections of teachers on teacher-reflection journals after the meeting, teacher interviews before and after practice lessons, and student interviews before and after practice lessons.

a) *Teacher journals after the reflection meeting:* One teacher wrote that she learned to teach "equal fractions" and various mathematical concepts related to fractions using different approaches. Another teacher wrote that she learned of the possibility that teachers misunderstood the conceptual complexity of certain key concepts that may have looked simple to them. She also learned the variations in terms of pedagogical strategies in relation to the abilities and uniqueness of different classes. The third teacher wrote that she learned how to help students to establish "concepts." We can consider the teachers' awareness of the issues on the conceptual clarity in the focus of the learning content, as shown in the journal writings (being conscious), while these issues have been implicitly "mediated" or "rejected" in the negotiation processes.

Engaging teachers in reflective practice 211

b) *Teacher interviews before and after practice lessons:* The teacher interviews are important sources of data used to reveal whether evidence can be found in the "perspectives" of each individual teacher on the key issue, that of the conflicting views on the role of pedagogy and learning content of the consultant on the one side and the teachers on the other side, because the "compromised solution" is rooted in the tension between these two conflicting views in achieving the object of the activity system. Some teachers' cases are shown in the following.

Teacher S, the team leader, categorically expressed his views on the function of the consultant in being assertive and probing. He uses the word "inch" to label the critical and uncompromising style of the consultant in "questioning" and "challenging" the traditional practice of teachers. The message in the interview also reveals a teacher dimension on maintaining social coherence in the team, indicating that the "style" of the consultant violated this important interactional principle among teachers. However, the mediating function of the perceived intellectually superior status of the consultant forced the teachers to submit. After the practice lesson, his view on the role of pedagogy and learning content in effective learning and teaching moved to another stage: he discovered that students could be very creative beyond their imagination when teachers are forced to vary their pedagogical approaches. He is also aware of the importance of mastery of the concepts in effective learning.

Teacher M, the panel head, stated that she could not imagine the collaborative lesson preparation would lead to the emergence of many creative ideas among teachers. However, she also explicitly expressed her concerns on the theoretical perspectives to the issue of teaching fractions. This concern may be her response to the consultant's orientation toward issues on the focus of the learning content. She is also well aware that different pedagogical approaches may lead to a mastery of different learning contents in mathematics. Her views on the issue of learning fractions appear to be aligned closely with that of the consultant. However, no evidence to establish a relationship between the two could be found.

The interview with Teacher M has shown that she is well aware of the issue on the learning content and the relationship between pedagogical variations and learning outcomes.

Teacher M: . . . indeed, teachers can discard the traditional practice and views . . . in particular I taught so many years and I had my own practice, after this experience, I discover we can take different views and approaches. Or some approaches have never been considered and imagined by me . . . I would change myself . . .

(Literal translation 004, reading 5:13–6:07, individual interview with Teacher M, May 2005)

212   Activity theory and curriculum leadership

Teacher O is one of the two teachers who implemented the newly revised lesson plan with the focus on the "compromised solution" – reorienting the focus of the practice lesson on the mastery of the basic concepts of fractions. In the interview before the practice lesson, she was well aware of the problem with the conceptual issues that were raised by the consultant. In the interview after the practice lesson, she confessed that she learned that she should stimulate student thinking by asking open-ended questions in her teacher training program, but she simply forgot to switch to the "espoused theory" and instead unknowingly followed the "theory-in-practice" (Paraphrase from the original 002, reading 3:09–3:52, *individual interview with Teacher O, May 2005*). She is also conscious and open about the function of the consultant, who was an outsider with little concern for the socio-political relationships among teachers who knew each other very well. "Maintaining a positive social relationship in the team becomes a priority in our discourse" (Paraphrase from the original 003, reading 6:17–6:58). Her reflections in the interview focused mainly on pedagogical strategies until her last monologue.

> *Teacher O:*   I would find examples from daily life about the concept of "less than one," using fractions or the other methods to express this concept . . . then we introduce the concept of equal fraction, distributing different shapes, asking them how they could divide them into four or eight equal shares . . . let them clarify their mind with some practice activities . . . the students failed to divide the shapes, they do not understand clearly, I should teach again in the next lesson.
>
> (Paraphrase from the original 008, reading 25:03–25:56)

She appreciated the opportunities to conduct peer observation, and became more aware of the problems that teachers faced.

Teacher G is another teacher who conducted the second practice lesson. Before the practice lesson, she was already aware of the problem with conceptual clarity in learning fractions (Paraphrase 001, reading 1:05–1:56).

After the practice lesson, the conceptual mastery is considered to be related to the pedagogical strategies used differently in the two practice lessons. One practice lesson adopted a traditional teacher discussion approach, whereas the other practice lesson adopted the activity approach, giving students the chance to fold different shapes of paper to move student conceptualization from concrete experiences to an abstract level of understanding the concepts of fractions (Paraphrase 001, reading 10:19–12:08). The students also attempted different types of "folding" without the teacher's instructions because the activity allowed students to adopt a new approach to a common task assigned by the teacher (Paraphrase 002, reading 12:19–13:07).

This step is essential because it relates to the real issue on the relationship between pedagogy and content knowledge, which is an appropriate sequence in learning a series of mathematical concepts on fractions (Shulman, 1986).

Engaging teachers in reflective practice   213

Student interviews before and after the practice lessons

In student interviews before the practice lesson, the 3D class students stated that they appreciated the pedagogical variations in Teacher O's lessons. They found these variations to be interesting and motivating. When asked about the practice lesson, they had the following to say:

Interviewer:	What did you learn in the practice lesson?
A student:	Fraction, percentage.
Interviewer:	Fraction, denominator, nominator.
A student:	These concepts have not been taught.
A student:	Square, histogram.
A student:	I made a mistake, one over two, I colored two, instead of one half
A student:	then I colored them all, and no fraction, we had fraction with circle.

(Paraphrase 002, reading 12:32–14:08)

This interview categorically shows that the students had a real problem with fractions and with the various activities and actions in the practice lesson. Some students had difficulty finding links and meanings among various types of actions and learning activities assigned by the teacher. In another class (3C), the students expressed their preference for learning activities. They liked games. After the practice lesson, some students expressed having difficulties in understanding fractions.

A student: I do not understand fraction and division bar, because a denominator carries a numerator and then one is "bigger" than the others.

(Paraphrase 003, reading 4:48–5:32)

A student: The triangle, folding, but not many students are able to fold successful, only a few were successful.

(Paraphrase 004, reading 15:42–16:13)

The interviewed students indicated that the two practice lessons were far from being successful in "teaching" the concepts of fraction. This observation could be aligned possibly with the concern expressed by the consultant stating that the real problem of learning lies in the conceptual clarity of the learning content instead of pedagogical variations that both practice lessons had shown.

Discussion

Knowledge creation models in teacher-situated learning argue that the engagement process allows the emergence of new ideas and innovations (Cochran-Smith & Lytle, 1999; Paavola et al., 2004). The application of the expansive learning cycle and key concepts of activity theory in the analysis of data derived from a teacher leadership project represents our first attempt to uncover the layers of meanings in understanding the complexities of the emergence and development of new and innovative ideas in subject-based curriculum development teams in schools. Three observations are significant to the theories of knowledge creation. First, the recreation of situated learning opportunities in teams shows the emergence of the compromised solution (new ideas to teachers) embedded in planning meetings, which were filled with tensions and conflicting views "softly mediated" by the team's efforts to maintain social coherence, instead of the search for real problems with effective learning. The divergence in views on the identification of the focus of the learning problem between the consultant and the rest of the team members highlight vividly the wide gap in "perspectives" between the two camps. The "compromised solution" was attempted in two practice lessons without significant success in leading students to master the key concepts of fractions despite the use of various pedagogical strategies by teachers. Second, the failure of the two practice lessons in achieving their pedagogical goal in the clarification of the concepts on fractions, in particular with the teachers being aware of the alternative approaches used by some students in folding paper, allows teachers to be aware of the priorities for learning content in effective learning. Third, the claim that knowledge creation models lead to emergence of new ideas and innovations should be qualified with due consideration for the effects of mediating artifacts, such as "divergence in perspectives," "priority of maintaining social coherence in teams," and "historical-genetic experiences embedded in traditional practice" on shaping the form and substance of the "newly compromised solution." Fourth, the effect of the Asian culture that prioritizes maintaining social coherence was apparent in the reflection meeting. The dominance of the interactional mode of discourse indicates that the transactional function has been subsumed and mediated mildly. However, when the priority for social coherence disappears, as in the case in individual teacher interviews, the preference for transactional mode reappears among all four teachers. The interviews explicitly show the reflective and apologetic tone of the teachers in recognition of their inadequacy in teaching the conceptual distinctions among fraction-related concepts in the practice lessons. This awareness of conceptual issues in the learning content and the appropriate pedagogical manipulations may become the achieved object of the activity system in the innovation project. This empirical study, with the assistance of the activity theory, illustrates that the complexity of knowledge creation models in teacher-situated learning is mediated (or facilitated or constrained) negatively or positively by various artifacts such as "cultural preference over social coherence" (the "How" artifact), "divergence in perspectives" (the "What" artifact), "recognition of issues with conceptual clarity" (the "Where" artifact), and "student failures in folding paper and students' new initiatives" (the "Why" artifact). A good reason exists for educators to revisit the established procedures and practices of these knowledge creation models in organizing teacher development and learning activities.

References

Benham, M., & Murakami-Ramalho, E. (2010). Engaging in educational leadership: The generosity of spirit. *International Journal of Leadership in Education, 13*(1), 77–91.

Bernstein, B. (1999). Vertical and horizontal discourse: An essay. *British Journal of Sociology of Education, 20*(2), 157–173.

Borko, H. (2004). Professional development and teacher learning: Mapping the terrain. *Educational Researcher, 33*(8), 3–15.

Borko, H., & Putnam, R. (1998). Professional development and reform-based teaching: Introduction to theme issue. *Teaching and Teacher Education, 14*, 1–3.

Calderhead, J. (1989). Reflective teaching and teacher education. *Teaching and Teacher Education, 5*(1), 43–51.

Campbell, A., & Groundwater-Smith, S. (Eds.). (2010).*Connecting inquiry and professional learning in education: International perspectives and practical solutions.* London: Routledge.

Chan, C.K.K., & Pang, M.F. (2006). Editorial: Teacher collaboration in learning communities. *Teaching Education, 17*, 1–5.

Chrispeels, J.H., Castillo, S., & Brown, J. (2000). School leadership teams: A process model of team development. *School Effectiveness and School Improvement, 11*(1), 20–56.

Cochran-Smith, M., & Lytle, S.L. (1999). Relationships of knowledge and practice: Teacher learning in communities. *Review of Research in Education, 24*, 249–305.

Elliott, J. (1991). *Action research for educational change.* Buckingham: Open University Press.

Engestrom, Y. (1987). *Learning by expanding: An activity-theoretical approach to developmental research.* Helsinki: Orienta-Konsultit.

Engestrom, Y. (1990). *Learning, working and imagining: Twelve studies in activity theory.* Helsinki: Orienta-Konsultit.

Engestrom, Y. (1992). *Interactive expertise: Studies in distributed working intelligence* (Research Bulletin 83). Helsinki, Finland: University of Helsinki, Department of Education.

Engestrom, Y. (1994). Teachers as collaborative thinkers: Activity-theoretical study of an innovative teacher team. In I. Carlgren, G. Handal, & S. Vaage (Eds.), *Teachers' minds and actions: Research on teachers' thinking and practice* (pp. 43–61). London: Falmer.

Engestrom, Y. (1999a). Expansive visibilization of work: An activity-theoretical perspective. *Computer Supported Cooperative Work, 8*, 63–93.

Engestrom, Y. (1999b). Innovative learning in work teams: Analyzing cycles of knowledge creation in practice. In Y. Engestrom, R. Miettinen, & R. Punanmaki (Eds.), *Perspectives in activity theory* (pp. 377–404). Cambridge: Cambridge University Press.

Engestrom, Y. (2001). Expansive learning at work: Toward an activity theoretical reconceptualization. *Journal of Education and Work, 14*(1), 133–156.

Gallimore, R., Ermeling, B.A., Saunders, W.M., & Goldenberg, C. (2009). Moving the learning of teaching closer to practice: Teacher education implications of school-based inquiry teams. *The Elementary School Journal, 109*(5), 537–553.

Garet, M., Porter, A., Desimone, L., Birman, B., & Yoon, K.S. (2001). What makes professional development effective? Results for a national sample of teachers. *American Educational Research Journal, 38*(4), 915–945.

216 *Activity theory and curriculum leadership*

Gee, J., Michaels, S., & O'Connor, M. (1992). Discourse analysis. In M. LeCompte, W. Millney, & J. Preissle (Eds.), *The handbook of qualitative research in education* (pp. 227–291). San Diego, CA: Academic Press.

Gronn, P. (2000). Distributed properties: A new architecture for leadership. *Educational Management and Administration, 28*(3), 317–338.

Gronn, P. (2002). Distributed leadership as a unit of analysis. *Leadership Quarterly, 13*, 423–451.

Groundwater-Smith, S., & Campbell, A. (2010). Joining the dots: Connecting inquiry and professional learning. In A. Campbell & S. Groundwater-Smith (Eds.), *Connecting inquiry and professional learning in education: International perspectives and practical solutions* (pp. 200–206). London: Routledge.

Hargreaves, A., & Shirley, D. (2008). Beyond standardization: Powerful new principles for improvement. *Phi Delta Kappan, 90*(2), 135–143.

Hargreaves, A., & Shirley, D. (2009). *The fourth way*. Thousand Oaks, CA: Corwin Press.

Hoban, G.F. (2002). *Teacher learning for educational change: A systems thinking approach*. Buckingham, Philadelphia: Open University Press.

Hopkins, D. (2007). *Every school a great school: Realising the potential of system leadership*. Maidenhead: Open University Press.

Hord, S.M. (2009). Professional learning communities. *Journal of Staff Development, 30*(1), 40–43.

Hord, S.M., & Sommers, W.A. (2007). *Leading professional learning communities: Voices from research and practice*. Thousand Oaks, CA: Corwin Press.

Knight, S., & Wiseman, D. (2005). Lessons learned from a research synthesis on the effects of teachers' professional development on culturally diverse students. In H. Waxman & K. Tellez (Eds.), *Improving teacher quality for English language learners* (pp. 71–98). Hillsdale, NJ: Lawrence Erlbaum.

Lave, J., & Wenger, E. (1991). *Situated learning: Legitimate peripheral participation*. Cambridge: Cambridge University Press.

Lee, J.C.K., & Feng, S. (2007). Mentoring support and the professional development of beginning teachers: A Chinese perspective. *Mentoring & Tutoring: Partnership in Learning, 15*(3), 243–262.

MacBeath, J. (2005). Leadership as distributed: A matter of practice. *School Leadership and Management, 25*(4), 349–366.

McCormick, R., Fox, A., Carmichael, P., & Procter, R. (2011). *Researching and understanding educational networks*. London: Routledge.

Meirink, J.A., Imants, J., Meijer, P.C., & Verloop, N. (2010). Teacher learning and collaboration in innovative teams. *Cambridge Journal of Education, 40*(2), 161–181.

Nunes, T., Schliemann, A., & Carreher, D. (1993). *Street mathematics and school mathematics*. Cambridge: University Press.

Paavola, S., Lipponen, L., & Hakkarainen, K. (2004). Models of innovative knowledge communities and three metaphors of learning. *Review of Educational Research, 74*(4), 557–576.

Papa, R., & Papa, J. (2011). Leading adult learners: Preparing future leaders and professional development of those they lead. In J. Papa (Ed.), *Technology leadership for school improvement* (pp. 91–108). London: Sage.

Piaget, J. (1953). *The origins of intelligence in children*. London: Routledge and Kegan Paul.

Rogers, A. (1996). *Teaching adults* (2nd ed.). Milton Keynes: Open University Press.

Rogers, A., & Horrocks, N. (2010). *Teaching adults.* Milton Keynes: Open University Press.

Schön, D. (1983). *The reflective practitioner: How professionals think in action.* London: Temple Smith.

Schön, D. (1987). *Educating the reflective practitioner: Toward a new design for teaching and learning in the professions.* San Francisco, CA: Jossey-Bass.

Shulman, L.S. (1986). Those who understand: Knowledge growth in teaching. *Educational Researcher, 15*(2), 4–14.

Shulman, L.S., & Shulman, J.H. (2004). How and what teachers learn: A shifting perspective. *Journal of Curriculum Studies, 36*(2), 257–271.

Spillane, J.P. (2006). *Distributed leadership.* San Francisco, CA: Jossey-Bass.

Spillane, J.P., Halverson, R., & Diamond, J.B. (2001). Investigating school leadership practice: A distributed perspective. *Educational Researcher, 30*(3), 23–28.

Spillane, J.P., Halverson, R., & Diamond, J.B. (2004). Towards a theory of leadership practice: A distributed perspective. *Journal of Curriculum Studies, 36*(1), 3–34.

Stahl, A. (2008). *New York State Grade 7 Math Test.* Hauppauge, NY: Barron's Educational Series.

Stein, M.K., Smith, M.S., & Silver, E.A. (1999). The development of professional developers: Learning to assist teachers in new settings in new ways. *Harvard Educational Review, 69*(3), 237–269.

Stoll, L. (2009). Connecting learning communities: Capacity building for systemic change. In A. Hargreaves, A. Lieberman, M. Fullan, & D. Hopkins (Eds.), *Second international handbook of educational change* (pp. 469–484). The Netherlands: Springer.

Stoll, L., & Louis, K.S. (Eds.). (2007). *Professional learning communities: Divergence, depth and dilemmas.* London: Open University Press.

Stringer, E.T. (2007). *Action research: A handbook for practitioners.* Newbury Park, CA: Sage.

Vygotsky, L.S. (1978). *Mind in society: The development of higher psychological processes.* Cambridge, MA: Harvard University Press.

Walker, C.L., Edstam, T., & Stone, K. (2007). *Two years, three kinds of educators, and four schools: Improving education for English language learners.* Paper presented at the annual meeting of the American Educational Research Association, Chicago, IL.

Yamagata-Lynch, L.C. (2010). *Activity systems analysis methods: Understanding complex learning environments.* New York: Springer.

Zeichner, K. (2005). Becoming a teacher educator. *Teaching and Teacher Education, 21*, 117–124.

11 Conclusion

SBCD has been with us for over 40 years, and distributed leadership has become popular in the last 15 years. However, the original form of SBCD lacks sophistication in structure and process. The concepts and principles embedded in the theory and the practices of distributed leadership are complementary to the practice of SBCD. Both can serve as a powerful agent of change in developing curriculum leadership among school teachers. The following sections summarize the experiences and arguments derived from the empirical studies reported in the previous chapters.

Re-conceptualizing distributed leadership

Diverse definitions of distributed leadership have been proposed, and having a consensus about what distributed leadership should look like is hardly possible. However, the origin of the emergence of its popularity among researchers and educators remains clear; educators and researchers have been less confident about the effectiveness of central agencies in delivering educational innovations and changes. Decentralization has become the trend of educational thoughts in policy and practice. Therefore, the shift in leadership practices, which are led by solo and concentrated leadership style of positional leaders to leadership practices that are widely contributed by formal and informal leaders and members of the institutions, becomes significant.

The diverse understanding of "leadership" and "distributed leadership" arises because of the following misunderstandings. First, "leadership" is closely related to the action word "lead," which requires a subject "who" and an object "what." This is a question about "who leads what." Thus, "who" must be a person who has the positional power and authority to lead an institution or a group of "followers" to achieve a task or a mission. "Leadership" must be about "someone in the authority or in the position that leads another person or a group of followers" to achieve a task or mission. Therefore, early research work in schools has focused on studying the characters or the styles of principals or other positional leaders and their impact on the culture, mechanisms, and student learning of institutions. However, with the passage of time, this view of individuals or heroic leaders has been considered inadequate to capture the complexity of the enactment of leadership practices in contexts such as schools. This new approach sees leaders as part of a complex relationship between leaders and followers in contexts. The heroic version of leadership practices has neglected the functional roles of followers in the achievements of tasks and the fulfillment of roles and responsibilities. The heroic view of positional leaders has neglected the reciprocal and mutual influences that each party has exerted themselves in the interactions and negotiation processes in the completion of roles and responsibilities. The latter aspect of leadership has interested many scholars in the last 15 years in leadership studies.

The lack of consensus in understanding distributed leadership is caused by the diverse understanding and interests of the concept of distributed leadership among major scholars who published substantially on this topic. Hallinger does not have a clear definition of distributed leadership, which is equivalent to other concepts, such as shared leadership and delegated leadership. Gronn sees leadership as emergent properties in work-related interactions and a network of mutual dependence, whereas Spillane views leadership as a form of social influence in interactions.

The lack of consensus in understanding leadership and distributed leadership in particular is evident in the empirical investigations and policies in the last ten years. Chapter 2 has a detailed review on the current literature, which shows that the majority of publications reports on co-principal, delegated responsibilities from principals, and co-leaders. The practices focus on "individual plus individual." The other projects and investigations focus on the principal-led leadership teams or teams of teachers. All the investigations and leadership practices are similar to leadership practices that focus on solo or concentrated leadership, which are expanded versions of a heroic view of leadership.

A new approach to leadership provides an alternative and sees leadership as a community of practices in which individuals contribute to its ultimate achievement. Ranks, status, and roles are clear. However, they merge in interactions and processes among members to achieve tasks and responsibilities.

The findings of the projects have illustrated the practices and effects of this new approach and show how leadership properties emerge in a form of leadership practices, which are collaborative and flattened in status. The findings also show that leadership styles of positional leaders mediate the mechanisms that restrict or allow the emergence of leadership properties among members in curriculum development teams. Moreover, the emergence of innovative ideas is mediated by the political and ideological considerations among members of curriculum development teams. All empirical studies reported in this book show the need to re-conceptualize leadership, leadership studies, and distributed leadership in ways that capture the essence of leadership as forms of "communities of professional practices" with a moral commitment to the goals and mission of institutions.

Curriculum leadership functions

Literature on leadership studies has listed a number of leadership functions, which are "instruct," "consult," "delegate," "facilitate," and "neglect." These action

220 *Activity theory and curriculum leadership*

words all require a subject "who," and an object "what" or "whom." These leadership functions are exclusively the responsibilities of those who assume positional leadership roles that allow them to instruct or delegate someone to complete said tasks. The findings in the studies reported in this book show that curriculum leadership functions are diverse. They include "guiding exploration," "re-orienting the direction of the discussions," "inviting contributions from all team members," and "reflecting on personal experiences." Studies found that members without positional authority exert influence in the direction of the discussion and in making the final decision. The findings also show that ordinary members are able to initiate new topics of discussions, change the focus of the discussions, and decide the outcomes of the discussion. These initiations exert critical influences on the outcomes of interactions and show that spaces for individual leadership practices are widely dispersed given the collaborative leadership style of the positional leaders. Therefore, the enacted leadership functions are widely distributed among members of the institutions.

Effects of distributed leadership in curriculum development teams

Studies found the indirect impact of distributed leadership upon student learning. However, the concept of distributed leadership in these studies is loosely defined and includes shared leadership and delegated leadership. Distributed leadership allows teacher engagement in a wide range of leadership functions. Therefore, empirical investigations show that distributed leadership has impact on teacher empowerment and the development of individual leadership capacity. The studies reported in this book present how leadership functions are enacted by a significant number of team members when teachers have less restrictions on participation and contributions in interactions. Therefore, distributed leadership practices serve as an agent of change and subsequent innovations in teacher empowerment and teacher curriculum leadership development. The SBCD mechanism and concept serve as an agential function in the development of teacher curriculum leadership. However, the ideological and cultural orientations between different parties in the curriculum development teams mediate the outcomes of the realization of the agential function of the SBCD mechanism and concepts.

A model of collaborative leadership in a distributed perspective

SBCD models have been proposed as structural mechanisms in the engineer of distributing curriculum leadership among teachers and have been regarded as change agents in the empowerment of teacher professional leadership. The SBCD models originated in Western democratic contexts and in countries where participatory democracy has been dominant. SBCD is a technical policy; hence, its proposal provides a general framework of procedure without detailed consideration about the effects of political, cultural, ideological, and leadership styles

Table 11.1 A summary of re-conceptualizing "distributed leadership" in curriculum leadership

	Collaborative Curriculum Leadership
Leadership style	Dispersed, flattened, delegated, democratic
Impact	Leadership functions and influence widely distributed among formal and informal members of an institution
Agential functions	Empowerment, development of potential leaders
Structural functions	Achieving institutional goals and missions
Discourse functions	Elaborated to allow emergence of leadership properties
Discourse patterns	Multi-directional and mutual reciprocal
Leadership functions	Initiations and contributions are widely distributed
Theoretical basis	"distributed cognition" and "activity theory" as conceptual lenses
Restrictions	Tensions between ideological orientations and pragmatic preferences among members of teams and institutions

Source: Created by author

upon the professional outcomes that SBCD has aimed at. The mediational functions of these factors, particularly in political and cultural milieu where power and hierarchical status dominate, have been neglected in the original formation of SBCD. The findings in the studies here all indicate that distributed leadership should be planned, designed, and evaluated while considering the complexity of the processes and interactions in its realization. A developmental perspective to view the relationship between solo and distributed is equally problematic when solo and distributed leadership, which are seen as a dichotomy of two extremes, are found to be misleading. "Dichotomy" and "developmental process" ignore the fact that both individual and collaborative leadership are necessary components in the effective realization of the mission and goals of an institution, which aim at bringing about change and innovations in pedagogy and curriculum. The experiences embedded in the studies over the years show that a sophistical design in the research on distributed leadership is necessary to show various forms of distributed leadership practices. An appropriate design can also show reliable effects on teacher and student learning. Hence, SBCD with a distributed perspective is an alternative for educators and educational researchers.

I propose "collaborative leadership" as an alternative to "distributed leadership" in developing curriculum leadership based on teams in schools, one of which is couched within our daily language of understanding and communication, and the other is likely to eliminate the confusion that the word "distribute" may cause for readers. Table 11.1 summarizes the essential elements in our understanding of "collaborative leadership" derived from our literature review as well as our empirical investigations reported in this book.

Index

Aas, M. 11
Abrahasen, H. 11
action research 57–8
activity theory: application of 180–1;
  distributed leadership and 11;
  expansive learning cycles 202;
  principles and analytical framework
  178–81
Adams, A. 99
Ahtaridou, E. 9
Anderson, S. 45, 137
Andrews, R. 129
Aspland, T. 46, 73, 117, 138
Atkin, M. 72, 116, 136
authoritarian leadership 33–4

Ball, D.L. 73, 115, 135, 138
Banks, M. 139
Beijaard, D. 155
Bell, B. 44
Benham, M. 153, 200
Bennett, N. 9
Bernstein, B. 203
Biggs, J. 65
Birman, B.F. 73, 74, 138, 153, 200
Black, P. 72, 116, 136
Blasé, J. 65, 66
Blitz, M.H. 13
Blom, S. 35
blurred leadership 38
Bolam, R. 99
Borko, H. 72, 80, 116, 136, 154,
  200, 203
Boyle, M. 142
Brabeck, M.M. 80
Britt, M.S. 49, 55, 116, 136
Brooker, R. 44, 46, 73, 117, 138, 183
Brown, J. 203
Bruner, J.S. 61

Bryant, D.A. 9, 19
Bullmaster, M.L. 129
Bunnell, T. 11
Bush, T. 11, 129
Buskey, F.C. 12

Calderhead, J. 203
Camburn, E. 148
Campbell, A. 153, 154, 200, 204
Campbell, T. 13
Carmichael, P. 153, 200
Carreher, D. 200
Carr, W. 44, 72, 116, 136, 182
Castillo, S. 203
Chan, C.K.K. 153, 200
Chen, D-T.V. 13
Chen, J. 9, 19
Chrispeels, J.H. 203
Cobb, C.D. 154
Cobb, V.L. 129
Cohen, D.K. 115, 135
Cohen, L. 118, 138
Coldren, A.F. 21
collaboration 59–60, 65
"collaborative leadership" 221
collective leadership 18
Collin, K. 9
"commognition" 201
communication pattern analysis 123–7,
  143–6
communicative networking patterns
  158–61
conflict issues 100–1
Conley, S. 135
consolidation 210–12
consultants 54, 79–84, 109, 128, 130,
  138–42, 184–90
coordination 17
co-principals 11

224 *Index*

Craig, C. 114
Crawford, M. 9
curriculum development teams: effects
of distributed leadership in 220;
formation and process 30–1, 66,
71–2, 136–7, 148, 154, 182–3;
leadership organization in 115–16;
leadership styles in 63–4, 75;
perception/experience of team
members 85–90; selection of 49–51
curriculum innovations: data collection
methods 31–2; developing teacher
curriculum development skills 34–5;
developing teacher curriculum
leadership 30–1; findings 32–6;
future research 36–9; impact of
school-based curriculum innovations
on teachers and students 70–111;
leadership styles and expanding spaces
for teacher learning 33–4; situational
and deep learning 35–6; stages 31
curriculum leadership: developing in
primary school 43–66; international
perspective 43–6
curriculum leadership functions/
patterns: discourse features of
169–71; distribution of teacher
participation in meetings 157–8;
effective model of teacher learning in
schools 155; English team 158–61,
162; establishing communicative
networking patterns 158–62;
establishing functional patterns
of the meeting discourses 162–8;
findings and analysis 156; General
Studies team 161–2, 168–71; nature
of 219–20; open questions open
invitations 167–8; participation styles
of other members 165–7; research
design and data collection 155–6

Dam, G.T. 35
Daniels, H. 178, 179
Darling-Hammond, L. 44, 47, 129, 182
data collection methods 31–2, 203–4
data interpretation 119
Datnow, A. 11
Davis, S. 14
Day, C. 9, 14–15, 17, 44, 57, 72, 134,
135, 137, 153, 182
Deacon, Z. 127
decentralization 134
deep learning 35–6, 93–6

Deppeler, J. 12
Desimone, L. 73, 74, 138, 153, 200
Devos, G. 13, 66
Diamond, J.B. 20, 154, 183, 203
Dimmock, C. 43, 45, 129
directive leadership 33–4, 64
discourse analysis: guiding exploration
120; inviting participation from
all members 121–2; reflecting
on personal experience 122–3;
reorienting direction of discourse
120–1; of team meetings 119–23,
130, 149
dispersed leadership 15
distributed cognition theory 21
distributed leadership: agential 11, 12;
changing leadership orientations from
positional to distributed leadership
practices 15–16; concept of 20;
critical analysis of reviews 19; cycle
38; decision making processes and 11;
definitions of 13–14, 16; dimensions
of distribution 12; from distributed to
hybrid leadership 16–17; distributive
approaches to leadership practices
135–6; effects in curriculum
development teams 220; effects of
13; efficiency and effectiveness of 11;
forms of 17, 18; leadership functions
5–6, 11–13, 14; multiple leaders as
a form of 11–12; multiple usages
of 10–11; nature of "distribution"
based on functions 12; principal-
led functions 11–12; properties in
practices 17, 18; re-conceptualizing
218–19; research papers published in
journals 10–14; scholars on 14–22; in
school-based curriculum innovations
75–9; in school organizations 14–15;
stages 12; structural 12; studies
18–19; summary of literature on 23;
team approach based upon 154
Donaldson, M.L. 154
Doppelt, Y. 99
DuFour, R. 99
Durrant, J. 73, 114, 134

Edstam, T. 153, 200
Educational Administration Quarterly 9
*Educational Management
Administration and Leadership* 9
educational principles 30
educational reforms 29–30

educational terminologies 57–9
Edwards, A. 190
Eemircioglue, E. 13
efficiency 99
Ekholm, M. 66
Elliott, B. 46, 73, 117, 138
Elliott, J. 44, 49, 182
Elmore, R.F. 135
Engestrom, Y. 31, 126, 154, 178, 179, 182, 202, 204
entire-school survey 52
ERIC database 10
Ermeling, B.A. 203
Evers, C.W. 45
examination 208
expansion cycle of learning 31, 204–12

Feng, S. 200
formal distribution 12
Foster-Fishman, P. 127
Foster, W. 135
Fox, A. 153, 157, 200
Frost, D. 46, 73, 114, 134
Fullan, M. 44, 45, 70, 80, 114, 115, 116, 128, 134, 135, 136, 177, 182

Gallimore, R. 71, 115, 135, 182, 203
Galton, M. 29, 43, 70, 114, 130, 135, 155, 157, 177, 183
Gamage, D.T. 177
Garet, M.S. 73, 74, 138, 153, 200
Gee, J. 141, 202
Gilbert, J. 44
Giles, C. 153
Glatthorn, A.A. 45
Glazer, E.M. 35
Glickman, C.D. 64
Glover, D. 11
Goddard, R. 115
Goddard, Y. 115
Goh, J.W.P. 13
Goldenberg, C. 203
Gordon, S.P. 64
Gronn, P. 9, 10, 11–12, 15–18, 203
Groundwater-Smith, S. 153, 154, 200, 204
Gunter, H. 87
Gu, Q. 14

Hadfield, M. 134
Hairon, S. 13
Hakkarainen, K. 130, 200
Hall, G. 114

Hallinger, P. 9, 10, 18–19, 45, 115, 129
Halverson, R. 20, 154, 203
Hammons, H.L. 12
Hannafin, M.J. 35
Hargreaves, A. 153
Harris, A. 9, 11, 20, 45, 46, 64, 66, 70, 71, 114, 117, 134, 135, 138, 177, 182
Hartley, D. 13
Harvey, J.A. 9
Haverson, R. 183
Hawthorne, R.D. 46, 182
Healey, K. 21
Heck, R.H. 18, 19, 45, 115
Hellekjaer, G.O. 11
Henderson, J.G. 46, 182
Hiebert, J. 71, 115, 135, 182
Hiruma, F. 148
Hitt, D.H. 45
Hoban, G.F. 154, 203
Hofstede, G. 130, 140
Holye, E. 84
Hopkins, D. 9, 70, 114, 134, 135, 177, 200, 203
Hord, S. 99, 114, 153, 200
Horrocks, N. 154, 203
Hosking, D.M. 16
Hospesova, A. 127
Hoyle, E. 196
Huggins, K.S. 12
Hulpia, H. 13, 66

Imants, J. 203
implementation 31, 32, 50, 208–9
incremental distribution 12
influence 16, 22, 53
institutionalization: of good practices for curriculum innovations 38–9; of structures for curriculum decision making 65–6
interactional patterns 143–6
interdependence 17
International Journal of Educational Management 9
International Journal of Leadership in Education 9
interviews: student interviews 52, 62–3, 74, 102–8, 213; teacher interviews 55–6, 58–62, 74, 75–9, 81–3, 191–4
Irwin, K.C. 49, 55, 116, 136

Jackson, D. 134
James, M. 157

226   *Index*

Jeffrey, B. 142
Johnson, R.B. 183
Jones, D. 13
Journal of Educational Administration 9

Keer, H.V. 13
Kelchtermans, G. 12
Kelly, A.V. 48
Kemmis, S. 44, 72, 116, 136, 182
Kennedy, K. 37
King, M.B. 73, 138
Klar, H.W. 11
Knight, S. 153, 200
knowledge creation model: critical
  features in teacher-situated learning
  204–13; new practice consolidation
  210–12; new solution examination
  208; new solution implementation
  208–9; new solution modeling
  207–8; Piagetian model 202; problem
  analysis through historical-genetic and
  actual empirical approaches 205–7;
  questioning, challenging, criticizing,
  and rejecting aspects of accepted
  practice 204–5; reflection meeting
  209; student interviews before/
  after practice lessons 213; Vygotskian
  model 202
Ko, J. 148

Lakomski, G. 45
Lambert, L. 66
Lamby, J. 13
Larsen, C. 11
Lasky, S. 148
Latta, R. 80
Lave, J. 21, 179, 201, 202
Law, E.H.F. 29, 43, 70, 72, 114, 116,
  118, 130, 135, 137, 148, 155, 157,
  177, 183
Lawton, D. 134
leadership: "collaborative leadership"
  221; definitions of 16; discourse
  features of 162–5, 169–71;
  distributed leadership 9–24, 218–21;
  focus of studies in school-based
  curriculum development 129–30;
  key consideration in curriculum
  development teams 37–8; teacher
  leadership development 130
Leadership and Policy in Schools 9
leadership organization 115–16
leadership style: characteristics of 171–2;
  English team 168

leadership styles: authoritarian 33–4;
  blurred 38; collective 18; consultants
  109, 128, 140–2; curriculum
  leadership development project
  63–4; directive 33–4, 64; dispersed
  15; effective 63–4, 109; expanding
  spaces for teacher learning and
  33–4; internal panel head 142–3;
  manipulation of 71–2, 75–9;
  mediation functions of 191–6; models
  of mediation of 196; positional 20;
  procedural 64; rotational 37, 39;
  rotational leadership 147; shared
  orientation 15, 18; single-handed 15;
  types of 33–4
LeChasseur, K. 154
Lee, J.C.K. 29, 37, 45, 130, 148,
  157, 200
Leithwood, K. 13, 45, 64, 114,
  134, 135
Leung, K.W. 45
Levin, B. 135
Li, C. 148
Lilijenberg, M. 13
Lima, J.A.D. 13
Lin, K.P. 114
Lin, T.B. 13
Lipponen, L. 200
Llewellyn, J. 29, 43, 177
Llewellyn Report 29, 34, 70
Lloyd, C. 115
Loucks-Horsley, S. 44
Louis, K.S. 45, 129, 153, 200

MacBeath, J. 12, 45, 46, 71, 116, 136,
  182, 203
McCann, P. 127
McCormick, R. 153, 154, 157, 203
MacDonald, B. 85
McKernan, J. 37
McLaughlin, M. 44, 47, 71, 114,
  115, 135, 182
McMahon, A. 99
Macpherson, I. 44, 46, 73, 117,
  138, 183
Manion, L. 118, 138
Marks, H.M. 129
Marsh, C. 45, 70, 114, 134, 177
Mascall, B. 13
Mayer, A.P. 154
Mayrowetz, D. 10, 11, 13
Mehalik, M.M. 99
Meijer, P.C. 155, 203
Meirink, J.A. 203

Melville, W. 13
Meyer, A. 137
Michaels, S. 141, 202
middle managers 147–8
Miettinen, R. 178
Mifsud, D. 11
Miles, M. 66
Miller, A.C.S. 46, 70, 114, 134, 177
mixed-method approach 12
modeling 207–8
Modeste, M. 13
Moos, L. 46, 182
Morley, I.E. 16
Morrison, K. 118, 138
Mullick, J. 12
multiple leaders 11–12
Murakami-Ramalho, E. 153, 200
Murphy, J. 129

Nesbit, C.R. 46, 70, 114, 134, 177
Newmann, F.M. 73, 138
Ng, D. 13
Nievar, M.A. 127
non-directive leadership 64
Nowell, B. 127
Nunes, T. 200

O'Connor, M. 141, 202
Onwuegbuzie, A.J. 183
opportunistic distribution 12
organizational leadership model 148
organization issues 99–100
Orphanos, S. 45
Orr, M.T. 45
Ovens, P. 46, 70, 114, 134, 177
Ozdemir, M. 13

Paavola, S. 130, 200
Pang, M.F. 153, 200
Papa, J. 154, 203
Papa, R. 154, 203
Park, V. 11
partnerships 38, 64–5, 148, 184
Piaget, J. 202
Pinyan-Weiss, M. 11
Piot, L. 12
Pitts, V.M. 21
planning, experimentation, and reflection (PER) model 72–3, 109, 111, 116, 118, 137–8, 201, 209
planning meetings 31, 32, 83, 118, 138–44
policy 29–30
Porter, A.C. 73, 74, 138, 153, 200

positional leadership 20, 64
pragmatic distribution 12
primary school curriculum leadership: data collection methods 51–2; discussion 63–6; educational terminologies in discourse 57–9; findings and analysis 53–63; goals and aims 46–7; leadership styles 63–4; professional attitude and curriculum decision making 60–2; professional conversations: 55–7; role of consultants 54; school aims and recent challenges 47–9; seed teachers/curriculum development teams selection 49–51; student interviews 52, 62–3; team spirit and collaboration 59–60
problem analysis 205–7
"procedural leadership" 64
Procter, R. 153, 200
professional attitude 60–2
professional development 55–7, 65, 91–3, 109–10, 182
professionalism 34, 35, 83
professionality 84, 87, 90, 130, 190, 196
Putnam, R.T. 72, 116, 136, 154, 203

Qiang, H. 129
Quality Education Fund 30, 181
Quinn, J. 80

Rayner, S. 87
reflection meetings 31, 32, 83, 91–3, 125–6, 144–5, 209–10
Retallick, J. 53
Reynolds, B. 99
Rieckhoff, B.S. 11
Riehl, C. 64
Risku, M. 9
Ritchie, G. 49, 55, 116, 136
Ritchie, R. 12
Roberts, A. 13
Robinson, V. 11, 115
Rogers, A. 154, 203
Ross, D. 99
Ross, V. 114
rotational leadership 37, 39, 147
Rowan, B. 148
Rowe, K. 115
Rudduck, J. 85

Salas, E. 17
Sammons, P. 14, 135

228 Index

Sandholtz, J.H. 64
Saunders, W.M. 203
Schliemann, A. 200
Schon, D. 44, 71, 116, 136, 154, 182, 203
school-based curriculum development (SBCD) 3, 34, 37, 220–1
school-based curriculum innovations: acquiring professional skills 91–3; curriculum development teams 71–2; data collection methods 74; deep learning 93–6; discovering student learning power 96–9; discussion 63–6; experience of team members 86–90; findings and analysis 53–63; focus of innovation 73–4; impact on teachers and students 70–111; leadership styles 109; managing 134–49; participating teachers concerns 99–102; PER model 72–3; professional development 109–10; role of consultants 79–84; student benefit 110; student conception of learning 106–9; student conception of teaching style 103–5; teacher engagement in curriculum decision making in 90–9; team leader selection process 71–2; understanding aim of innovation by team members 85–6, 89
School Effectiveness and School Improvement 9
School Leadership and Management 9
Schunn, C.D. 99
Sergiovanni, T.J. 45
Sfard, A. 200, 201
shared orientation leadership 15, 18
Sharma, U. 12
Sherin, M.G. 71, 115, 135
Sherrill, J.A. 80
Shouse, R.C. 114
Shulman, J.H. 154, 177, 178, 203
Shulman, L. 71, 115, 135, 154, 177, 178, 203
Silk, E.M. 99
Silver, E.A. 204
single-handed leadership 15
situational deep learning 35–6
Skilbeck, M. 3, 4, 34, 37, 44, 70, 134, 177
Smith, M.S. 204
Snow-Gerono, J.L. 99
socio-cultural activity theory 21

Soder, R. 129
Somech, A. 127
Sommers, W.A. 153, 200
Sparks, D. 44
Spillane, J. 114
Spillane, P. 9, 11–12, 20–2, 136, 183, 203
Stahl, A. 201
Stein, M.K. 204
Stenhouse, L. 44, 70, 114, 134, 177
Stigler, J.W. 71, 115, 135, 182
Stoll, L. 99, 153, 200
Stone, K. 153, 200
Storey, A. 11
Stoten, D.W. 13
strategic distribution 12
Stringer, E.T. 154, 203
student interviews 52, 62–3, 74, 102–8, 213
Sugrue, C. 53
SWOT analysis 49–50, 51, 54, 55–6

Talbert, J. 71, 115, 135
Tashakkori, A. 74, 119, 156
Taylor, A. 135, 137
Taylor, J.E. 148
teacher curriculum leadership: developing 30–1; developing skills 34–5
teacher development 44, 182
teacher interviews 55–6, 58–62, 74, 75–9, 81–3, 85–102, 191–4
teacher leadership development 130, 149
teacher learning 33–4, 51, 53, 98–9, 154, 155, 201
teacher learning model 201
teacher participation 33–4, 46, 53, 65, 90–1, 98–9, 114–15, 121–2, 128–30, 157–8
team meetings: communication pattern analysis 123–7, 143–6; discourse analysis 119–23, 149; distribution of teacher participation in 157–8; interactional patterns 143–6; visual data analysis 118–19, 127, 139
team spirit 59–60, 79, 127, 130
teamwork 65, 79
Teddlie, C. 74, 119, 156
Thomas, S. 99
Tian, M. 9
Ticha, M. 127
time constraints 101–2

Timperley, H.S. 183
Torrance, D. 12
Townsend, A. 12
Troman, G. 142
Tschannen-Moran, M. 115
Tubin, D. 11
Tucker, P.D. 45

university faculties 38, 64–5, 148

Vandenberghe, R. 66
Van Keer, H. 66
Verloop, N. 155, 203
Vescio, V. 99
visual data analysis 118–19, 127, 139
Vygotsky, L.S. 202

Wahlstrom, K. 45
Walker, A. 129
Walker, C.L. 153, 200
Wallace, J.D. 46, 70, 114, 134, 177

Wallace, M. 99, 196
Walsh, M.E. 80
Wan, S.W.Y. 29, 72, 114, 118, 130, 135, 137, 148, 155, 157, 183
Ward, E. 99
Welton, A.D. 154
Wenger, E. 21, 179, 201, 202
Wisc, C. 9
Wiseman, D. 153, 200
Wong, K.C. 129
Woods, P. 142
Woods, P.A. 9, 12, 13

Yoon, K.S. 73, 74, 138, 153, 200
Yuen, J.H.P. 13

Zajda, J. 177
Zeichner, K. 153, 200
Zhao, M. 148
Zuberi, A. 20, 21